THE
TEXAN AND
DUTCH GAS

KICKING OFF THE EUROPEAN
ENERGY REVOLUTION

Douglass Stewart
&
Elaine Madsen

Order this book online at www.trafford.com
or email orders@trafford.com

Most Trafford titles are also available at major online book retailers.

Print information available on the last page.

ISBN: 978-1-4907-9698-7 (sc)
ISBN: 978-1-4907-9697-0 (hc)
ISBN: 978-1-4907-9700-7 (e)

Library of Congress Control Number: 2019912599

Trafford rev. 08/28/2019

www.trafford.com
North America & international
toll-free: 1 888 232 4444 (USA & Canada)
fax: 812 355 4082

Table of Contents

v	Foreword
vii	Introduction
1	Chapter 1—In at the Creation
7	Chapter 2—Preparing for Takeoff
12	Chapter 3—Stewart's Startles
21	Chapter 4—A Stirring in the Netherlands
27	Chapter 5—That Fellow from New York
33	Chapter 6—Oldenzaal After All
47	Chapter 7—Is That a Gas Pipe, Jan?
61	Chapter 8—Startling Jersey and Shell
72	Chapter 9—A New Player for the Team
83	Chapter 10—Government Matters
98	Chapter 11—Family Chronicles
111	Chapter 12—Brussels, Beyond, and Home Again!
128	Chapter 13—The Dutchman from Casablanca
141	Chapter 14—Stewart Interrupted
149	Chapter 15—The "Uitsmijter" Solution
169	Chapter 16—Stonewalled! Battered in Belgium, Foiled in France, Undenkbar in Germany
181	Chapter 17—Success Breeds Control
190	Chapter 18—Ascending the Export Mountain
205	Chapter 19—Scaling the German Summit
221	Chapter 20—Stewart Passages
233	Epilogue— Finishing the Kickoff
234	Back to the Uitsmijter Solution
237	Appendix Essay 2006
241	Afterword

243   Reunion at the Stewarts' Fiftieth Wedding Anniversary Party

245   Biographies

249   Index of Persons Referenced by Country

253   References

255   Acknowledgments

257   About the Co-Author

Foreword

The determined young man on the cover of this book stepped onto Amsterdam's Schiphol airfield in October 1960 with no idea he was taking the first step on a journey that would alter the economic and social landscape of several countries, bring great wealth to the Dutch nation, and spread environmental benefits across Europe. That young man is Douglass Stewart.

This book is his memoir of that journey, a behind-the-scenes look at the 1960 discovery of what was at the time the largest natural gas field in the world. The book is also about the team of young men with whom he worked and how, under the radar of two of the world's largest oil companies, Esso and Shell, they succeeded in launching what would become Europe's energy revolution.

This book highlights the way in which the lives of Stewart and three of the team members crossed one another in the geography of World War II without actually meeting until they were brought together on that same geography in the peaceful pursuit of bringing Dutch gas to Western Europe.

Mapped by Stewart's economic and engineering vision and his entrepreneurial spirit, the team slipped their corporate bonds to interact with the farsighted government of the Netherlands, of nearby countries and with the giants of European industry.

At the beginning of their journey, no market existed for such a volume of natural gas, no pipelines to transmit it such long distances, and no ready-made appliances with which to use it. In less than five years, pipelines were constructed, the first gas was transmitted, conversions were under way, coal mines began to close, and Europe's energy revolution was in full swing.

I have been an eager tourist exploring the route traveled by Stewart and his team, and the pleasures of bringing this story to life have been many. My encounters with Stewart's coworkers, friends, and family have enlivened my work. He has been a patient and challenging collaborator. I wish for you, our readers, pleasures of your own in your journey through his story.

—Elaine Madsen—

Introduction

This book is based on my personal experiences together with information obtained from interviews and conversations with associates involved in the Dutch natural gas development between 1960 and 1965. The dialogues in the book consist of direct quotes from taped telephone and personal interviews as well as dialogues reconstructed from my recollections of the general sense of various encounters that took place with a number of key people who participated in the early days of the natural gas business in Europe. I apologize to those whose names are not mentioned, but this book deals only with those with whom I was closely associated. The story is not just about business dealings but also about digresses to the personal life and experiences of people involved in the challenging negotiations that led to the formation of the Northern European natural gas distribution and marketing organizations of the last forty years. The book also harks back to the involvement of some of the persons in World War II.

Fortunately, because the management of Esso and Shell consisted primarily of oil people and not gas people, and because everything was new in the European natural gas business, we early birds had the freedom to be entrepreneurs with few fetters from our top management or from government. We dealt with enormous resources, important governmental officials, high stakes, and tough negotiations, especially with the existing entrenched coal gas monopolies in Belgium and Germany. In particular, former president Charles de Gaulle gave us a hard time in France.

I have a great admiration for the Dutch people and their government, which was farseeing in their grasp of the problems and opportunities that arose with the discovery of the Groningen gas field. The past forty-five years of successful and profitable functioning of the gas arrangements stand witness to their wisdom.

As we succeeded in our efforts and the project began to look big, profitable, and important, we were gradually brought under the bureaucratic governmental and oil company webs of control and red tape. Nevertheless, Dame Fortune grants to only a few the opportunity to be in at the creation of such a vast profit-making enterprise. We made the most of it!

—Douglass Stewart—

—Chapter 1—

In at the Creation

For eons, the possibility of Europe's energy revolution lay dormant beneath Dutch soil until the day a Dutch engineer's drill bit exposed it. A tall young engineer from Texas revealed the means by which that revolution would be set in motion. His name was Douglass Stewart.

In October 1960, Stewart was at his desk in the Rockefeller Plaza offices of Standard Oil Company of New Jersey, working on graphs for a report he was preparing about the potential of an oil field in Venezuela. That report would be someone else's responsibility before the day was out. Fate had, on this day, elected Stewart as one of the individuals to be in at the creation of a dramatic change in the energy industry of Europe.

Stewart looked up from his work to find his boss, Dawson Priestman, standing in the doorway of his office.

"Shell's been holding back on a discovery in the Netherlands," said Dawson. "It's got Bill Stott so stirred up he's called in the whole Jersey board this morning. We need you to sit in on this one, Doug."

Priestman, like all the old-timers, still referred to the company as Jersey, even though it was already known as Esso. Bill Stott was Jersey's vice president of marketing. His calls for interdepartmental meetings generally had the air of a summons about them; however, a meeting that required the attendance of the entire board was not an everyday event.

On their way to the sixty-fourth floor, Priestman explained to Stewart that the meeting was about a discovery of natural gas rather than oil. Stewart was puzzled.

"When did that blow in? Did I miss something?" asked Stewart.

"Vasquez wanted to keep you on Venezuela. Stott was on our backs, so he and I dug into it ourselves," replied Priestman.

The announcement of the discovery had been an immediate red flag to Priestman and to his producing coordinator, Siro Vasquez. Alert to the possibility of the way that such a discovery could impact the production department, Vasquez quickly contacted the Esso producing advisor, who had just returned from his annual visit to NAM, an acronym for a fifty-fifty Esso/Shell exploration partnership in the Netherlands—Nederlandse Aardolie Maatschappij. In the advisor's opinion, NAM had certainly not been forthcoming about the size of the new discovery in the way Esso had a right to expect. Vasquez and Priestman took the information and their concern to Esso's marketing director, Bill Stott. His speculation turned at once to how such a large natural gas discovery might affect Esso's European oil markets. Since there were no European pipelines to transport the gas and no manufacturers of appropriate household appliances to make use of it, no matter how big the discovery was, it wasn't likely to generate any immediate problem. Nevertheless, Stott agreed the situation did require examination. Within hours of the three men's discussion, Stott had called for the full board meeting.

In 1960, Jersey dominated Shell in worldwide significance except in the public consciousness of the Netherlands, where Shell was one of that country's largest and most prestigious businesses, having ties to the crown going back more than a century. There, Jersey had only a small market share and a small refinery. The fifty-fifty NAM exploration partnership of the two giants had been established in 1947, but it was operated virtually autonomously by Shell.

Priestman made a succinct comment on Shell's attitude about the partnership. "Jersey's influence with Shell in Holland extends about as far as approving budgets once a year."

That was about to change. On this day, no one, least of all Doug Stewart, knew Stewart was about to become a major player in bringing about that change. He and Priestman passed John D. Rockefeller's old rolltop desk in the long hall just outside the awe-inspiring Jersey boardroom. Beneath its high oak-lined ceiling, it was dominated by a thirty-foot long oval-shaped mahogany conference table, which filled half of the room. High on the far wall at the end of the room, John himself, from within the ornate frame of a very large oil painting, scowled down on everything. When Stewart and Priestman stepped inside the boardroom, they found that about twenty others had already arrived. The board members were being carefully ushered directly to their seats at the table. Priestman and Stewart were shown to seats along the wall.

This was not Stewart's first board meeting; he'd made presentations on a number of other occasions. This one, though, would alter the course of his career.

The agenda for this morning's meeting included a presentation by the producing division advisor, who had just completed his annual tour of Europe. It was his responsibility on these tours to visit affiliates in each of the European countries in which Jersey had an ownership stake. Handouts for everyone at this meeting included a translation of an October 14 Belgian newspaper article that reported remarks by Belgium senator Victor Leeman:

> *During a debate on European energy policy at Strasbourg, Belgium's Senator Leeman announced that an enormous natural gas field containing reserves of 300 billion cubic meters, the equivalent of 1.7 billion barrels of oil, had been discovered by NAM.*[1]

News of the discovery appeared in Dutch newspapers on October 17. On October 18, unknown to Esso, Shell Netherlands dispatched a letter to J. W. de Pous, the Dutch government's Minister of Economic

---

1   Subterranean Commonwealth by Wolfe Kielich.

Affairs. The letter suggested a "new arrangement" for a "new situation" with respect to "important additional volumes of natural gas."

The discovery of this "new situation" was certainly not new to Shell Netherlands. They had actually known of it for more than a year. To be precise, they'd known of it since July 22, 1959, at 6:33 a.m., when a natural gas flow had been confirmed by drilling in the Schlocteren area of the country. Moreover, further drilling near the area of Groningen had revealed the extent of the discovery. The means by which this information found its way to Belgium was widely discussed but was not revealed for many years. Jack Rathbone, Jersey's chairman of the board, was a commanding presence wherever he was and nowhere more so than when he was presiding at the head of that mahogany table. His first question was not addressed to Stott, who had requested the meeting, but to the advisor from the producing division. "I have to hope this Belgian newspaper report is not all we're going to hear about this. Is there any documentation for these extravagant numbers?"

The advisor rose to address the group. "There's plenty of speculation about how Leeman knew, but it's to his advantage in that kind of meeting to make it sound as spectacular as possible because it implies Shell and, therefore, possibly Esso, is hiding something."

The first visual the advisor brought up on the view graph machine was a map of the Netherlands, and he directed everyone's attention to the Groningen area in Northern Holland as he continued. "Shell's silence about what's going on up there is suspicious on its face. I could not get thing one out of anybody at NAM. Shell is our partner, but they are not acting in that capacity. Particularly, they're playing the size of these discoveries very close to their chest. I got absolutely no estimates from them as to the magnitude of these new finds. I was permitted only a brief one-day review of NAM's operation and the plans they have at their producing office in the Oldenzaal area. Off the record, one fellow made it clear to me that whenever natural gas discoveries are made, Shell downplays it. Their primary business is oil. Natural gas is nothing more than its by-product. They get rid of it to the state at the wellhead for the lowest purchase price."

At this point, Bill Stott reminded everyone how, in the past, Jersey had also made the presumption that natural gas had only limited marketing possibilities and sold its natural gas at the wellhead. The folly of that presumption had become highly visible in Jersey's bottom line in the mid-1950s. At that time, sales of natural gas in the United States accelerated in a remarkable fashion. Gas utility companies had purchased natural gas cheaply at the wellhead and then made large profits by moving it into the home heating and cooking markets, severely undercutting Jersey's U.S. heating oil markets.

Stott was adamant in pointing out that while the dominant fuel in the Netherlands was still coal, Jersey had a rapidly growing market share in fuel oil. In his opinion, a large cheap source of natural gas at the kind of low prices it commanded in the United States could suddenly not only disrupt the emerging oil markets in the Netherlands but would also affect the rising market share of fuel oil in neighboring countries.

Stott emphatically agreed with Shell. "Natural gas is nothing but a pain in the neck and will do nothing but hurt our oil business," he said. "They're right to downplay it."

The advisor responded candidly, "It may be difficult to downplay several billion cubic feet, sir. My own estimate is that subsequent discoveries could take us far beyond that number. Shell's running NAM, and we don't have anybody on the inside to tell us if there's a threat to profit or not."

Stott retorted that there was very little likelihood of profit for the company in pursuing natural gas. He was apparently unaware that Stewart had already been instrumental in a case in Texas that proved that natural gas could absolutely be very profitable to Jersey.

Siro Vasquez called everyone's attention to the fact that the two companies actually had a producing sharing agreement on any discoveries in the Netherlands that dated back to the 1930s. Not being forthcoming about the size of the discovery in the way Jersey had a right to expect was certainly an appropriate cause for alarm.

Vasquez went on to explain how he and Priestman scoured the files for whatever information might be there regarding the Netherlands discovery. They found several reports sent over the course of several years regarding oil drilling efforts, but there was no report giving even a hint of the magnitude of the natural gas find, even though the discovery had been made the previous year, in 1959. Vasquez felt strongly that the missing information was a red flag the board could not ignore. With publication in the newspapers, it was getting bigger by the hour. He then underscored the advisor's comment that what was needed was someone on the scene in the Netherlands to get facts that would enable the board to elect a course of action in the matter.

Rathbone recommended that the board follow the counsel of Vasquez and the advisor. They needed to get somebody overseas to NAM who could give them some answers. The board agreed. Rathbone asked Vasquez if there was anyone available who could handle the assignment.

"Our man Stewart has the background to ferret out the facts," Vasquez said. He turned to face his "volunteer." "Can you leave tomorrow, Doug?"

At Humble Oil, a Standard Oil subsidiary in Texas, Stewart's achievement in recognizing and documenting a hitherto unrealized natural gas profit had been what propelled him to New York. Since his arrival four years earlier, his value to the company had been steadily marked by regular raises and promotions, most recently to the post of assistant manager in the production economics department, which was what made him an obvious candidate for the Netherlands assignment. Even so, Vasquez's question was as surprising to Stewart as a skyrocket in a rainstorm. Without hesitation, however, he responded, "I can."

Chapter 2

Preparing for Takeoff

I n 1960, Jersey's management was committee-driven so that major decisions would have input from every level. Corporate activities were designated as "upstream" and "downstream" both in-house and in its annual report. Upstream produced product for the company and included the producers, geologists, production economists, engineers, and operating people. Those designated as downstream included the departments of transport, refining, marketing, finance, and economics, concerned primarily with transporting and marketing the upstream product.

There was little association between these two groups except at the very top level, and an unspoken undercurrent of superiority had taken root in both. Upstream people regarded themselves as the "real" oilmen because of their hands-on experience out in the oil fields developing and producing the product upon which the corporation depended for its existence. Downstream's view of its superiority was based on the belief that they were producing the capital upon which the corporation depended for its main profit.

Since any new petroleum discovery was an upstream responsibility, it was properly one of their engineers who would evaluate this one in the Netherlands. Stewart's upstream designation would one day have unforeseen consequences, but on this day, the appointment was, for him, a welcome and exciting challenge.

Before he did anything else, Stewart went straight to his desk and called his wife, Jane. "Jane was always supportive of my career and readily went along with whatever changes or resulting moves came about because of new assignments," recalled Stewart. "She had the same spirit of adventure that I do. She was delighted that I had been selected for this important assignment, and she had only one question: 'How long do they want you to stay?'"

Stewart had no more of an idea of how long he'd have to stay than he did about what he'd actually do when he got there. But he was going to be as prepared as possible by taking with him as much background information as he could assemble in a day. He went directly to the office of Martin Orlean, an analyst who prepared energy forecasts for Jersey's coordination and petroleum economics department.

According to Orlean, "Esso's earlier decision to sell natural gas at the wellhead meant Esso had not been able to protect its other petroleum products and could not hold the home heating and cooking market against the shrewd moves of the gas utilities in the United States, who had given away free gas heating units and hauled away the old ones. Once a utility hooked up a heating customer to their gas grid, the gas utility companies then had that customer for the life of the house."

From others in the economics department, Stewart got a clearer understanding of Esso's involvement with Shell and how they were connected to this discovery of natural gas. The intriguing thing about this connection was that for a very long time, Shell seemed to have forgotten about, or maybe just wanted to ignore, their producing agreement with Esso in the Netherlands dating back to the '30s. At some point in the past, a Jersey man walked into Shell's office and reminded them about Esso's interest.

On September 19, 1947, the Nederlandse Aardolie Maatschappij was formed with BPM (Bataafsche Petroleum Maatschappij, a subsidiary of Shell in The Hague) and Standard Oil of New Jersey (Esso), each participating for 50 percent. Esso's partner in NAM, Shell/Royal Dutch Shell Group, was actually two companies. The Shell Transport and Trading Company, headquartered in London, owned 40 percent of the "group," and the Royal Dutch Petroleum Company, headquartered in The Hague, owned the other 60 percent. Both these companies shared the same board of directors, with London concentrating on the marketing end of the business and The Hague office running the worldwide exploration and production functions. For the purpose of simplification, these combined companies will be termed "Shell."

As Stewart examined the files they revealed, there was no question that NAM was being operated by Shell as if it was a wholly owned subsidiary, even though 50 percent of it was owned by Esso. To the Dutch people, NAM was regarded as a Dutch company with great political influence, partly because of Shell's historic ties to the Dutch royal family and, moreover, because Shell was a major employer of the Dutch people.

What really caught Stewart's attention was the Dutch petroleum law. This law had one foot in the sixteenth-century Spanish law and the other firmly planted in the Napoleonic Code of 1810. European precedents for this were first established by the fourteenth century in Spain, when the Spanish king required that two-thirds of any exploited minerals be paid to him. By the reign of Philip II in the sixteenth century, this appropriation was reduced to one-fifth of the net value of the minerals extracted.[2]

In the eighteenth century, Napoleon occupied the Netherlands, ostensibly to protect the country from Spain and England. In actuality, Napoleon drained the country of her resources[3] and codified that Spanish precedent with a law that declared, "The government has inalienable/imprescriptible rights/eminent domain over mineral wealth of the country."

In their 2003 article, "A New Mining Act for the Netherlands," Dr. Martha Roggenkamp and Dr. Christiaan Verwer elaborated on the background of the establishment of that Dutch Mining Law: "Napoleon

---

2   Mining Law: Bridging the Gap between Common Law and Civil Law Systems by Cecilia Siac, attorney-at-law at Tormina Consulting, Inc., from a paper presented at the Canadian Bar Association in April 1997.

3   The Embarrassment of Riches and Patriots and Liberators: Revolution in the Netherlands 1780–1813 both by Simon Schama.

was in favor of ownership of the minerals . . . running with the ownership of the land. The legislators wished to apply a different system in which important minerals were owned by the state."

Somehow those nineteenth-century legislators prevailed, and the law was established under which the crown (the state) awards the rights to minerals through an Act of Concession, and the state has the right to apply all sorts of conditions. The article noted the new mining act did not apply to petroleum concessions awarded before 1965, such as the Groningen concession. A new mining law of 2004 replaced the old Napoleonic law.

In 1960, however, it was the Napoleonic law that prevailed. The rights to any discovery made by NAM's drilling belonged to the Dutch State.

The files in Jersey's economic department revealed to Stewart a fact he regarded as particularly singular. The Dutch government had only granted to NAM an "exploration drilling Permit." Before Esso/Shell's NAM could derive any financial benefit from the new discovery, they would have to apply for, and be granted, a "production concession" from the government. Stewart immediately realized this circumstance gave the government a great deal of leverage in any negotiation. It also meant that Shell, as a partner to Esso, could not negotiate for that all-important producing concession without Esso. He also discovered in the files that matters regarding natural gas were the province of J. W. de Pous, the Dutch Minister of Economic Affairs, a man who would be revealed to be a significant and powerful force in the months ahead.

Armed with the information he'd gathered, Stewart left the office a little early to pick up a few things in preparation for the trip. "From my army days, I knew that Europe would be cold and damp at that time of year," said Stewart, "so I rushed into a store on my way to the train and bought a lined trench coat similar to the one I had during the war. I also bought some toys and games for the kids to keep them amused while I was away."

That evening, Grand Central Station's great marble expanse reminded him of the marble palaces he'd seen in Europe as a young lieutenant in charge of military convoys during World War II. During those years, he'd seen the grandeur of those palaces humbled by war's deviltry and destruction. He had not been back to Europe since the end of the war and wondered how far recovery had progressed in Europe's great cities.

In the rocking, rundown New Haven Railroad, Stewart was oblivious to the dirty and uncomfortable cars, which at that time never seemed to be repaired. He was even oblivious to the stale cigarette smoke that always lingered annoyingly in the air. His thoughts were occupied by the unknowns of the task before him. He kept turning over and over in his mind all the information he'd taken in that day and pondered in what direction the assignment would take him.

One thing was certain: Stewart had no intention of limiting his inquiry to ascertaining the bare bones of the size of the Groningen discovery, nor was he going to limit himself to reporting only what problems might occur with Shell.

I didn't like the idea of returning to the board only to tell them they had a big problem," he said. "Although my assignment was only to determine the size of the discovery, I decided that when I got to the Netherlands, I would try to get a better fix on just exactly what the possible markets there might be for all that natural gas. I resolved right then and there to come back and startle Jersey with some ideas for what they might do about it."

—Chapter 3—

Stewart's Startles

Although marketing was a downstream responsibility, Stewart had never been one to limit his thinking to corporate pigeonholes when solving a problem. At Humble Oil, Jersey's Texas subsidiary, it was his practice at least four times a year to seek out and identify a dormant situation or problem within the company. He would explore the parameters of such a problem and devise not only a solution but also a means through which the company could employ the solution for a profit. He would then propose that solution to management with what he called his Quarterly Startle.

It was the unparalleled success of one of those "Stewart Startles" that brought him to the attention of Jersey's New York producing division. At Humble, he had been recognized as an experienced reservoir engineer with a proven track record in analyzing drilling and gas reservoirs that would return significant profits.

Harold Wright, a retired career oilman in Houston, worked with Stewart when he was a district reservoir engineer for Humble's operation on the King Ranch. To Wright, Doug was a man who stood out. "Doug was a big good-looking guy, very outgoing, and extremely vigorous, which was how I thought of myself. But about half the time, I'd be folding up, and Doug would already be out doing something different. There has always been something worldly about Doug. He had kind of a cosmopolitan attitude. It may have been his experience abroad in the war, although he never really talked much about that. There was just something about him that told you he'd been around a lot."

Still friends today, Stewart describes Wright as a man of principle. "I first met Harold in 1948, when he had just started Humble's drilling rig training program, same as I had done. Wright never hesitated to tell anybody, at whatever level, what he thought. When I was in New York, I offered him a job in my department because I knew he was the best man for it."

According to Wright, his Houston boss attempted to dissuade him from taking Stewart's offer. "I got a call from the chief engineer down in Houston telling me that if I took the job with Stewart in New York, don't even wonder about coming back. But of course, I did take it and never looked back."

Wright took the job because of his confidence in Stewart, which had been established during their shared experience at Humble. "In those early days, Doug and I had the responsibility for analyzing underground oil and gas reserves in order to develop the means to increase recovery and maximize profits from production. While we were there, a substantial amount of natural gas was discovered in South Texas. It was not just in the areas where Doug and I were, but in fact, it was all over the whole King Ranch. At that time, natural gas was selling for something like a nickel, and it just wasn't worth putting in pipelines. It was burned off to get rid of it or, more commonly, just left unproduced in gas reservoirs underground."

Although natural gas wasn't viewed as marketable, it nevertheless was a useful by-product in the process of extracting oil. Only 15 to 30 percent of the oil in underground rock formations could actually be recovered. It was the natural gas in these formations that provided pressure to help push the oil to the wells. This natural gas was composed of methane and was wet with various hydrocarbons, such as propane, butane, and natural gasoline, which condensed to liquids underground and could be lost as pressure decreased because of oil and gas production. This phenomenon was called retrograde condensation. This decline in pressure could be reduced through "gas recycling." This was a process in which dry gas was pumped into one end of a reservoir and swept out the other end. This drove out gas liquids, such as propane and butane, which actually did have market value. This process really wasn't reliable or very economical because if the pressure in a reservoir failed, the gas liquids would drop out in the reservoir and couldn't be recovered. Even when they were saved, these liquids did not pay for the cost of that gas reinjection, so recycling was not done because the process was not cost-effective.

In 1955, there were large unutilized wet gas reserves in the King Ranch area. Stewart was then head of the Southwest Texas division and was in the process of thinking up his next "Quarterly Startle" when he recognized some unexplored possibilities in that recycling process.

"I knew these gas caps contained a lot of rich gasoline as well as propane, butane, and other hydrocarbons," he recalled. "I thought that if there were only a way these things could be taken out economically, surely a bigger market for them would open up."

Conventional thinking at that time was to leave these liquids in the ground until sometime in the future, when all the oil in the field was produced. That could mean waiting as long as twenty years before pipelines would be laid down to recover those liquids and for the gas to have a market. If those liquids could be reclaimed in the present, they could be trucked to market without that long wait and without the need for pipelines.

Although he had an idea of how reclamation of those liquids could be done, Stewart knew "the powers that be" first needed to be "startled" by the possibility of financial return. Without such a prospect, they would not consider making the investment required to make those marketable liquids accessible.

Stewart put the concept of "present value" on the table. "The oil companies had not yet begun to utilize the idea of present value. That is the current value of money as compared to getting the money ten, twenty, or thirty years down the road. I didn't invent the idea, but I knew they weren't really thinking about the present value of those liquids in the ground. I got some data from our field people about all our different reservoirs and, together with an assistant, put together a report that showed if we could cycle these reservoirs, recover the gas liquids, and then sell them, the present value would be $100 million more than if we waited and produced the gas twenty years later. In today's terms, that would be something like half a billion dollars. I prepared the whole thing in report form, with maps, economics, and everything."

What Stewart was proposing was no less than the construction of the world's largest gas recycling plant. Preparing his "Quarterly Startle" to explain this bold and original idea was consuming so much of his time that Dawson Priestman, his boss, demanded to know what was going on.

"Doug, what are you doing? I haven't heard much from you lately."

His response certainly got his boss's attention. "How'd you like to make a hundred million bucks?"

"How's that?"

"Hold on a minute," said Stewart.

He went back to his office, fetched his report, and laid it on his boss's desk.

"He came back startled, indeed!" said Stewart.

"Doug, this is wonderful," his boss said. "We're having a meeting of the supervisors next week, and the people from Humble headquarters are coming down. Can you present this?"

Stewart had a clear recall of how the Humble executives reacted to his presentation. "All the big shots from Houston came down, and I made this presentation. They really liked the whole idea, but then they went back and talked to their experts. Humble had a gas division in Houston, which was supposed to be doing what I'd done on my own. This wasn't their idea, and not surprisingly, they tried their darndest to shoot holes in my study. But they couldn't do it."

Wright recalled that not everyone at Humble was enthusiastic about Stewart's ideas.

"What they really didn't like was that, in effect, Doug went around them by giving the study to his boss first. He'd skipped the division head and presented it right to the bosses without going through their red tape."

Wright described the atmosphere in which they worked at Humble as highly competitive. "Humble only hired people who were in the upper 10 percent of their engineering class. This made for a very competitive pot of real sharp people vying for limited opportunity. Now when Doug came up with the idea of how to get the liquids out of the natural gas, it was not something that hadn't ever been thought about or tried someplace, but Doug is an original thinker, and what he proposed had just never been tried on the scale or by the means he dreamed up. Doug was the one who recognized the possibilities. With him, you're dealing with a guy who's a little bit smarter than you are. And he doesn't just have ideas. He has this ability to come up with ideas nobody else has thought of. That was part of Doug's strength—and part of his problem. He was a little bit better than the other pretty sharp people. The only way some of them knew how to react to him was to try and bring him down. His gas plant proposal was kind of a controversial project there for a while."

The biggest challenge for Stewart was convincing his superiors that the construction of such a massive gas recycling plant, for which there was no precedent, was actually merited and, furthermore, that it was sound, both fiscally and technologically. Another engineer was called into Corpus Christi, and working together, they created "A Study of the Fields in and on the Vicinity of the King Ranch."

What Stewart had to get through was not just corporate red tape. He had to get them to see how he'd expanded his own original idea. If the company decided to build this recycling plant, they could get the liquid components not only out of the natural gas but into the market as well.

Wright explained, "We started off cycling three hundred million cubic feet a day, a big chunk. But about the time that this cycling was getting along, Humble was running out of the gas they sold in the Intrastate Gas System, which was mainly from East Texas."

Stewart recognized that to continue serving that market, Humble needed to bring some of that South Texas gas up north. There was the possibility of a big market in Houston. A power plant that generated electricity by running on natural gas instead of oil or coal was much cheaper to build and run. If Humble combined the operations of cycling with pipelines to transport the dry gas, they could serve that market.

Stewart's "Startle" showed the company how to tie all the King Ranch fields in together.

"What they would have to do was construct a massive gas plant and lay down two pipelines, one from the King Ranch straight into Houston and the other one into Corpus Christi," said Stewart.

This study substantiated Stewart's original presentation, and Humble started construction.

Wright had a vivid memory of what that plant came to be. "The thing grew to something over a billion cubic feet a day, which was probably the biggest gas plant in the world for several years. There are bigger ones around the Middle East and places like that, but for a long time, the King Ranch gas plant was the granddaddy of them all."

Now that Stewart's Startle had not only been recognized but was going to be fully realized, he did not wait around for a pat on the back but began right away, looking for the next opportunity to advance his career. What he decided to do was threaten "not to quit."

"I didn't really want to leave Humble, but with the leverage I had because of the gas recycling plant, I thought they really wouldn't want me to leave," said Stewart. "There was another small oil company nearby operated by a former Humble division engineer. I knew this guy was looking for an engineer, and I knew my boss knew him. So I talked to my boss and indirectly implied that these other people were interested in me, and what did he think about it? Within a month, I got a big promotion and was made assistant division engineer in charge of all reservoir engineering. In effect, they created a new job, gave me another title and a raise too."

About six months later, the manager of producing economics in Jersey's New York office was in town and was interested in recruiting an assistant. He asked Stewart if he'd be interested.

"I called my wife, Jane, and asked if she would like to go to New York," said Stewart. "She said, 'Whatever you want to do, I'll go.'"

It was 1957. Stewart was assigned to Dawson Priestman's office as assistant manager of producing economics. On his first day there, Priestman invited him to a meeting of the heads of the producing coordination department to hear a report from two of the department's roving advisors who had just returned from Yemen, seeking an oil exploration concession there. This meeting gave Stewart his very first look into the exotic world of international oil exploration. To begin with, he found himself sitting at that table with Lewis G. Weeks, Standard Oil's chief geologist, who was famous for his worldwide geologic experiences and for his publications about worldwide future oil reserves. Stewart had read much of Weeks's work. Also attending the meeting was the head of Jersey's engineering department, two other geologists, and Paul Temple from the legal department.

"I felt a little awed in the presence of all these worldly businessmen," said Stewart, "and the more I heard that day, the more my Texas background felt just a bit homespun."

Siro Vasquez began by explaining that the advisors had taken the trip at the unofficial behest of someone in Washington to preempt a group of Russians who were reportedly seeking the same concession. Standard Oil wasn't too enthralled with the geologic prospects in the location but sent the advisors to verify whether the possibilities were real.

The advisor who had apparently been the head of the group that went to Yemen began by recounting how grateful he was for having heeded the advice of someone who had already traveled to Yemen to take a good supply of canned goods. He explained they otherwise might have starved to death because what was available there was very sparse and strange unlike anything they'd ever encountered before.

On arriving in Yemen, the advisors were driven to the compound of the sheik. They were put in the visitor's quarters, essentially just a bare room in which to sleep with an open doorway leading to a small courtyard. In the middle of the courtyard, a sheep was being roasted over an open fireplace. Facing them across the open fire, they could see a similar room, already occupied by the Russians. One look at the flies crawling on the food that had been set out for them sent the advisors, and the Russians, to find alternatives. The Russians hadn't come as well prepared, so the Americans shared some tins of canned sardines with them.

Several days went by with little to do and no indication of when they would be granted an audience with the sheik. The Russians disappeared one day, and still, they were told to wait. Finally, the meeting was arranged to take place in the sheik's palace, which turned out to be very dusty and un-palace-like. As they were being ushered down a hallway, they were assailed by the sound of roaring lions, live ones rushing up to bars that, thankfully, kept them caged.

Through the bars, on the other side of the lion's cage, there was a doorway leading to what they assumed was the sheik's harem as anyone wanting to get in or out of whatever was in there had to get past the lions, which certainly sounded hungry. The advisor speculated that there must have been an adjacent room into which the lions could be lured for feeding, allowing the sheik safe access to his women.

Ushered into the sheik's presence, the advisors found him sitting at the opposite end of the room. He seemed to be half-blind and appeared sickly. The sheik greeted them through an interpreter, who explained the purpose of the Americans' visit to the sheik. The sheik thanked them and said he would think about it. And that was that. That was the meeting! According to Stewart, "Jersey never did get that concession, and neither did the Russians. Years later, Hunt Oil Company did and found a sizable field."

It took several weeks before Stewart located a house so that Jane and the children could join him. Every morning he walked by NBC's window, through which he could see Dave Garroway and the cast of the *Today's Show* as it was being telecast across the country. A huge crowd on the street is now a daily feature, but in 1960, the cameras panned at random to pedestrians passing by, and Stewart waved at Jane, who was watching the show back in Texas.

As Stewart recalled, his move to New York brought many changes to the young Stewart family, including a big raise in pay. "Ten thousand dollars seemed like a lot of money, but once we were living in Connecticut, everything was much more expensive. We had less usable funds left over than we ever had in Texas. I have a chart somewhere that shows how I plotted my available funds. I think it was down to about $150 a month."

Three years and several raises later, Stewart was dispatched to the Netherlands. Just before leaving the house for the airport that morning, he received a mysterious call from the Esso Travel Office. The Refining Department wanted him to carry a package to Holland. Just before he boarded the KLM flight to Schiphol Airport, the package arrived. It was a cardboard box two inches high and twelve inches square. Stewart was instructed to be careful not to jar or crush this box.

Thinking it must contain some delicate refining instruments, he asked, "What's in it—in case the Customs Inspector asks?"

"Wild turkey eggs," he was told. "The refining manager wants to incubate them there and start a flock of birds on his shooting lease in Holland."

"I never did find out if they hatched," said Stewart. But what was on its way to hatching in Holland was Stewart's discovery, in a little townhouse not far from The Hague, that would let the curtain begin to rise on Europe's energy revolution.

Chapter 4

A Stirring in the Netherlands

Across the Atlantic, lest expectations exceed reality, the prudent Dutch Minister of Economics, J. W. de Pous, had been reluctant to move too quickly to act on, or comment on, the unexpected publication of information about the natural gas discovery or even upon the speculation generated by Senator Leeman's announcement. The news coverage had pushed the matter to sudden public attention before the government had formulated any plans.

Over time, the ten trillion cubic feet of gas, which was thought to be an extraordinary amount at the time, was going to prove to be a very conservative estimate.

For decades, a Dutch engineer named H. A. Stheeman was convinced something geologically extraordinary would be found in the area of Schlocteren and Groningen. His certainty was not shared by his NAM colleagues. In 1955, Stheeman's faith came near to validation when he and his crew began drilling near the village of Ten Boer, uncovering a gas show at a depth of about ten thousand feet. Unfortunately, that success was immediately threatened by the impending catastrophe of a natural gas blowout. A safety valve in the drilling equipment had malfunctioned. According to Wolf Kielich, in *Subterranean Commonwealth*, it took two weeks before the exhausted Stheeman and his heroic crew got the pit under control.

But for the failure of that safety valve, the dramatic changes the Groningen discovery would one day bring to many nations might have been launched right then. Instead, the Groningen discovery had a life of its own, unfolding in other directions that would not bring Stheeman recognition.

Even if the drilling had been successful that day, it was unlikely that the energies of NAM would have been directed to the new discovery. That year, the petroleum industry was thrown into resolving the crisis generated by the unprecedented and dangerous blocking of the Suez Canal in Egypt. Weekend driving was curtailed throughout the Netherlands. The increased cost of the long, hazardous journey that oil tankers were forced to make around Africa meant oil and gasoline prices skyrocketed around the world, and consumers were faced with abrupt and critical shortages. Maximum effort was spent by the oil companies to ensure an uninterrupted flow of petroleum products to the industrialized world. The event at Suez turned out to be both a flash point and a wake-up call. This was history's first reminder of mankind's increasing reliance on the Middle East for this finite resource.

In the early morning hours of July 22, 1959, Stheeman and his team had permission to resume drilling for gas at Schlocteren. Without mishap this time, they were rewarded with a very high pressure flow of natural gas. By mid-August, further testing in other areas near the town of Groningen indicated that something extensive might be present. Oddly, this new probability generated no particular activity or excitement, although permission for further exploration was planned. This lack of urgency was not due to neglect but to the fact that in Holland at that time, natural gas was considered to be a low-profit fuel. Even when subsequent tests suggested the amount of gas was beyond the ordinary, no particular estimate was issued. Routine information about the testing was transmitted to Shell and Standard Oil offices in the Netherlands and the United States, but no reports were published.

In *Subterranean Commonwealth*, author Kielich quoted the explanation of NAM director J. M. P. Bongaerts, who was Stheeman's successor. "Don't forget, at that time, there was a great deal of pessimism in the large oil companies. Their philosophy boiled down to first, make 200 percent sure of exactly what you've found before you let it be known. Not so surprising really because during these years, a number of promising finds were made elsewhere in the world, particularly in Libya, where the actual results turned out to be less than a quarter of what was expected."

NAM's lack of attention to the possibilities of the Groningen discovery was a grave disappointment to Stheeman. In Kielich's book, T. H. Tromp, former Minister of Public Works and a friend of Stheeman from student years, recalled Stheeman's great disappointment. "I followed the complications between Stheeman and Shell at a distance. He was disillusioned, a little embittered. He never got much publicity. He spent a lifetime occupied with the natural gas question, but he was never taken seriously by Shell and his colleagues."

Nearly a year went by with no significant action by NAM, primarily because natural gas accounted for less than 1 percent of the fuel market in Holland. The prime fuel for both domestic and industrial use was coal, with fuel oil fast moving into second place. Oil companies anticipated that fuel oil would soon outdistance coal. There simply was, as yet, no market for natural gas. Little public attention for the discovery was generated, with the exception of a few lines in a local newspaper noting that the size of the flame from the natural gas being burned off was visible miles away in the city of Groningen.

At Esso's Nederland Haus in The Hague, however, serious notice was about to be given to that natural gas discovery. On this October morning, Esso's Jan van den Berg parked his Vespa scooter in front of the imposing structure. The most common means of transportation for people of every social class in Holland was the bicycle; even the queen rode one to her office. Jan had moved up to a motorized scooter some time ago, and he was really excited. Today was going to be the last day he'd be riding that scooter. His wife, Ciny, was going to pick up their first new car, a Volkswagen. They had not agreed on the color. He was leaving it up to her. Jan wondered if he would come home to find a quiet, conservative color befitting a serious businessman or if it would be that bright yellow she favored, which seemed just a little "proud" to him.

In his early thirties, Jan was a dapper man of small stature but a man big in personality, intellect, and expertise. He was manager of Esso Nederland's Economic Group, and his expectation for that day was to put the finishing touches on the annual energy report he was preparing for Jersey's office in New York. Jersey required every affiliate to prepare a detailed countrywide breakdown of fuel use by type of fuel and category of customer for both total consumers and for Esso sales. The reports, known as the Red and Green Books, also forecast oil product demand and sales for the next several years.

To make his report as accurate as possible, Jan had researched many industry and government publications. He had gained considerable knowledge of industrial energy uses and also of the fuel uses of the Dutch people. Jan was very pleased with what he'd accomplished for this year's report, particularly its accuracy and depth.

The information he'd collected brought into sharp focus the ways in which his and Ciny's living circumstances exceeded those of the average Dutchman. Jan's Esso salary permitted him to rent a relatively new two-story townhouse in Wassenaar, a suburb of The Hague. Though it was small, he and Ciny had two bedrooms upstairs, with a washbasin in each. Downstairs, there was a combination living room/dining room and a kitchen. There was no heat source upstairs at all; warmth was provided by heat rising up the stairwell from the coal stove in the living room. Jan had traveled widely throughout the Netherlands and was well acquainted with the way people lived in the cities and farms lying below sea level. The North Sea's wind and rain drove bone-numbing dampness across the English Channel for many months of the year. For families who could afford it, kitchens like Jan's had what was called a geyser, a kind of small hot water heater. The heater burned town gas, which was a fuel manufactured from coal at the municipal town gas works. Town gas was very expensive, so Jan and Ciny only used it to heat water and for the cooking stove. There was a bathtub in the house, but it had to be hand-filled from the hot water geyser.

Only about 5 percent of Dutch houses had central heat from coal or heating oil and kerosene. For the rest, central heating was out of the question because of the expense of town gas. Most Dutch homes still used kerosene or anthracite coal in heating stoves, which were messy, did not heat much of an area, and often went out at night. Sometimes when Jan's coal stove burned out, it got so cold upstairs water actually froze in the bedroom sinks.

In his office the next day, Jan pulled himself away from musing over his good fortune to put the finishing touches on his report for Jersey. Just as he picked his pen, he was interrupted by a call from the general manager, Coen Smit, who wanted to see him immediately. As Jan cooled his heels in Smit's outer office, he couldn't help thinking that if he'd just been allowed to stay at his desk for that half hour, he would have been finished with the report.

Finally ushered into the cathedral-like room, he found Smit relaxed on his comfortable couch under the tall stained glass windows. Smit handed Jan the local October 17 newspaper headlining the story about Senator Leeman's announcement of the natural gas discovery. There was no room between Smit's rapid-fire questions for Jan to slip in an answer.

"Do you know anything about the natural gas business or what it'll do to our oil markets if this thing is really the size they're reporting? Jersey must be worried about it because they just phoned to let me know they're sending over one of their reservoir engineers to look into this. You and Cees van der Post are to give him every assistance in any way you can."

Jan left Smit's office relieved he wouldn't have to pull this together alone. Cees van der Post was about two years older than he and was a graduate engineer with Esso's LPG (liquefied petroleum gas) marketing group. Cees was well regarded, both within the company and by clients, for his energy and technical ability. Jan knew Cees could provide information on that market.

Jan was not familiar with natural gas himself, but he knew his department had amassed information on every energy market in the Netherlands. Esso sold propane and butane in liquid form to several of the town gas manufacturers, which was then reformed into low-BTU town gas. Jan and Cees worked late that night, laying out a plan for rounding up everything in both their departments. Although it would mean working late the next night as well, they were sure they would be prepared for their first meeting with the American. By the time Jan got on his scooter to go home, it was already dark, and the chill of that October evening seeped through his jacket. The new Volkswagen would be waiting for him, but what color would it be?

The yellow answer was sitting in front of his little townhouse. Ciny was waiting inside to see how he felt about her choice. Jan paused outside, wondering how she was going to feel about his being late for dinner two nights in a row. Not only was yellow fine with Jan, but Ciny was also fine about Jan being late again. In fact, when she found out about the American, she suggested that Jan ask him home to dinner. Perhaps he'd like to find out about Dutch cooking, she said.

The next day, as Jan and Cees assembled the information for the American, they voiced aloud the concerns they shared about this visit. "How is this fellow from New York who knows nothing about Dutch markets going to be able to take in everything we've assembled fast enough to apply it to the problem at hand?"

Chapter 5

That Fellow from New York

As Stewart's plane descended toward Schiphol Airport, the green patchwork of fields and red roofed houses lined up along the canals came into view. Passing through customs was far more perfunctory than it has become in our hypervigilant day. The customs inspector, who spoke little English, wanted to know exactly what was in the box Stewart was handling so very carefully, just as Stewart had anticipated.

"I opened the box for him," said Stewart. "He took one look at those brown speckled eggs, listened to my explanation, and immediately summoned the agricultural inspector, who also spoke little English. I doubt they grasped what I was saying about incubating them, but the inspector finally threw up his hands and waved me through."

Outside the terminal, Pres. Coen Smit's big black Chrysler limousine was waiting. Willem, the uniformed driver, was a blond giant who spoke to Stewart formally in Dutch-flavored English.

"When Willem kept nodding respectfully as if I were important, I was sharply reminded of my responsibility to accomplish something definitive," said Stewart.

It was early morning. A thin fog hanging over manicured meadows dotted with cows. The scene seemed to have been artfully arranged in a kind of still life, posed for Stewart's appreciative eye. Unlike the barbed wire fences in Texas or the stone walls of Connecticut, Holland's fields were defined by narrow canals. The simplicity of a farmer carrying hay to his barn, in the very practical wooden shoes that protected his feet from the damp ground, prompted the surge of excitement Stewart always felt when he found himself in places he'd never seen before.

Willem delivered Stewart to the quaint old Hotel de Wittebrug on the outskirts of The Hague. The room was an enormous high-ceilinged chamber. There was a very large bathroom housing a voluminous dragon-footed tub. Unlike the modern ones back home, this one was large enough to accommodate Stewart's big frame.

"Outside the window, I could hear what sounded like a little circus calliope," said Stewart. "I looked out, and there, below me, was a little man cranking away on a beautiful white organ on wheels. It looked like a little old-fashioned upright piano, with gilded flowers and decorations very like those on a circus wagon. The man looked up at me and smiled, took off his cap, and held it out. I tossed him a few of my newly acquired Dutch coins. I wasn't sure of their value, but he bowed deeply and resumed playing with a big smile. I thought of how much Jane would have loved that moment."

Since he had been up all night on the plane, Stewart was relieved when he phoned Mr. Smit's office. "I wouldn't be meeting him until the next day. Smith thought perhaps I'd need to catch up on my sleep after such a long flight. It had been long, but my excitement was not ready to give in to sleep right then. I looked out the window and across the way, along the canal. The scene before me was like a painting come to life. An easy breeze wafted a few leaves into the water as a bicyclist rolled by. How could I sleep? There was so much to see and so much to think about."

Stewart had to get out and see what scenes lay beyond the hotel. "There was no time or energy for a real tour, but I walked into a residential area first. The memory that stands out for me from that walk was my surprise that in The Hague, there were real houses, just like the ones in Manhattan. These were brick, with white stone around the windows. Sometimes they were neatly packed together, one after the other and right against the street, with no yard in front. At every turn, I kept wishing that Jane were there with me to see it too. I dared to imagine that somehow the task at hand would be extended, that I'd have to come back and Jane would be with me. That night, I fell asleep easily, confident I would find what I needed to bring back to Jersey.

"I slept well and rose that morning to my first Dutch breakfast. Spread before me was a feast. It was a cold breakfast consisting of all kinds of thinly sliced Dutch cheeses and ham, boiled eggs, and two or three kinds of bread, including a rough, very thin dark brown one, which was very tasty with cheese."

Willem was there promptly at 9:00 a.m. to take Stewart to Esso Nederland Haus. As they came to an intersection, Stewart saw a massive dark red brick fortress of a building rising from across the park. It dominated the area, in much the way Standard Oil dominated the world petroleum marketplace. Willem explained that the Dutch called the building the Esso *kirk*, the Dutch word for church. The structure had been built by an architect who specialized in designing churches. It had big stained glass windows and a single steeple. It was not the typical pointed steeple but something like the mounded top of Notre Dame.

Inside, Stewart was a bit awed by President Smit's office. "I had never seen an office like this. It was a cavernous, high-ceilinged room with stately stained glass windows. Mr. Smit was a tall, blond, handsome man in his late fifties who strangely looked almost like Willem's brother."

Smit's genial greeting put Stewart immediately at ease. Smit had already arranged a meeting for them with the general manager of Shell Nederland in Rotterdam. Smit reiterated pretty much what Stewart had heard from the Esso advisor back in New York. Shell had not only expressed reluctance about Stewart's visit, but they also had not agreed that he could go out to NAM's office in Oldenzaal, a small town near the German border. While that certainly sounded less than positive, waiting out front was a big black Shell limousine to take the two of them to Rotterdam.

When Jan and Cees found out the American had already left and they were not to meet him until he returned from Rotterdam, they were more than a little disappointed. They were really proud of all the information they'd been able to assemble so quickly and had translated it into English for Stewart's convenience. They couldn't help but wonder when, or even if, they would have the chance to present their carefully assembled report.

As the car approached Rotterdam, Stewart wondered about the condition of the harbor. From his wartime tour of duty, he knew both its harbor and the heart of the old city had been destroyed by German bombing in May 1940. Although fifteen years had elapsed since the end of the war, he was surprised to find Rotterdam was still rebuilding. "As we came to the heart of Rotterdam on that day, I got my first look at what I have come to regard as one of the most moving war memorials in all of Europe," recalled Stewart. "In the center of the square stood a monumental and haunting metalwork commemorating the horrors of the 1940 bombing that obliterated the center of the city and forced the surrender of the Netherlands."

Stewart and Smit entered the modern Shell building, which was impressive in a different way from Esso's old and somewhat dowdy Esso kirk. They were ushered into the office of Baren Scheffer, the managing director of Shell Netherlands, who smiled distantly as Smit introduced the American.

"As I discussed with you yesterday, Mr. Scheffer," began Smit, "our Mr. Stewart would like to go out to Oldenzaal to take a look at the NAM geologic data and talk to their people—tomorrow, if at all possible, so he can report back to our New York people promptly."

Scheffer wasted no time in declaring where he stood. "So, Mr. Stewart, you think you are a gas expert. Our own gas experts from London have already studied this matter, and we've made our decision. We plan to sell some of the gas to the State Gas Board for manufacturing what we call town gas. As this is such a small market, we plan to make the main outlet for the gas our electric power plants. Your New York producing advisor was just here last month and visited Oldenzaal then for our annual budget review. We see no need for your visit to NAM."

Stewart didn't wait for Smit to respond on his behalf. "Well, sir, I don't consider myself an expert, but our advisor was not so sure as you about those markets or of the size of those reserves. Jersey's New York board sent me over here to visit with NAM and to talk to your people so I could gather a few facts. I would certainly appreciate the opportunity to go out there."

Scheffer's demeanor was courteous, but the chilly detachment dripping from his attitude made clear the presence of the two men from Esso was an interruption in his day that was keeping him from more important duties. "As I just said, gentlemen, we don't feel a trip to Oldenzaal is necessary. We're sorry you've come all this way, but do let your office know they will continue to receive our periodic reports as usual."

Without another word, Scheffer summarily punched a button on his desk, and a secretary appeared to escort the men out.

Stewart's mood was understandably discouraged. Smit was smoldering at the insult of Scheffer's rude dismissal. Smit was not only Scheffer's corporate peer, but he was also the embodiment of Esso in the Netherlands and Shell's partner in NAM. One particular comment of Smit stood out in Stewart's memory: "New York's not going to take this lightly."

Douglass Stewart landing at Schiphol in November 1960. When he returned to New York, he would not just tell Esso that they had a big problem regarding the Groningen gas discovery, but he was also going to "startle" them with a creative solution.

The Esso Haus in The Hague, nicknamed "the Esso Kirk" or church because of its design with a steeple. Many windows were also stained glass.

—Chapter 6—

Oldenzaal After All

B ack at Esso Nederland Haus, Jan and Cees were puzzled. Smit's secretary advised them that the American had gone back to his hotel and that the expected visit to Oldenzaal might not take place at all. They couldn't help but wonder if this meant all the effort the two of them had spent assembling data for their visitor had been in vain. That the trip to Oldenzaal might not happen wasn't really much of a surprise to them. Everyone in the office was well acquainted with the fact that Shell operated NAM as if Esso didn't exist.

The two men wondered just what this American from New York could get out of Shell that a friendly Dutchman couldn't. Was he a paper-oriented, theoretical fellow, or was he an engineer with hands-on field experience and technical smarts enough to squirrel something useful out of Shell? In time, Jan and Cees would come to know that Douglass Stewart had hands-on experience and also skills in engineering, economics, and negotiation that would prove very useful in his next encounter with Shell.

Stewart had entered the University of Oklahoma masters program in petroleum engineering after he returned from the war in 1945. His thesis proposed a possible secondary recovery program utilizing gas reinjection in a major new oil field located near Oklahoma City. He explored the fact that because there was little exact information and data on the field, it needed both the science and the art of interpretation, as well as foresight, to develop economic programs that could increase recovery. Stewart drew the conclusion that if a successful program could be carried out, it would more than double the profit from the existing field.

On the basis of his thesis and his top grades, he was recruited and hired for the petroleum engineering staff at Humble Oil in Texas. It was then Humble's practice to start their new engineers in the oil field gangs as common laborers, called roustabouts. It was also Humble's practice at that time to build a company camp wherever a major discovery occurred, so they had little camps all over South Texas.

Humble Oil colleague Harold Wright had his first encounter with Stewart at just such a camp. "I first met Doug when he was down in Humble's Kingsville, Texas, district. He was about a year or two ahead of me and already an engineer when I got down there. I was put on a drilling rig, just as he had been when he first got there. Like a lot of Humble's camps, Kingsville was forty miles from everywhere, in all directions, nothing but mesquite brush for miles and miles and miles. In some camps, there were no real roads, just sand pack, which was quite a trick to get a vehicle through. And the heat was a killer."

Stewart did more than complain about that heat. With his characteristic resourcefulness, he figured out something that actually hadn't been tried before.

"There was no such thing as air-conditioning in the offices on the King Ranch, but I figured out something to give mine a break," said Stewart. "Maybe it was termites or whatever, but the buildings were up on stilts, so there was a cool breeze wafting through the shade underneath. My office was at the back, so I got some very large boxes, filled them with wood shavings, and dripped water through that then set up a fan to pull that air through then opened the windows so that the cool air underneath would come back into my office. I had the coolest office in the whole building. It looked kind of weird, but nobody ever said anything to me about it because it worked."

Humble provided no individual housing for its crews. Stewart slept in the bunkhouse, ate in the dining hall of the roustabout's boardinghouse, and was assigned to digging ditches, joining pipe to wells and doing repair work. The usual gang consisted of a foreman and three roustabouts with a two-ton flatbed truck, on which was loaded a removable steel welded "doghouse" with all the tools inside, which would be unloaded at each new location. The gang then did all the oil fieldwork.

Stewart vividly recalled his experiences in that job. "There was no outlet for the natural gas. It was burned off as it flared from a freestanding pipe from the oil wells. The company used steam rigs then, which were less efficient than diesel, but the steam rigs could be run on the free natural gas, and these rigs were therefore more economical. One of our jobs was to lay the gas lines from the tank batteries to the location where the next well would be drilled. It was hard work, but we young engineers got a feel for this hands-on side of the oil business. In particular, we learned to work with and understand the guys in the field."

After working on the gang for about three months, he was transferred to the company's drilling rig roughneck gang. These wells were drilled round the clock by three shifts of five men, supervised by the "pusher" and each gang led by the "driller." The worst job, and second most dangerous, was the roustabout, who had to throw the chain around each drill pipe connection as the pipe was spun to fix the joint. The young engineers started with the midnight shift and got the first job of spinning the chain. When Stewart graduated from spinning to the derrickman position (high aloft to rack the pipe in and out of the hole), he didn't last long.

"I was relieved of my job as derrickman when I accidentally dropped a wrench ninety feet down to the derrick floor," remembered Stewart. "No one was hurt, thank God, but that may have been the reason that the next week, I was promoted, at last, to a job as junior field engineer in the field office."

One of his first tasks in that job was to learn about how gas was delivered to the homes of the workers in the company camp. "Every week I had to check the pressure regulators at the main station to ensure that the gas was being delivered at the proper pressure and to replenish the container of Calodorant, the skunk-like odorant that is added to methane. Methane has no natural odor, and this unpleasant smell is added as a safety measure so that residents will be instantly aware that they have a gas leak."

One day as Stewart poured out the stinking liquid into the plant container in his coveralls, some of it slopped down his pants leg. Because he was dealing with the stuff all day, his nose had become immune to the odor, and he didn't realize he was a walking "gas leak." After his shift, he rushed off with another young engineer to the nearest small town, which was about forty miles away, to see a movie. Shortly after they had settled into their seats, someone cried out, "Gas leak! Everyone out!" This resulted in a mass evacuation of the theater. Stewart and his friend exited the theater with the rest of the crowd without bothering to confess that the source of the "gas leak" was a certain junior engineer.

⋇

Back from Rotterdam, Stewart sat in his room at the Wittebrug Hotel preoccupied with finding a way to turn Shell's dismissal around. Going back to New York with nothing to report, except that he'd been booted out of Scheffer's office, was a scenario not on the Stewart horizon when he stepped off the plane. No matter what idea he tried out on himself, everything ended up spelling "failed assignment."

When the phone in his room rang a few hours later, Stewart half-expected more bad news, but instead, it was Smit delivering some very welcome news, with just the slightest hint of triumph in his voice. Just as Smit had declared, New York had not taken Scheffer's dismissal lightly. On Smit's return to his office, he had contacted Jersey's president, Monroe "Jack" Rathbone, to report Scheffer's haughty dismissal. Rathbone phoned Scheffer's boss, Shell's general manager, in London. Smit didn't relay to Stewart exactly what transpired in that transatlantic phone call; he simply informed Stewart, "There'll be a Shell car at your hotel tomorrow morning at nine to take you out to Oldenzaal. You'll spend the night, and they'll get you back here the following day. I'm sure you know we're all eager to see what you bring back."

Delighted at this turn of events, Stewart reflected on the day's roller-coaster shift in prospects. His thoughts kept drifting back to the city's war memorial and the way in which it spoke so eloquently of the event it had been created to memorialize. The human form of the monument might almost have been molded from the very rubble of the bombing by hands made of raw fire. The heart of the figure had been torn from its torso. In agony, its arms implored the heavens for having its heart obliterated by the savage and deliberate bombing of a defenseless city and its innocent civilians. A total of 800 people lost their lives, and more than 78,000 were left homeless on that unforgivable day. The monument still stands as an unforgettable rebuke to the inhumanity of the destruction and as a tribute to the unconquerable spirit of the Dutch people.

This vivid image of Rotterdam's wartime tragedy dropped like a stone into the pond of Stewart's memory, and ripples from it turned his mind to the destruction he'd seen firsthand in the English cities of London and Liverpool during the war.

***The Liverpool docks had been rendered nearly useless by the German parachute mines, which rained down upon the city beginning in May 1940. As an ordinance engineer, Stewart understood all too well what the bombs were created to do.

"These insidious things were designed to detonate near the surface of the water, sending out concussion waves that devastated whole city blocks nearby. The spirit of those people in the face of all this was immensely heartening to see."

Stewart and his brother Francis had been out hunting in Norman, Oklahoma, when they heard about Pearl Harbor on the car radio. Already an officer on active duty, Francis returned at once to Fort Sill.

Because of a serious bout with pneumonia, Stewart failed in his first two attempts to follow Francis into active duty. Instead, he enrolled in ordinance officer training as an engineering student at Oklahoma University, where he was prepared for responsibilities in the vast organization that developed war equipment and delivered supplies to the frontline troops. Graduating from the university as a second lieutenant, he was named "outstanding ordinance engineer" and was immediately accepted into active service. After a brief rifle training course, he was assigned to the 944th Motor Vehicle Distribution (MVD) company.

In Bristol, England, Stewart attended Bomb Reconnaissance School, where he learned how to find and dispose of mines and bombs. His brother Francis's battalion had just arrived in nearby Wales, and the two of them were able to see each other twice before Stewart was deployed. Sent first to Northern Ireland and then on to Tidworth, England, Stewart's company remained there from May to July for the vast buildup of men and material for the coming D-Day invasion.

"My job was to take a special detachment of about forty men to the docks in London each day and pick up vehicles arriving from the States," said Stewart. "At this time, London was under siege from the new German V-1 and V-2 rocket bombs. The sight of such devastation on people's homes was a sobering reminder of why we were so very far away from our own families."

About a month after D-Day, Stewart's company was ordered to the marshaling yard at Southampton to board a ship for France.

"We sailed in convoy and arrived off Omaha Beach on July 4. It was night when we anchored, and there was a full moon. The beach was a pale strip of white sand under a cliff stretching across the horizon. There were no lights. We could hear motors running and see antiaircraft fire in the distance. We clambered down the sides of the ship on ladders onto landing craft that carried us to the beach, where we camped in a nearby field. Years later, when my brother and I finally got around to talking about what had happened to us in the war, we found out we'd landed on that beach at the very same time and had been only 1,500 feet apart."

Because of a great storm, all the many Omaha Beach piers, which had been put in at such great cost in men and gear, had all been washed away. Without piers, the ships bringing in the vehicles to be unloaded had to anchor offshore. The sailors lowered the jeeps, tanks, and trucks onto what they called Rhino barges. These were actually just giant steel boxes bolted together to make a barge about the size of an Olympic swimming pool, powered to shore with two outboard motors. The barges were then rammed onto shore at high tide. The army was in action only miles away and was desperately in need of every vehicle as quickly as possible. As soon as the tide went out, Stewart and his men were able to swing into action.

"I commandeered a bulldozer and, as soon as the tide went out, started scooping the wet sand into a ramp while my team hopped onto the barge to prepare the vehicles for operation. By the time the ramp was ready, the men could drive everything right off the beach to the vehicle assembly park. The dangers of the land mines I had so recently been studying in the safety of an army base were immediately transformed into the stark reality of the mortal remains of a soldier who had just been blown apart. If any single one of us had been inclined to complacency, that was dispelled by the grim task of gathering up what remained of him into a body bag.

"I took a couple of the men and our mine detectors and swept the field. There were a number of unexploded bombs and mines, which I put in a crater and blew up. Under those circumstances, there is no time to take in the shock of the suddenness of having people you laughed with, ran with, and learned with being so very gone. That stays, festering there behind the force of having to keep going. It's as if it all goes away in the white-hot moment of what you're doing yet never lets go of what it leaves in the back of your brain."

Yesterday they had been living, breathing young men, but now they were returned from the front as a cargo of war dead, heaped onto the backs of two half-ton trucks on their way to becoming gold stars in their mother's windows.

A temporary cemetery was established near their company. Stewart went to pay his respects. "Nothing in an ordinary man's life prepares one for the first sight of death on so massive a scale. The bodies of boys who died in field hospitals were naked. Those who died in the field were still in uniform, some frozen in grotesque positions. It was rumored the Germans were using gas shells, so we were cautioned to keep our gas masks handy. One night I woke to the cry of 'Gas!' I couldn't find my mask at first. There is no way to describe that kind of gripping fear.

"By nightfall, everybody was dropping from exhaustion. Although we were never directly fired on, we spent every night in foxholes because the German planes flew over on their way to bombing missions we could hear from miles away."

The St. Lo breakthrough came on July 25. All day, the sky was full of allied planes on the way to the front near St. Lo. Stewart and his men were convoying trucks to the Cherbourg area and saw the vast armada of planes. Stewart's detail stayed on the beach until September, and he received a third commendation for their performance on the beach. His company was then ordered to form a motor pool in Paris.

※

Just as everything on that Normandy beach had been unpredictable, Stewart was now in The Hague on this morning in 1960, on his way to a new set of unpredictable events. He awoke eager to get to them. He'd packed a small bag for the overnight stay and prepared a list of questions to take with him. Downstairs, in the spacious De Wittebrug Hotel dining room, he once again marveled at the Dutch breakfast array, so unlike the American bacon and eggs he was used to.

At precisely 9:00 a.m., Stewart stepped outside to look for the Shell car. It was there all right, but it wasn't just a car. It was a big black limousine, out of which popped an elderly but very spry gray-haired gentleman wearing a tweed jacket and a decidedly sprightly attitude.

"Welcome to the Netherlands, my friend," said the older man. "I'm the coordinator for the European geological exploration ventures. I haven't been to Oldenzaal myself in over a year, so I can tell you I am as anxious as you are to learn about NAM's gas discoveries. We know Esso feels they haven't been brought up to date on the finds, and I don't wonder. Sometimes even we have to pry information from them."

Though Stewart was put at ease by the gentleman's genial greeting, he could tell the man was quite formal, and at first, Stewart found little common ground with him as a fellow businessman. Gradually, the Dutchman began to relax and related how he had served Shell in many foreign countries in pursuit of oil and had spent many years in Indonesia. When Stewart shared a little of his own background in the American oil fields, his companion began to let go of his formality.

When Stewart spoke of having crossed the Limburg province in the Southern Netherlands during the liberation in 1945, he was, for the first time, confronted with the deep gratitude so many Dutch felt for what Americans did to release Holland from five years of oppression. Stewart was to encounter this many times in the coming years. This was not always conveyed with a rush of words but rather, as in the case of the geologist, with simply a look, a moment of profound wordless acknowledgment that said what words have no power to convey.

The geologist went on to relate some of the hardships his people had experienced during the war, particularly in the period just before the British and Americans arrived. Stewart had been only dimly aware that in Indonesia, many Shell people and their families had been held prisoner by the Japanese. The geologist spoke particularly about the father of a Shell man he knew who had been imprisoned for several years and treated brutally before his release at the end of the war.

When the two men moved to the common ground they shared as scientists, the geologist opened up, telling what little he did know about the Groningen discoveries. During the several hours of the drive, Stewart was very appreciative that his new Dutch friend took the time to point out the history of interesting sites on the way. The changing types of farmhouses from area to area, the town squares, the unusual haystacks, the local customs, and the different types of mills were all so different from anything in America and, truth to tell, secretly thrilling. Stewart felt no need to hide his keen interest and appreciation.

The first town beyond The Hague was Gouda. Crossing a small canal, they came upon the town square. Before them was a small gray gothic structure called a Stadhuis (city hall). It was bedecked with red and white shutters and a lacelike facade, which seemed to have been dropped out of a fairy land. The structure had three large pointed towers and no less than six small ones. Tall round-topped windows with a band of statues ranged across its facade. An intricately designed double staircase led to the second-floor entrance.

The geologist explained that the Stadhuis dated back to the year 1450 and that there were many others just like it all across the Netherlands. Some were even larger and more ornate. Behind this Stadhuis stood a dignified yet elaborate small square two-storied building from the 1600s. It was adorned with a charming bas-relief showing the weighing of cheese. Stewart's first thought was *What a shame the lovely stone is all blackened by soot.* When he looked more closely at the building, he realized that the cheese being weighed, even back in the 1600s, was the famous round red-robed Gouda cheese known all over the world.

Stewart's companion carefully corrected his mispronunciation. "You say it this way, my American friend. It is 'Howda,' not 'Gooda.'"

Further on, they came to the ancient city of Utrecht, with its 350-foot-tall freestanding domtoren (church tower) rising through three-tiered lacelike ornately windowed steps. There was a crown on top of the tower instead of a steeple. Canals curved their way everywhere through the town and were well below street level. The canals were crossed by bridges made of handlaid brick and white stone. Bordering the canals and streets were well-kept red brick buildings, all decorated with white stone in zebra-striped layers.

Stewart mused about the way Holland's ancient, lived-in history seemed to speak of itself at every turn. "The Netherlands is so different from the States in the way it honors its history, but then they have so much more of it than we do."

Fifteen years had elapsed since war marred the pastorale of this beautiful countryside, but in several of the towns they passed through, the restoration of war's destruction was still not completed in many buildings and churches. The geologist recommended that if Stewart ever returned to the Netherlands again, he should be sure to visit the famous "Open Air Museum" near Arnhem, to where typical houses, windmills, and drawbridges from both ancient and more modern times from all over Holland had been moved and reassembled to maintain for future generations a tangible record of their past. At Arnhem, there was also a memorial to the men of the Allied forces who had lost their lives in a vain attempt to end Holland's occupation in September 1944.

The geologist's generous narrative made the hours evaporate.

At the NAM office in Oldenzaal, a large group of geologists and engineers were waiting for them. Today's all-very-friendly-and-open reception was very different from the rejection Stewart had experienced the previous day in Rotterdam. Particularly gratifying for Stewart was meeting NAM's head geologist, Dir. H. A. Stheeman, whose drilling discovery put Dutch natural gas in the headlines.

"Stheeman was obviously very proud of his company and especially of his most recent discoveries at Schlocteren and Groningen," said Stewart. "He took me into a large conference room with maps all round showing the various salt dome formations. There were probably at least ten people in there, all very open about the various discoveries they'd made. Their theory was that the gas they'd discovered so far was underneath these formations. Just according to the maps I could see, there must have been about twenty-five of them scattered out over a wide area, and they were only then drilling their third well."

Despite all the amiability, the fact that no one from Shell had made even a rough estimate of the possibilities underscored Stewart's belief that the probable reserves were much greater than anything NAM had officially given out.

"I wrangled a small map of the salt domes out of them and also obtained data on pressures, sand porosity, and other pertinent data to make my own calculations," said Stewart. "I thanked them for their many courtesies as my mind raced over the possibilities just from what I could see on that little map right there in my own hands."

The magnitude of what he saw on that map can only be described as stunning. Even on a conservative basis, the proven reserves were not just the sixty billion cubic meters the Shell engineers were talking about. This looked more like six or seven times that much. It was very late when the geological meeting concluded. Stewart and the Shell geologist from The Hague left the office and stepped into a frosty October evening. As the big Shell limousine sped them away, Stewart's head was swimming with numbers and possibilities. "Suppose there were even more salt domes than Shell itself yet knew about? Or what if all the damn things were connected? This thing might be enormous. To my knowledge, there was no gas formation anywhere near as thick and of such quality, with the possible exception of those in the Middle East."

The early estimate of something approximating ten trillion cubic feet of gas would be far eclipsed by future drilling. Stewart knew he was looking into a once-in-a-lifetime opportunity.

The limousine brought the two men to a small two-story quaint inn on the outskirts of Oldenzaal. It was late in the season, and the two men were the inn's only guests. Stewart was given a small room upstairs with only a washbasin and no bath. Downstairs was a dark but cozy dining room. He and the geologist sat in front of its welcoming fireplace to compare notes. The geologist insisted they share a traditional Ginever, a strong Dutch liquor Stewart was surprised to discover was made from potatoes.

The Shell geologist wouldn't venture even a guess as to the size of the natural gas finds but did agree that these early discoveries augured well for more reserves. Stewart chose not to venture his own excited speculations. Their conversation turned to the difference between Shell and Standard Oil.

Although Shell had about twice as many employees, Jersey made more annual profit than Shell. Stewart came right out and asked the geologist what he thought was Shell's business objective, expecting to hear of a goal similar to the 15 percent return Jersey aimed for. To his amazement, the Dutchman replied, with great sincerity, "I think the purpose of Shell Oil is to make a good living for its employees." The geologist noted that Jersey always appointed a local man as head of its foreign affiliates, while Shell, on the other hand, usually placed either a Dutch national or a British national as manager of its foreign affiliates. It was also Shell's policy to use some nationals in other executive positions for political reasons. In his opinion, Shell was therefore more politically connected in many countries than Jersey. He surmised that because Shell had two head offices, this could explain why they tended to use more people.

After a heavy dinner of venison and hare with braised potatoes and brussels sprouts, topped off with a cognac, the two said their good nights and went upstairs to their rooms. Stewart realized he'd made a blunder. Unlike an American hotel, there was no toilet in his room and no men's room to be found anywhere on the floor. There was only a door with "OO" on it, which did not open. Quite uncomfortable by now, he remembered there had been a restroom downstairs near the bar, and he stumbled down in the dark for relief. Next time, he would check the essential facilities out first.

The next day's return trip to The Hague was just as interesting as the trip the day before. All the way back, the geologist continued his narrative, pointing out more of the history of the Netherlands. The limousine stopped first at Shell's office in The Hague to drop the geologist off. As the car circled the block to head back to Stewart's hotel, he was confronted with the unexpected sight of the Dutch geologist, still smartly hatted in his natty fedora, peddling home on his bicycle.

The following morning, in the Esso offices, Stewart had his first encounter with Van den Berg and Van der Post.

"Jan and Cees, of course, were all prepared and quietly began to set out all the facts and figures they'd assembled," said Stewart. "I apologized for not being able to read Dutch and thanked them for going to the trouble of putting it in English, but I was not in a quiet state of mind. I was bustin' to tell them what I'd come away with from Oldenzaal."

The two Dutchmen recognized a charming paradox in Stewart. There was about him a kind of Savile Row urbanity, which was immediately tempered by the down-home folksiness of his disarming "Call me Doug." The reveal of his intellect and his steely grasp of economics followed as quietly and incisively today as it did then. Whatever Jan and Cees may have known about Stewart's engineering background dissipated as soon as he spread before them the map of Groningen that he'd wrangled from the NAM geologists. Their own enthusiasm was quickly ignited by what he related next.

"The possible gas reserves could be even larger if more of those salt domes are productive," explained Stewart. "I can't wait to compare these possible reserves and production with the available markets."

He went on to describe the impact study they'd need first. It would have to take into account a wide range of discovery quantities and identify what kind of markets the gas could reach and at what prices.

With the material that Cees and Jan had assembled, they could see how the potential matched up with the local Dutch energy markets for the previous year. The energy consumption sectors were divided roughly one-third each to households, industries, and power plants. Town gas was only an insignificant 1 percent of the energy sector. They found Stewart's conclusion both startling and dismaying.

"I realized right then and there that if everything that wasn't on wheels could be somehow suddenly converted to natural gas use at the current rate of energy consumption, there was already enough gas to displace all the oil and coal markets for something like twenty-five years," said Stewart.

If the gas went only to the Dutch power plants, as Shell proposed, these plants were the lowest priced market, and this was also the market where Esso was a large supplier of fuel oil. Stewart had to take a step back.

"If I stopped at that assumption, it meant I'd be going back to tell Downstream Jersey their oil markets would disappear. I was looking at one big problem."

When Stewart accepted Jan's invitation to dinner with him and his wife that evening, he had no idea the solution to that big problem would be waiting for him right there in Jan and Ciny's tidy little townhouse.

—Chapter 7—

Is That a Gas Pipe, Jan?

Jan's wife, Ciny, picked up Stewart and her husband in her brand-new yellow Volkswagen. They drove out to Wassenaar, a suburb of The Hague. In the center of town, the streets radiated away from a magnificent old windmill built in 1688.

Stewart thought the town must have grown up around the mill itself. "Wassenaar was a lovely place, quite different from the densely crowded apartments and townhouses where most of the Dutch people lived," he said. "We drove past large thatch-roofed houses standing alone among tree-lined gardens and avenues. When they explained to me that this was where the executives from Aramco (Saudi Arabian Oil Company) and other oil companies had their homes, I frankly envied them."

While Ciny was cooking dinner, Jan showed Stewart around the house, which was furnished with fashionable modern teak wood. At the end of the room was a dining table, upon which was a Persian rug of the kind one would ordinarily find on the floor. Displaying these beautiful handmade creations this way was a Dutch custom Stewart had never seen anywhere else. On top of the rug, in the center of the table, was a beautiful black pewter coffee server. Stewart immediately thought how Jane would have admired it if she'd been along.

Jan explained that there were different kinds of servers identified with different areas in the Netherlands. "That one is from the town of

Groningen, right near the very gas field that we've been talking about all day."

As they enjoyed the traditional before-dinner Ginever, Stewart noted that the living and dining area were warmed by a glowing coal stove set in the fireplace. He wondered why they didn't use gas for heating the house.

Jan explained, "Doug, it's just too expensive. The town gas first has to be manufactured from coal. It's about $2.88 in U.S. dollars. The same amount of fuel oil costs only about thirty American cents, and electricity costs as much as town gas."

At that moment, Stewart's glance lit on a round one-inch pipe with a bull plug sticking out of the floor behind the stove. He jumped and walked over to the stove. "Jan, is that a gas pipe?"

"It is," replied Jan. "Every house in the Netherlands is piped for town gas. It's been in the building code since the early 1800s, when gas was used for lighting before we had electricity. We have pipes upstairs too."

"Jan, that's it! There's the answer to the big problem. If the whole system could be interconnected, the natural gas could be piped direct from Groningen into every household in town. We've done it in the U.S. Why can't it be done here?"

Just then, their conversation was punctuated with a loud *kaboom* from the kitchen. Jan explained the sound was made by the town gas geyser that heated water every time the hot water faucet was turned on. There was no other hot water in the house unless it was heated on the gas stove.

Ciny came from the kitchen, inviting them to sit down to dinner. When Jan told her what they'd been discussing, she recognized immediately what it would mean to Dutch homemakers.

"That would mean we could have hot water right in the house, all the time, in a proper bathtub," she said excitedly. "I wouldn't have to have that dirty, sooty coal traipsed into my house every morning for that stove."

Jan smiled knowingly at Ciny. "And it would mean you wouldn't have to be shivering all alone every morning while you wait for me to get that stove fired up."

Stewart's mind immediately raced beyond that single household. "Think about this," he said. "If we could convert all the homes to natural gas at about the same price as heating oil or coal, homeowners would throw away all those stoves. They'd have clean, efficient gas heating."

The town gas in Jan's house went through ancient cast-iron pipes at low pressure. Natural gas had twice the energy equivalent at the same pressure; the lines had probably been built for a much larger capacity than the small amount now used for cooking and water heating. Stewart recognized this was a solution just waiting to be implemented.

Jan saw even larger implications. "What about all our small industries—the greenhouses and pottery plants?"

Stewart picked up Jan's idea and ran with that one too. "Jan, with gas reserves as large as we know we've got at Groningen, for the market potential we can see here in the Netherlands, just think, there's that same market next door in Germany and Belgium. Shell's idea about dumping this to power plants is small potatoes. There might be a big market out there for natural gas at the top end of the energy market. We could get three or four times the value there than we can ever get at power plants."

The next day, Stewart, Van den Berg, and Van der Post poured over the data that was readily available right there in Esso's Hague offices with the intensity of diamond cutters. Although it would take several years to convert all these cities and the individual consumers to natural gas, the proven gas reserves were more than sufficient to supply the household and small commercial consumers in the Netherlands. It was certain the reserves far exceeded what was being speculated at Groningen. The recognition of the untapped market beyond the Netherlands, in German and Belgium, kept growing in Stewart's mind. Dare they imagine even beyond?

The task of finding all they needed to know about the possible markets and about pipeline systems in the Netherlands and in the other countries loomed before them. Just where were the glass and pottery factories, the greenhouses, and the manufacturing plants, not only in the Netherlands but also in Germany and Belgium? In the answers to those questions lay a natural gas market that had never before existed.

Questions rolled out of Stewart's mind as if it were on fire. How much gas would a typical household use if it converted to gas, and assuming the price was right, what volume would be consumed in winter as compared with summer? What pipelines already existed? Who owned them? What trunk lines would be necessary? What would it all cost? What would be the impact on Jersey's general interest profits if one type of market was penetrated as compared with the other?

Jan and Cees had answers for him every step of the way, but so much else hung in the balance beyond those answers. They would have to deal with the reaction of the Dutch government, not just for the magnitude of the gas discoveries but also what these brand-new and potentially huge markets for the gas would mean to them.

If this vast new marketplace became a reality, NAM's partners, Shell and Esso, only had an "exploration license." They could not get the gas out of the ground unless the government granted them a "producing concession." The terms for that concession would have to be negotiated. Lastly, who or what entity was going to sell the gas in those new markets?

Beyond all this, Stewart recognized another and much more immediate question had to be dealt with. "I wondered how we would convince Shell that selling the gas to an industrial market was not the best solution. And how about Jersey itself? I'd have to convince our own company before any of this potential could be exploited. I was going to need more help before I reported back to the Jersey board. I was not about to go back and present problems without a solution. I wanted to bring to them the biggest startle I had ever presented."

Stewart laid out a work schedule for Jan and Cees that would keep them busy gathering the data for the next week. As he left Holland, Stewart was confident he would be asked to return and was confident that when he did, everything he needed would be there.

Back home in Connecticut, the Stewart children, especially little Jane Ann, loved the Dutch chocolates and the little wooden shoes he brought home for them. He was straightforward with his wife about the possibility for the next trip to be an extended one.

"Jane wasn't overjoyed with the idea that if Jersey was as interested in everything I'd learned as I thought they'd be, it would mean I'd have to return to the Netherlands," he said. "As always, she encouraged me to do whatever my job required, but the question was, for how long? I couldn't even speculate on that."

When Stewart showed Jane the two little ceramic Dutch houses that he'd gotten from the airline, she was fascinated with the workmanship. That one day those two little houses would grow into a very long row of them sitting on their mantelpiece was something she could not know at the time but which the future had in store for the Stewarts.

On Monday morning, the train ride into Manhattan seemed much longer than usual. Stewart was full of excitement about what he was bringing back from the Netherlands to share with Priestman and Vasquez.

But Priestman did not greet him enthusiastically. "What took you so long?" he demanded. "We thought you would be back in three days."

Stewart described for Priestman what the situation was, but even when he looked over the information Stewart put on his desk, he was not electrified. Stewart made up his mind that the next time he presented the facts, it would be in a way that would generate a much more positive response.

The producing department arranged a meeting with the heads of transportation, marketing, and economics so that all the downstream departments could become involved and be fully informed. It was agreed Stewart needed to go back and get the complete picture of what they had to deal with. Since Martin Orlean had been such a help before his first trip, he asked for, and got, permission for Martin to go along as well.

After assuring Jane he would be back as soon as possible, Stewart was once again on his way to the Netherlands. In Esso's Hague offices, Orlean, Van den Berg, Van der Post, and Stewart began digging into the data together. They compared case studies of alternate plans involving different gas prices and different market approaches, including Shell's plan for the gas to go to power plants.

At the other end of the scale, opposite Shell's idea, was Stewart's "premium market" approach in which the oil companies would sell the gas to the high-end market within the Netherlands. This meant all the households, greenhouses, and small industries would be served first.

Only then would the surplus gas be exported to all available and similar markets beyond the borders of the Netherlands.

Oil companies gave no thought to the ultimate consumer at that time. Stewart knew that had to change. "If the amount of gas at Groningen was as large as I was sure it was, there would be plenty available for export. Instead of selling to a middleman at the wellhead, we should be selling at the city and industry gate."

No pipelines existed on the scale that would be needed. Stewart knew Esso and Shell would have to build them, first from the wells to the border of the Netherlands and then beyond. Those pipelines would make the market theirs.

"We would sell the gas through our own pipelines to all those waiting cities and industries in Germany, Belgium, and France."

What would be required to obtain approval for an operation on the scale of this massive undertaking would be cost estimate documentation and projections into the future that would take into account such things as market growth and construction delays. Stewart was as sure the economics of the study they were designing would succeed in selling Jersey on his premium market approach as his recycling proposal had sold Humble.

All this data had to be cranked out by hand on mechanical calculators. The computers of the day, such as they were, filled whole rooms. In any event, none were then available in the Netherlands offices. The boldness of Stewart's proposal was exceeded only by the magnitude of the task, particularly in trying to project the costs of the necessary pipelines. In answer to Stewart's request for technical engineering experience, Jersey sent Paul Miles of the Pipeline Group to help develop those costs.

As the days and weeks ground on, the separation from Jane and their children put Stewart in an increasingly dark mood. He'd already missed Halloween for the first time. He'd been so busy he didn't even know until two days later that the young senator from Massachusetts was now the president. He even missed Thanksgiving.

Like a buzzing mosquito you hear but can't find, Stewart couldn't dispel the possibility that this study was not going to be completed in time for him to be home for his wedding anniversary on Christmas Eve or for Christmas morning with the kids. He hadn't yet written to Jane about this, yet as sure as he was thinking about it, he knew Jane would be too.

"In order to lift our spirits, Martin and I took off one weekend for Amsterdam," said Stewart. "The weather was as gray as our mood. Even when the bright lights of the city went on, nothing penetrated that funk until I happened upon a little shop, trying to find something to show Jane how much I appreciated the good sport she was being about the way my time away from home just kept stretching on. Right there on a shelf behind the counter, I spied an amazing coffee server, something like the one I'd seen at Jan's house. I bought it right there on the spot. We still have it. Finding something for Jane that she would immediately recognize as unique definitely improved my mood." With a little lighter heart, Stewart returned to the Esso kirk, where the hard work of the four men began to coalesce in a really positive way.

In Jan van den Berg's contribution to Wolf Kielich's *Subterranean Commonwealth*, he refers to Cees, Stewart, Martin, himself as "the Esso Four."

According to Profs. Aad Correlje and Geert Verbong in their study of the Dutch gas system "The Transition from Coal to Gas: Radical Change of the Dutch Gas System," "This approach represented a completely new vision on the role of gas in energy markets, pricing strategies and the relationship between public and private activities."

Not only was Stewart's premium market idea a clear plus for Jersey sales, but it also maximized advantages for the Dutch government. They would receive a far greater revenue stream from taxes and royalties if they sold the gas this way than they would ever receive if they followed Shell's plan to dump the gas to power plants. All Stewart had to do was prove it.

Just when things seemed to be going smoothly, what seemed like a huge problem came from a totally unexpected source. They were advised by a Jersey lawyer that all the gas at Groningen had already been sold to the State Gas Board. Years earlier, NAM had entered into a contract with the State Gas Board (SGB) to sell all discovered gas to them at prices far below what could be realized through Stewart's premium market approach. Stewart immediately recognized that this contract meant Shell and Esso would find themselves wiped out of their oil markets by their own discovery.

"Worse, the contract called for an even lower price if larger reserves were ever found," recalled Stewart. "There was a take or pay clause that required the State Gas Board to prepay for gas offered by NAM and, if not used by the board in any year, forced them to dump the gas at a low price. The premium value and qualities of the gas would thus be squandered in under-boiler burning, where fuel oil or coal would have sufficed. I wondered if maybe we could just buy the State Gas Board company from the government, then we'd be selling to ourselves and could tear up the darned contract."

This revelation made it much harder to find a way of entering the gas transportation and marketing of gas beyond the wellhead. Nevertheless, Stewart prodded them to complete the report to the Jersey board.

"I felt optimistic that we had a good chance to make some sort of deal. We presented our premium market plan to bring the gas to the general public in their homes at competitive prices and at the same time increase the profit from the gas to the government while improving the public environment."

The oil companies had both the motivation and the capital to provide the investment in pipelines as well as the experience and engineering capabilities to make it all happen. Stewart set aside the task of burrowing the premium market concept through the labyrinth of government channels and turned to the more immediate task of convincing Jersey. The Esso Four worked intently to complete their detailed report and recommendations for Stewart to take back to New York.

At that same moment, Shell was already busily engaged with those very government channels and still behaving as if it did not have a partner. On December 8, without advising or consulting with anyone from Esso, Shell's London chairman, John Loudon, and Lykle Schepers of Royal Dutch met for their first informal discussions about the Groningen discovery with Minister de Pous and Prime Minister J. Zilstra.

On December 9, Bob Milbrath, a Jersey marketing executive, was scheduled for a visit to Esso Nederland. Milbrath's visit would be a kind of dry run for their report and for the biggest Startle Stewart had ever presented.

"We all sat anxiously around the big boardroom table in the Esso kirk as Coen Smit and Bob Milbrath arrived," said Stewart. "When I handed Milbrath the two bound volumes we'd prepared, he was a little taken aback. He'd probably only been expecting a routine report about the possible size of the gas reserves."

Those two volumes documented the benefits to Esso and to the Dutch government of every aspect of Stewart's premium market approach. They not only set out the possible gas reserves but also proposed alternate marketing and economic possibilities, with everything supported by technical data. In addition, the team offered proposals for solutions to every problem raised.

Stewart began his presentation, his eyes on Milbrath. "Mr. Milbrath, we estimate that NAM may have found one of the largest gas fields in the world. The way that these reserves are utilized can, on the one hand, cause a disruption of the oil industry and waste the value of the resource or, on the other hand, can bring greater profits from the gas and optimize its value. NAM currently has only an exploration license and must apply to the government for a producing concession. Further, NAM has contracted to sell all of the gas it finds in the Netherlands to the government-owned State Gas Board for town gas manufacture at a low price. Shell has proposed that it sells the excess gas to power plants and heavy industry, which are also low-priced markets. We see better market opportunities here in the home heating and special light industry market. These are markets in which Jersey does not participate in the United States because there, we only sell at the wellhead. To benefit from these new markets, which we are calling the premium market, we propose that, in addition to obtaining the producing concession, Esso and Shell also participate in gas transportation and marketing beyond the wellhead.

If these gas reserves prove large enough, additional benefits and revenue possibilities could be obtained from exporting extra gas to neighboring countries at a premium price."

The team then made their formal presentation, documenting Stewart's statements. No one spoke for a moment. Stewart's eyes were still on Milbrath. He could see that Milbrath was not only "startled," but he was also enthusiastic. Milbrath proposed they go immediately to Paris because he knew that Wolfe Greeven, a Jersey director, just happened to be there. Milbrath called him right there, and Greeven agreed to a meeting in Paris the next day.

The team repeated their presentation in Paris. Director Greeven was also so startled he personally arranged for a Jersey board meeting the next week in New York.

To Stewart, all the hard work of the Esso Four had not only just paid off, but his ideas were also assured of the kind of consideration that had to happen if he was going to be allowed to follow through on them.

"I couldn't have had a better endorsement than having Greeven put that board meeting on the calendar," said Stewart. "I had achieved everything and more that I set out to do. At that moment, though, my thoughts were not about what it was going to be like when I presented the plan to the Jersey board. All I wanted to do was get out of there and go home. I'd never been away from Jane that long in our entire marriage. By the time I got on that plane, I was starting to feel like only half of me was there. All I could think of was that I'd be able to be home for our Christmas Eve anniversary and Christmas morning with the kids. Jane would already have the house full of Christmas, that I knew for sure. I spent the hours of that interminable flight back home in memory lane, remembering how Jane and I met and started our family."

Stewart had met Jane when he was working at the King Ranch. The Texas A&I University was nearby. He and another young engineer went to one of the A&I dances, in Stewart's green convertible, of course, which was always attractive to the girls. They eagerly anticipated meeting some of the coeds.

However, at this dance, it was not a coed who attracted Stewart. He was watching a tall, slender girl dancing with someone else. When that particular number was over, Stewart introduced himself to the lively, statuesque beauty and learned that her name actually was "Lively," Jane Lively. She was there to visit her two sisters, one of whom was a student, during the school's break for Washington's Birthday. Her other sister turned out to be married to a young man who was a clerk, living at the same Humble Oil camp where Stewart bunked. Always enterprising, Stewart looked that fellow up first thing the next morning and got himself invited home to dinner after work that day.

Harold Wright knew the Stewarts from the very beginning of their courtship. "It wasn't long after Jane and Doug met that there was only one girl in Doug's green convertible. First of all, Jane was just a standout person. Picture a girl who is a striking blonde and relatively tall with a good figure. Add to that her natural grace and a sense of elegance, mixed with a decided air of practicality. She'd fit in wherever she was. Doug was a leader, so was Jane."

As Stewart drove up to the house of his coworker for the dinner to which he'd wrangled an invitation, there was Jane. "She was in pigtails, blue jeans, and no shoes, dancing in the driveway with her sister," he recalled. "She accepted my invitation, and that night, we drove to a nightclub in Corpus Christi for our first date. We were the best and worst dancers on the floor because we were the only dancers on that slow Monday night.

"At that time, Jane was working in the corporate office of Braniff Airways and living in San Antonio. All summer long, we commuted the 150 miles between there and Kingsville. Jane and I got married on Christmas Eve in her church in San Antonio. Our honeymoon was in Houston, so I could attend an advance reservoir engineering school for selected engineers. This was just fine with her. In all our years together, she was always interested in everything I was doing. Just as an example, she was right beside me once when I had to go check out an oil well blaze.

The man who was crawling up to the wellhead to stop that fire with a sack full of dynamite was Red Adair. Many years later, it was Adair's company that was responsible for ending the oil well fires in Kuwait after the Gulf War. I had to call him myself once when I was assigned as Esso Eastern's coordinator for Australia, and one of our wells had blown out in the Tasmanian Gulf."

$$\mathrm{X}$$

Stewart looked out the window of the plane to see the moonlight illuminating the Newfoundland winterscape of frozen lakes and icebound fields below. The twinkling lights of the Eastern Seaboard bloomed into view.

"Somewhere down there in that winter night was Connecticut and my family," he said. "For a moment, I was overwhelmed with how long I'd been away and how very deeply I missed them.

"After the flight finally set down, the cab drive out to Connecticut seemed even longer than the flight. There had been a big snow, and the snowplows had raised waist-high mounds all along the highway. Did the snowplows get off the highways and into the towns yet? What if the cab couldn't get up the narrow road to the house?"

Just then, the cab rounded the curve, and there was Jane, snow swirling around her, shovel in hand, clearing the way.

"I got out and took that shovel out of her hand, and we dragged my suitcase into the house together, laughing with every step. I was so glad to have her back in my arms I didn't want to let go of her. The kids were already in bed, so they didn't get their little surprises until the next day. Jane did like that coffee server!"

Decades later, Stewart's admiration for his wife is undiminished. "I truly didn't know what a great person Jane was until after I married her. She was always the organizer of parties, dances, card games, and church affairs. She became a women's group leader in every town to which we ever moved. Whether I brought home executives, ambassadors, or a well digger, Jane always had just the right touch.

"After I retired from Exxon, I started my own natural gas business in Houston. As it grew in success, I was home a lot more. Jane kept our lives ever interesting by planning trips to exotic places like New Guinea and South Africa. Jane was a great partner and my best friend for the next fifty-three years."

*In December 1961, four of the Dutch gas study
team members joined an Esso party.
Back row left to right: Paul Miles, third from left, Jan van den Berg.
Front row: Douglas Stewart and Martin Orlean.*

Jan van den Berg after he became manager of gas sales of Gasunie.

—Chapter 8—

Startling Jersey and Shell

The next Wednesday, Stewart was back in the Jersey office, with John D. Rockefeller looking down from his painting as he rose from his seat at the boardroom table and presented his "startle."

"Gentlemen, in accordance with your instructions, I visited the NAM offices in the Netherlands, and after your intervention, Mr. Rathbone, they were very forthcoming. They showed me everything they knew about the geology and data from the drilling wells. From my analysis, the proven reserves are very large, probably in the order of 350 billion cubic meters or 12 trillion cubic feet of gas. In terms of oil, this is larger than the recent finds in Alaska. The gas sand is of superior quality, and in the area of the discovery wells, it is 1,000 feet thick with unusually high porosity. If the scattered wildcat finds are connected, this field could be several times larger. With the help of some of the excellent Esso people in the Netherlands and our own Martin Orlean, who will explain the economics for you, we have developed a plan to utilize this gas in a very profitable way by selling it to the household and light industry markets as a premium fuel rather than adopting Shell's plan to sell it at a low price to power plants and heavy industry.

"In order to avail ourselves of the optimum price that these new premium markets will develop, Esso should adopt a new policy regarding natural gas. We won't just sell it at the wellhead. Instead, we can participate from the wellhead all the way to the consumer. We can demonstrate to the Dutch government how natural gas, sold as a premium fuel, will greatly accelerate its revenue through the taxes and royalties they will receive. This will enable the government to improve living standards for its citizens. The natural gas will also reduce the use of coal, which soils homes and fouls the air wherever it's used. Gas surplus to the Dutch premium market can help at the same time to improve the country's trade balance by exporting the surplus gas at the premium price. Beyond Dutch borders, Esso could dominate the same untapped market of householders and light industry that exists throughout Western Europe. If we invest in pipelines and marketing efforts in those countries by selling to select industries and municipalities ourselves, Esso will be at the vanguard of a new business with a profit potential so vast it can hardly be calculated because it has never before existed on the European continent."

Orlean and Stewart then graphically presented the study findings that documented Stewart's claims:

1. Probable proven reserves are 100 billion cubic meters. Ultimate resources may exceed 350 billion cubic meters, the equivalent of 2 billion barrels of oil (a discovery about the size of Alaskan reserves).

2. At the premium price, about half the gas would be consumed in the domestic Dutch market, and half would be available for export into the same markets in nearby countries.

3. It is Shell's preference to have large industrial and power plants consume most of the gas at a low price, where it would primarily displace fuel oil. Instead, it is technically feasible to deliver the gas to the much larger market of householders and commercial consumers as a premium market fuel, primarily displacing anthracite coal.

When Chairman Rathbone asked for comment, Bill Stott was positively enthusiastic about natural gas. This new proposal would attack coal and not his fuel oil market. It would, if adopted by the board, give control of the newly proposed business to his marketing department, not the producing department, which would have put the effort in Vasquez's domain. Others who commented seemed highly in favor of the recommendations. Milbrath said that he personally would go over to The

Hague and London the first week in the new year to help convince Shell of the new approach.

Rathbone thanked Stewart and Orlean for their work and indicated that the board would be waiting for Shell's decision. Priestman wasn't too happy to lose Stewart, but he thought it might be for only another few weeks. Stewart knew better. It was going to be a long haul to convince Shell to embrace the new idea and perhaps an even greater challenge to convince the Dutch government to grant the producing concession that would make it all possible. It could turn out to be even more difficult to convince the government of the unprecedented step of allowing a powerful commercial enterprise, like the two oil giants, into the gas marketing and pipeline business in their country.

Stewart and Orlean returned to The Hague to assist Esso's Dutch president, Coen Smit, in negotiations with the Dutch government to obtain the NAM producing concession. Jersey recognized that Shell, as the operator of NAM, would lead those negotiations. It would be necessary to find a way either to buy out the State Gas Company or to form a new company with the state as a shareholder in some manner.

The question of how to make that happen was left open. Even if these Dutch goals were achieved, it was clear to Stewart that Jersey wanted to be free of Shell in selling the gas beyond the Dutch border. He knew the export countries would be another huge challenge to meet.

"A new 'startle' about export opportunities was already forming in the back of my mind. As we left the room, I looked up at John D.'s portrait, and I swear he seemed to be smiling a tiny bit," said Stewart.

Former colleague Harold Wright, who had by now moved to the New York Jersey office at Stewart's request, recalled another significant and powerful change Stewart advocated and ultimately achieved. "I was in New York during the time Doug was in Holland. In addition to getting the thing organized, and in getting the premium market concept on the table, he accomplished something even more important. He insisted on getting fuel equivalent pricing for natural gas on the table. At the time, natural gas was being sold by the oil companies in the U.S. at far less than its true commodity value compared to other fuels. Fuel equivalent pricing was a complete turnaround in the way natural gas had been priced for years. He had to overcome a huge amount of indifference and outright objection to his ideas, but I'll tell you one thing, if Doug was in a group, he wound up running it."

It was only a week until Christmas, but Jersey wasted no time. Shell was the first hurdle. One of the Jersey board members contacted Lykle Schepers, director of Shell/BPM in The Hague, and made an appointment for Stewart and Coen Smit to meet with him the first week in the coming year.

Stewart was overjoyed that he and Jane would be celebrating their anniversary together. When Jane chose to wear the Dior suit she'd worn on their honeymoon, which still fit her perfectly, Stewart responded in his old army officer's uniform, which he just managed to squeeze into.

New Year's Eve that year was especially fun for the Stewarts. They arrived home from a party with barely enough time for Stewart to scramble out of his old uniform and get a cab to the airport. He grabbed a bag, hurriedly threw things into it, only to look up and find Jane standing there in the doorway of their room, corsage still in place, calling his attention to the bag she'd already prepared for him.

On the plane, Stewart dozed a little and then woke to review notes for the Shell presentation. He knew he had to convince Shell of his plan as much as he had Esso's board. It was Shell's London office that had compiled the marketing study upon which Shell based its erroneous conclusion to sell the Dutch gas to power plants. Pointing out the flaw in Shell's position had been part of Stewart's presentation for Esso. Repeating that in the presentation to Shell would be putting a spotlight on Shell's shortsightedness in its own house. Would they become defensive, or would the audaciousness of it bend them Esso's way?

The work of converting Shell to the premium market plan began in the rambling old yellow limestone Shell/BPM building in The Hague. Smit, Stewart, Orlean, and Van den Berg were shown into the office of Lykle Schepers, one of the most influential industrialists in the Netherlands. The team made essentially the same presentation to

Schepers as they had made to the Jersey board, refuting Shell's conclusion about dumping the natural gas to power plants.

Lykle Schepers's cordial response put to rest Stewart's concerns. Schepers listened attentively and, without a moment's hesitation, made his recommendation that Stewart and his team go to London immediately, assuring them he would make the necessary appointment for them with Shell's management. This not only put the Esso team directly before the real Shell decision-makers, but they would also be there under Schepers's aegis.

On the way to London, Stewart recalled that the last time he'd been there, he had arrived on board the *Queen Mary*, which had been transformed into a troopship, and London was under attack by buzz bombs.

As the car sped them through the miles of suburbs between Heathrow and London, he was presented with a far happier view than those wartime memories. The rubble-free streets of London were now fronted by restored and newly constructed buildings. The monuments to Lord Nelson in Trafalgar Square and to Eros in Piccadilly were no longer covered over with sandbags and wooden frameworks to protect them from the nightly buzz bombs but were now gloriously open to their pigeon companions. In the face of those old memories, London's congested traffic, black taxis, and bright red phone booths were signs of welcome.

The next morning, the team was ushered into Shell's vast boardroom, where they presented their ideas and their conclusions regarding the flaw in Shell's study. A lively discussion followed with Shell's gas marketing experts. They, of course, did not want to let go of their own position, and neither did their immediate superiors, who'd assumed that position was the final answer.

Although there was some heat to this exchange, the Esso team followed Stewart's lead and did not respond defensively but simply returned again and again to the facts that Shell's people had never considered. Once Stewart and the team finished, none of the senior executives attempted to dissuade their people from justifying the idea of dumping the gas to power plants at low prices, but no one did so.

Stewart knew Schepers had been convinced of the soundness of the team's argument in The Hague, or he would never have arranged the meeting. Had he given Shell's London executives some sort of heads-up? Certainly, the Shell technical people appeared to be losing their resistance to the Esso plan.

Suddenly, the discussion came to an unexpectedly abrupt halt and most certainly on a high note as far as Stewart and the Esso team were concerned when the Shell chairman simply announced to the meeting, "Well, unless someone has a better idea than the Esso team, let's adopt their plan."

Thirty years later, in a letter to Stewart, Van den Berg recalled that announcement as a just reward for all their labor. "Of all the things we experienced, I think that was the most exciting moment for me."

The immediate issue for the team now was how to approach the Dutch government. Shell not only agreed to the Esso plan, but they also initiated the effort by contacting Prime Minister Zilstra and Minister of Economic Affairs de Pous to advise them NAM wanted to discuss a new arrangement. A meeting with de Pous was set up for mid-March.

A joint Shell/Esso task force in was formed in The Hague and given the assignments of converting the Esso team's report into the Dutch language and preparing a proposal regarding joint Esso/Shell participation in the gas business. Esso's Coen Smit and Shell Nederland's new managing director in Rotterdam, J. C. Boot, would be the primary contacts with the government.

A small question popped into Stewart's head. "I did wonder, just a little, whether the rudeness to Smit and me from Shell's previous director in Rotterdam, when we first tried to go out to Oldenzaal, had anything to do with this new face heading Shell's Rotterdam management team. But I never got around to asking."

A. H. Klosterman, a pipeline engineer, headed Shell's team. Stewart headed Esso's, which included Van den Berg, Van der Post, and Orlean. This was a familiar process for Stewart, not unlike being on detached service in the army, that is, heading up a handpicked team assembled to arrive at a specific solution.

"I knew it wouldn't be sufficient to just tell the Dutch government, 'It's been done in the U.S. You can do it here,'" said Stewart. "We needed to present solid information that would document the actual investment required to set up a city gas network in the Netherlands. We had to be able to predict real-situation price levels for both wholesale and retail consumers." Stewart's expertise in economics had been key in his presentation to Humble for the King Ranch gas recycling plant, and it had been key in his presentations on the premium market approach to Esso and Shell. He was equally certain that presenting the economics of this new idea to the Dutch government would be what would carry the day.

He advanced his idea to Van den Berg and Van der Post first. "You two are involved day to day in the energy supply here. Is there any way we can develop some sort of a model that would give us some kind of predictability for the different kind of consumers we might have? I mean, is there some town nearby where we could look at the economics of their present gas grid and somehow project what usage might be if they converted? I think we could use a projection like that as a base to extrapolate usage for 'X' number of years to come."

Cees knew where to find it. "I know the perfect town. It's but twenty minutes from Schiphol—"

Jan didn't wait for him to finish; the two of them kept finishing each other's sentences. "Hilversum!"

"Ja," said Cees, "I know him, the town gas manager. We've been selling him propane to increase his gas supply for a couple of years."

"They have got about twenty thousand householder customers and—"

Cees finished Jan's sentence for him. "Some small industries. If we prevail on him for his cost data and the plan of their pipe networks, we could get a good fix on both wholesale to the town and retail to the householders."

Just what Stewart was hoping for. "You think he'd work with us?"

No sooner said than done. Just as Cees picked up the phone, Stewart sounded a note of caution. "Can you swear him to secrecy?" Jan and Cees were taken aback by that idea, but Stewart had a sound reason for it. "This could be a political hot potato. The press could interpret our trying to assemble this information to mean that Shell and Esso are planning to take over the gas business when we haven't even been granted a producing concession. If the politicians take it that way, all the numbers in the world won't mean diddly. What we put together has to show, in the most powerful terms possible, that the government and the country can truly benefit from what we're talking about." Jan and Cees both felt their man at Hilversum was technically astute and that he was also a man of honor who would understand the need to work quietly. Cees immediately got the Hilversum manager on the phone, and the response couldn't have been better or quicker: "Ja, you come down here. We have been reading about this natural gas. When can we get some?"

Now it was Cees who sounded the note of caution. "Not so fast. There's none to be had yet. First, we study what the possibilities are before any gas can happen. We want to come to you at Hilversum first to see how we can make it work. The only thing you have to do is not talk about it until we get a picture of how to make it work for householders and small towns first. If we don't do it that way, the politicians will jump all over us. So what say you about doing it that way?"

The Hilversum manager was as good as his word. The next week, the four Esso men descended on the little city of Hilversum. In a way, its population turned out to be the perfect test case for the study because it was a city ahead of its time. For centuries, it had been a center for textiles, but by 1961, the postwar boom was already moving the city toward its present status as the media center of the nation. Even its Frank Lloyd Wright prairie-influenced town hall, situated on a large tract of land that included a lake and a fountain, was already speaking the language of the future.

Stewart was quietly impressed with the town and with the gas works manager. "He was really enthusiastic about his city being the example for the whole of the Netherlands. He kept all our work secret until we could meet with Minister de Pous so that the government could have all the data it was possible to assemble. Then the government's own experts and officials could examine it. They could determine for themselves whether or not the plan was feasible."

Once again, Stewart and the team were face-to-face with a myriad of meticulous calculations that would have to be done by hand on old-fashioned mechanical calculators. Nevertheless, with the Hilversum manager's cooperation, they were able to assemble a detailed model of how natural gas could be introduced into a typical Dutch city, along with the probable costs and price structure.

More importantly, the Hilversum study projected the ways in which demand would grow over the course of a fifteen-year period. With but a few modifications in cost and price estimates, this study has withstood the test of time. In 1988, Gasunie cited the study presented by the Esso Four as "the foundation stone of the success of the natural gas industry in the Netherlands."

Stewart's team was not only developing the Hilversum study for the Dutch government, but they were also hard at work kicking off export studies on Germany and Belgium. By mid-January, Milbrath was satisfied that plans for the export studies were ready to go. A meeting was arranged for Monday, January 23, with the board of Esso's 100 percent-owned Esso A. G., their German marketing affiliate in Hamburg.

On Friday the twentieth, in The Hague, Milbrath decided to review what Stewart and the team would present in Hamburg over an early dinner. When they decided to head out to the vacation town of Scheveningen, Stewart was delighted they weren't expected to work through the weekend.

"It was a clear day," Stewart said. "The North Sea's bone-numbing chill whipped into us as we stepped out of the taxi, but I was not going to miss the opportunity to walk out onto Scheveningen's famous seawall."

Despite the icy winds, the others joined Stewart to explore this amazing construction marvel. It was built to withstand twenty-foot tides and the force of the sea's winter gales, which, on that day, sent the seagulls soaring along the updraft. The men hadn't decided on where to have dinner, so they ducked into the nearest bar for a Ginever.

By now, Stewart's experience with Ginever had expanded. "Ginever's best drunk straight, very cold on a very cold day, of which the Netherlands provides plenty. Martin describes it as a kind of Dutch Tequila."

Since Stewart had led all the team presentations so far, Milbrath told them that on Monday, after his introductions, he would turn the meeting over to Stewart and Orlean. The men stepped outside to brave the icy winds just long enough for them to reach what Stewart recalls as Scheveningen's most famous Indonesian restaurant, the Bali. He'd never experienced anything like it.

"The walls featured authentic native paintings and puppets from Indonesia. Our senses were assailed with the pungent odors of the spices and tangy, almost oily, aroma drifting in from the kitchen. Out came exotic dish after dish: flavored rice, coconut, plain and fried, satays on skewers, peanut sauces, and fire-breathing pepper sauces, some red, some yellow, and some black, all smelling of dried fish. In fact, the worse things smelled, the better they tasted. There must have been twenty-five different dishes, accompanied by shrimp and kropok bread, all to be washed down with golden rich Dutch beer."

After dinner, the men moved to the smoking room to enjoy cigars, cognac, and coffee.

"Good thing I had the rest of the weekend to rest up and to get the smell of the restaurant out of my coat," said Stewart. "Fortunately, it was only Friday, and we had the weekend off to explore The Hague's historic surroundings."

Stewart eagerly anticipated Monday morning's meeting but had not a clue about what the team's reception would be. "This was a Jersey affiliate, and if the mother company wanted something, they could jump. But on the other hand, an affiliate could also drag its feet and just make themselves look busy."

In this case, the mother company wouldn't be asking the affiliate to embark on a tried and true opportunity. It was instead being given an invitation to step off into uncharted territory for a product that didn't as yet even have pipelines through which it could be transported. What the team did know about Esso A. G. was that they had responded quickly when Jersey decided to put them into fuel oil sales after the war, and they had quickly become very successful at it.

Unless Hamburg could be convinced to initiate these studies, everything Stewart believed could be accomplished would remain conjecture. Fortunately, the key to convincing them was already on the scene. His name was Hans Löblich, the head of their energy sales department. He and his family were looking forward to their long-planned skiing weekend in Bavaria. The visitors from The Hague were about to spoil that.

—Chapter 9—

A New Player for the Team

Hans Löblich was a tall, blond intellectual with eclectic tastes in his early forties. He had a steely and mathematical turn of mind with an unerring ability to deflate the pretentious or pompous. He also had an unexpectedly quirky sense of humor, combined with an uncanny ability to artfully translate complexity into readily understandable terms without losing the true character of the original.

At just about the same time the Esso Hague team had decided to prepare for Monday's meeting over dinner in Scheveningen, Löblich was reviewing a letter he'd dictated earlier to a steel mill in the Ruhr. He was proposing a new process in their operation that could increase the efficiency of the blast furnaces and coincidentally replace coal with Esso fuel oil. His recent workload had been heavy, and he had been away from home far more than he liked. He was looking forward to leaving his office early that day as a way of making up to his family for those long hours. When he left home that morning, his wife, Gisela, and their teenage girls, Gabi and Monika, were full of enthusiasm, chattering about what they were going to pack for their upcoming skiing trip. Just as Hans was setting his signature to the letter, his secretary stepped into the office. Eager to leave, Hans handed her the letter, pushing back in his chair to do so, only to be interrupted by her apologetic but firm voice. "I'm so sorry, sir, but Herr Kratzmuller needs you in his office right away."

Dreading a delay, Löblich headed downstairs.

Kratzmuller was a no-nonsense type person, and with only a preliminary nod, he unwittingly pronounced the end of the Löblich family's ski trip. "Löblich, we have an important group from Jersey arriving Monday from the Netherlands. They want to meet with us to discuss a large find of natural gas there and whether there are markets for that gas in Germany. We need to have as much information for them as soon as possible on the coal gas industry here and on any natural gas production in Germany. I want this office to be seen as completely knowledgeable about all of it when they arrive.

"You must be prepared to answer whatever they ask. I hope you didn't have plans for the weekend, but this is an emergency."

Löblich's courteous reply bore not a hint of disappointment. "Nothing I can't put off."

Hans grimly returned to his office to call Gisela with the bad news, hoping she would soften the girls' disappointment by reminding them that at this time of the year, the snow really could last a few more weeks. The past few days of unexpected and unseasonable rising temperatures did nothing to encourage his own hopes on that score. It was going to be a very long weekend.

On Monday morning, The Hague team drove to Schiphol airfield to catch a small Lufthansa plane to Hamburg. A dense fog hovered at ground level, and Stewart was apprehensive of the weather. When the fog lifted slightly, the little plane taxied down the runway. From the air, he could still see nothing of the ground, even when the descent for Hamburg began.

"The sight of tall smokestacks sticking above the fog prompted a prayer that this pilot knew where the runway was," said Stewart. "There was no ground to be seen until we were only feet above its darkened, damp surface."

January had painted Hamburg's entire landscape in muffled tones of gray. From the Esso A. G. limousine, the drive along the Alster River revealed few remaining scars of the Allies's fire bombing that destroyed 50 percent of Hamburg's residential areas and 40 percent of its industrial region and laid 80 percent of its harbor facilities to ruin. Instead of devastation, Stewart was confronted with the resourcefulness with which the city had restored itself to prosperity. "Our hotel, the Vier Yartsizen (Four Seasons), was part of this energetic and attractive rebuilding and restoration," he said. "All of the nearby buildings were soot-smudged white or gray stone with little shops fronting the sidewalks. Busy people were hurrying to work, but there was little traffic, for there were few automobiles then."

Stewart stepped out of the limo into the unmistakable penetrating odor of burning coke, which prompted him to wonder if Hamburg had ever experienced anything akin to London's coal-based killer smogs of the early '50s. (He later determined this had not been the case in Germany because the dominant fuel there was coke, not coal, as had been the case in England.) During his recent visit to London, his attention had been captured by a news story recounting the grave effects of that deadly smog. He had later turned up substantive data about the effect coal had on cities in which it was the prevalent household and industry fuel.

"The debate about whether or not coal smoke affected human health ended the winter of 1952–53 in London," said Stewart. "On December 8, cool air from across the English Channel settled over the Thames Valley and did not move. Within a week, 3,000 more deaths than usual had occurred. The medical essayist David Bates, then a young physician with experience in wartime medicine, recalled in a *Frontline* report by Devra Davis on PBS that officials could not imagine that the environment could produce more civilian casualties in London than any single incident of the war. In sheer scale, this disaster could not be ignored. In one week, 4,703 people died, compared with 1,852 the same week of the previous year. Bates recounted the reluctance of officials to accept that so many people had suddenly dropped dead merely from breathing dirty air, noting that 'the public realized this earlier than the government of the day.'"

"One Member of Parliament put this episode into context when he asked Harold Macmillan, then Minister of Housing, 'Does the Minister not appreciate that last month, in Greater London alone, there were literally more people choked to death by air pollution than were killed on the roads in the whole country in 1952?"[4]

Armed with that background, in subsequent presentations, Stewart began pointing out the way natural gas eliminated even the possibility of such a disaster. Stewart was certain marketing efforts should include this information in materials designed to explain the benefits of natural gas to the average householder. He was equally convinced the information was of such importance it should be included in the presentation to the Dutch government. Looking at the Hamburg skyline, Stewart said to himself, "These folks need us and our gas."

That morning, Hans Löblich walked into Esso A. G. earlier than usual and with everything at his fingertips for the meeting with these Jersey men from America. This was in no small measure because he had had the unequivocal support of his family over the weekend despite their disappointment over the delayed ski trip.

That Monday morning meeting proved to be memorable both for the level of those present and for the depth of the Esso team's presentation. The A. G. people attending were Löblich; the deputy chairman, Dr. Theel; and Dir. Kratzmuller. Dr. Geyer, Esso A. G.'s managing director, chaired the meeting and introduced the visitors.

Representing Jersey management were Stewart; Paul Temple, a lawyer from the New York producing department; Martin Orlean; and Bob Milbrath.

Milbrath began the meeting. "As you may have heard, our 50 percent-owned affiliate NAM, operated by Shell, has made a large discovery of natural gas in the Netherlands. Jersey feels the discovery of this large gas field is going to be of great significance, from both a production profit standpoint and for its future impact on marketing. The Shell board in London just approved our team's basic ideas for marketing the gas in Holland. Our Jersey team is already at work assisting Shell's Dutch affiliate team in negotiating with the Dutch government to obtain the producing concession for the end use of the natural gas."

---

4   Frontline: History Today, December 2002, by Devra Davis.

With that, Milbrath introduced Stewart as the Jersey team project manager. Stewart repeated the presentation he'd made in London and New York, but this time he included a little history of the discovery itself. He also explained his premium market value concept and Jersey's desire to participate in gas transportation and marketing. "Although it is presently unclear how the export gas will be sold, we are already proceeding with our own studies to determine that. As far as we know, Shell is unaware of our intention, and they are not yet looking to export markets. Their plan to dispose of the gas by selling it to power plants at a low price, in competition with fuel oil, is shortsighted in the extreme. We at Esso can determine where the gas distribution companies are in Germany. What are their rights? What are the prices and size of the potential premium energy markets that can be penetrated by natural gas? Let us be the ones to find out if Esso can lay its own pipelines. At this moment, I cannot say whether Esso can market its share independently from Shell or NAM. For the present, that is our hope, and we will proceed as if that is possible. Jersey made a mistake in not getting into the distribution of natural gas in the U.S. We do not have to repeat that mistake in Europe."

Löblich recalled how impressed he was that Stewart already knew natural gas was being produced in North Germany. The questions Stewart asked about the area were right on the money. What Löblich found particularly surprising was that Stewart made such forthright declarations about Esso's marketing independence.

"If it is economically feasible, Esso fully intends to participate in the pipeline transportation and sale of natural gas here in Germany," Stewart continued. "We want to set up a marketing study group here in cooperation with your office, but I cannot stress too strongly the need to keep our exporting intentions completely secret, even from other Esso departments, in order not to arouse the coal gas distributors. We don't want interference from any source during our negotiations. Even though we are in joint negotiations with Shell for the producing concession, we are not informing them of our export hopes."

Even more surprising to everyone was Stewart's caution regarding the coal gas industry. Until those involved in the study had all the answers, they were to speak to people in that industry only as if Esso were discussing the possibility of supplying naphtha (LPG) or liquid natural gas imported from Africa.

"We must not telegraph to anyone what we are hoping to accomplish here until we have the facts and know just what we can really do," warned Stewart.

Milbrath thanked Stewart for his comprehensive presentation and turned the meeting over to Herr Kratzmuller, who introduced Löblich. No one at the meeting had any idea of the labor Löblich had expended over the weekend to address the group, but the range and depth of his presentation evoked Stewart's admiration. Löblich's summary of the German gas business provided answers and apt references to the questions Stewart had just posed. It also amplified everyone's image of what they would have to deal with if they were to be successful in exporting the Dutch gas.

All the main players in Germany distributed the low-BTU town gas generated from blast furnaces, cokeries, or small-town plants, especially those manufacturing gas from coke for town distribution. Germany's main gas distributor was Ruhrgas, which was then owned by various steel and coal interests.

Löblich pointed out several difficulties the company was facing. He noted, in particular, the efforts of Ruhrgas. "Ruhrgas is aggressively trying to expand their gas territory and sales. They are presently in conflict with smaller distributors in the south of Germany." In the Dusseldorf area, the most prominent distributor was Thyssengas, which was then owned by Baron Heinrich Thyssen-Bornemisca of Germany's famed industrial family. Others included Saarferngas and Gas Union in Bavaria, along with smaller local gas distributors like Weser Ems and a few others, such as one in Hamburg itself.

Löblich continued. "We already have some contacts with gas distributors through sales of LPG. There is an already sizable central heating market in some German cities that are presently fueled by coke and heating oil. There will certainly be much larger premium markets here in Germany than in the Netherlands."

Stewart was especially delighted at the recognition of his premium market plan. He had anticipated the group would respond positively, but instead, Dr. Geyer, Esso A. G.'s general manager, interrupted Löblich with a decidedly negative tone, speaking directly to the Jersey group. "We should also tell our American friends that all the entities Herr Löblich has cited are deeply entrenched in our society. The large steel and coal companies that own them have been here for over a hundred years. They have great political influence. They won't hesitate to engage to protect their interests. In my judgment, Mr. Stewart, you will have difficulty in getting beyond the Dutch border. But if you have wishes for us to study the possibilities anyway, we will cooperate. We have great confidence in our Herr Löblich. He pioneered our entry into the fuel oil business. It is he who will work with your team."For Stewart, the choice of Löblich to head the new study team was the most significant development to come out of that meeting. "Hans had a unique ability to synthesize vast amounts of data without the benefit of modern high-speed computers. Because of his broad marketing experience within Germany and his many connections, he played a key role in the development of our export program. Hans was simply the right man in the right place. He had at his fingertips, or within his working purview, the ability to ferret out just the facts we needed to validate our ideas in this new business of exporting and marketing natural gas in Germany."

On their way back from Hamburg, the group mulled over what they had accomplished in their meeting.

Milbrath felt good about the reaction of the German board to the presentation, but he had been affected by Dr. Geyer's caution. "You guys did a great job, Doug. There's no doubt their board grasps the potential for what could happen here with natural gas. But I think Jerry Geyer knows what he's talking about on the coal and steel people and their political clout. I think opposition will be fierce. I wouldn't be surprised if it even got ugly, Doug."

Stewart had a much more positive point of view. "Bob, before that even gets a chance to come to the surface, the studies their board authorized today will help us find ways to overcome whatever obstacles the gas distributors throw at us. If there's a weakness in their dike, we'll find it. We've got the money and the know-how to do it."

Orlean's skeptical nature did not easily succumb to Stewart's ever-present optimism. "What about their guy, Doug? This Löblich seems pretty quiet. You really think he's got the stuff to turn out what we need fast enough?"

Stewart's response was decisive. "Martin, as soon as I zeroed in on what particular markets we needed, Löblich came right back with an estimate on the size they might be. It's obvious he knew we'd ask that question. He'd done his homework. Didn't you see his reaction when Geyer raised his doubts about the old guard? I could see the man's mind turn over from across the room. He's ahead of Geyer already. When we put in front of those guys the kind of profits our study will reveal, it'll drown out any objections they can dream up."

Orlean wasn't giving in. "You're so cocksure of every damn thing, Doug. Tell us what happens if Shell finds out about these studies before the concession is secure."

Stewart retorted, "Slow down, Martin. Shell can't go after that concession without us at their side. They're not going to blow that just because we're ahead with some marketing possibilities."

Milbrath took another tack. "We already know the German gas distributors are not thinking of householders as a primary market. A bigger concern may be that the coal industry and these cokerie plants making coal gas are not going to just step aside. There may be some effort to cast a cloud of doubt, maybe even outright suspicion, in the minds of the hausfraus about the safety of natural gas."

Although the international environmental movement would not be launched for another decade, Stewart was already ahead of that curve. "If they pull out that tactic, it can be thrown right back in their faces. Smoke from coal-based fires mixed with fog turned into a killer smog in England twice in just the past ten years. I heard about it when I was in England last month. There's a ton of stuff archived about it."

When Orlean said he vaguely remembered something about it in the news, Stewart sharply pointed out, "It may have been only a news story in the States, but it was for damn sure more than that here. If these old coal boys even try to create false doubt about natural gas, our reminder to European housewives and mothers of what coal fire smog did to children and old people just across the English Channel will create a backlash coal can't begin to answer."

Milbrath wondered how that argument would apply to the industrial market. Stewart had an answer. "Shell has already declared that industry is where they think the gas should go in the Netherlands. If they even want to get into export, that's the market they'll go after too. So, Bob, my argument works there too. How many English factories with coal-fired boilers had to shut down during those killer smogs?"

Orlean's skepticism had not dissipated. "Doug, you can't honestly think we can sell this on the basis of cleaning up the air instead of on financial savings?"

Milbrath had had enough discourse. "Forget that stuff. We've got a bigger problem than dreaming up marketing scenarios. Shell has never taken Esso seriously in this fifty-fifty deal. They're running the show in Holland as if we don't exist."

Stewart countered, "Bob, it's only Dutch territory up to the border."

"And?"

"That gas isn't going anywhere without pipelines, and if they're Esso pipelines, we buy it all at the border, and the whole rest of Europe's our baby."

Orlean couldn't buy it. "Doug, you can't really think Jersey's board is gonna bite the size of that pipeline bullet on their own?"

Stewart did. "We show that board we can lock up the major gas companies and distributors with exclusive contracts. We've locked up the whole damn market. So Shell controls Holland. We'll be so far ahead of them beyond that border. Esso will see the kind of profit we're talking about justifies that pipeline bullet. Who can't see that?"

Milbrath's own pragmatism interrupted this time. "Doug, it's not conceivable anyone can make all those contacts and get the kind of commitments you're talking about without a word leaking to Shell."

Stewart had a clear strategy in mind. "Okay, Bob, maybe not indefinitely, but if each company we approach thinks they're the only one getting the gas, they'll keep quiet, especially when we hint they'll be getting it in Esso pipelines."

Milbrath concurred. "When Shell sees we've got the customers, they'll be on that export bandwagon in a New York minute."

Orlean's concern continued. "Doug, we don't have a producing concession, we don't have pipelines, we do not have one single German company on the line. What customers are we talking about?"

Stewart could not resist. "How about Belgium? It's right next door." Stewart wasn't just joshing with Orlean. He was dead certain about what needed to be done. "I have not a shred of doubt about where to go with this. The plan would increase the benefits for all concerned."

Stewart says he was "so damn sure I knew how to make it work, that I sometimes got a little testy with those who didn't share my enthusiasm," but he also recognized his certainty about customers beyond the borders of Holland was only conjecture unless the team succeeded in convincing the Dutch government that the highest and best use of their newfound natural gas would come through exporting what was not needed for domestic use. Their presentation to the government needed to bring it to the realization that achieving the best price for their gas in export would result in revenue so vast the government would be able to benefit its people to a degree never before imagined.

Even if Stewart and the team were able to convince Esso that the size of the market warranted the massive investment in the pipelines required, and even if the two giants came to an agreement to cooperate in marketing the gas beyond the borders of the Netherlands, the government had the power to elect to do everything themselves. The fact remained that Esso and Shell couldn't even take the gas out of the ground until the government made its decision.

Holland was still living within the constraints of recovering physically, economically, and psychologically from all that had befallen it during World War II. The Golden Age that once defined the country was but a memory. Its future, and the promise of a new Golden Age, was on the horizon of the many decisions that would come before its government. For the two companies, and for Stewart and his team, all issues paled beside two very vivid questions for which none of them could command an answer. To what entity, and when, would the Dutch government grant the producing concession?

—Chapter 10—

Government Matters

T he seventeenth-century "Golden Age" of the Netherlands refers to the most prosperous era in its history. Successive waves of foreign domination altered its social and economic circumstances, measuring the ebb and flow of the country's economic decline in succeeding centuries. The discovery of the vast natural gas field at Groningen heralded the possibility of a new Golden Age of prosperity, dignity, and recognition.

This fresh economic flowering was set in motion under the sage guidance of J. W. de Pous and the members of the government committees he appointed. In his role as Minister for Economic Affairs, the significance of this man and his leadership must not be underestimated. Prof. Arne Kaijser describes de Pous's level of influence in the introduction to his selection of *The Governance of Large Technical Systems*, created for Routledge Studies in Business Organizations and Networks, edited by Oliver Coutard:

> *As the Minister for Economic Affairs, de Pous had considerable power. His general responsibilities covered industrial and energy policy. He had strong influence over the Dutch State Mines . . . his trump card in the negotiation process was that, in accordance with Dutch mining law, he was responsible for granting the production concession for natural gas that NAM wanted to secure. He realized at an*

early stage that the Groningen gas matter was the biggest issue his ministry had ever handled. He chose to involve only a handful of staff members at the ministry, to minimize the risk of important information leaking out. His closest collaborator in the gas matter was L. G. Wansink, who was responsible for daily contact with the other players throughout the negotiations.

Wansink's importance in the government's negotiations with oil company representatives was highlighted in Professor Kaijser's article "From Slochteren to Wassenaar: the Creation of a Natural Gas Regime in the Netherlands, 1960–1963."

Looking back, Stewart recognized that everyone, including himself, was overly optimistic about the timing and progress of negotiations with the government. "We not only were incredibly optimistic. We were also naive and cheeky to think that we (Esso and Shell) could quickly arrive at a deal with the government. This was a program that would affect the lives of every Dutch citizen. There were two and a half million households that had to be converted, thousands of small businesses, industries, town gas grids, and hundreds of million of Dutch guilders would have to be invested in pipelines and gas wells. The great care and intense deliberation with which de Pous and the government committees entered into the decisions cannot be overestimated."

The most profound task before the Shell/Esso work group was the creation of a presentation for the government that had to be rendered with sufficient clarity and substance that it would convince de Pous and his committee that their proposal truly served the people's greatest good. Stewart was certain the government would respond positively to the Hilversum study. The team's presentation had to make an unequivocal demonstration to the government of the immense value that the combined technological expertise, experience, and capital of Shell and Esso could bring to the project. He also urged the team to give priority in the report to the ways the premium market concept optimized the value of the natural gas in the marketplace.

In the midst of the team's discussions about the different means of presenting their case, the most compelling point came from Jan van den Berg. He believed passionately that presenting the very personal and powerful needs of the ordinary Dutch household was of paramount importance. Jan was adamant in his conviction that this would most powerfully illustrate for the government, as nothing else could, how the very future of the country and its citizens could be changed for the better.

"There's no question the economics are powerful, but we also need to get the government to be thinking what it's going to mean to everyday people to have this natural gas in their houses," said Jan. "We should make the government think of how ordinary people will be able to regulate the temperature in different rooms, how they'll be able to have, at long last, central heating instead of stoves in different rooms. Those heating units are inexpensive, so our people will save on building costs and oil tanks, not to mention the clutter and soil of coal. You've been living in America like that all your life, Doug. You can't even imagine how it is for us here."

Jan was right. Life was very different for the average Dutch household before the arrival of natural gas. According to Josina Droppert of Leiden, "We had a wooden storage shed at the back of the house where we kept the black coal. Every year, before winter, we bought as much coal as we needed to get through the winter. It was delivered in cloth sacks, carried on the shoulders of the deliverymen.

"We had one stove for the whole house, which was situated in the back room. That room could be shut off from the front room by sliding doors. When it became very cold, that was the only room we lived in. Upstairs were the bedrooms, without any heating at all. Frost was always on the windows, and as children, we undressed downstairs when it was very cold.

"The stove was always burning, day and night, although at night, the heat was turned down. That required skill because I remember that sometimes the fire went out at night, and then my mother was frantic.

"A friend of the family made a steel pipe with little holes in it at the flat end, and a hose was attached to the other end from the gas stove upon which we cooked. You opened the gas and lit the flat end so you had quite biggish flames. The flat end was then put in the stove. Of course, before that, the stove had to be emptied of old ashes and filled with new coal, a very dirty job.

"You could not touch the stove when it was really burning, but as a little child, I did not believe the warnings, so my parents let me burn my finger!

"When most households switched from coal to natural gas, we were not the first to have it because we did not have much money."

Jan van den Berg's eloquence and sense of urgency illuminated the issues before the team in a very particular way, convincing everyone these benefits should have a prominent place in the presentation.

Jan also pointed out something that, years later, proved to have been enormously prophetic. "In the western part of our country, it's not only the coal stoves in houses that produce lots of soot but the fuel oil in the greenhouses—maybe more so. If they were instead powered by natural gas, it would be a boon to the agricultural industry. If more greenhouses are built, our people will have better food all year round."

At that time, every adult in the country had vivid memories of the war and particularly the deprivations of the winter of hunger, in which thirty thousand Dutch citizens lost their lives. The use of gas in greenhouses would improve the quality and availability of homegrown produce and would be powerful factors in the team's presentation.

In Exxon-Mobil's spring 2002 publication *The Lamp*, writer Shelley Moore reported, "Over the years, the gas revolution stimulated new industries. The area between Rotterdam and The Hague, for example, is known as the 'glass city' for its landscape of gas-heated greenhouses. These facilities have made the Netherlands a major exporter of tomatoes, cucumbers and other produce that normally flourish only in warmer regions of the world."

Stewart credited Van den Berg's ideas as significant factors in the government's ultimate acceptance of the team's presentation. "Because of Jan's awareness of, and concern for, the daily lives of his fellow countrymen, our next presentation to the government underscored in a profound way the life-changing societal and personal benefits of bringing the natural gas first to the homes of the Dutch people and then to light industries such as greenhouses."

That presentation to the government also proposed that NAM should be the entity to which the producing concession be granted, and NAM would develop the producing facilities. In addition, the presentation proposed that NAM would sell the gas to a 100 percent-owned Shell/Esso distribution system. This system would deliver and transport the gas throughout the Netherlands, selling it to the Dutch householders and to industries and municipalities as well. Although the proposal specified that NAM would also export the gas, the process for exportation was not spelled out.

Once the now combined Esso/Shell team, consisting of Stewart, Van den Berg, Van der Post, and Martin Orlean from Esso and Shell's A. H. Klosterman and his colleagues, had completed the presentation in English, Shell prepared the Dutch translation. By mid-March, the presentation was ready. To Stewart's surprise, Minister de Pous accepted their invitation to come to their presentation in Esso's Nederland Haus instead of a government building.

Because of Shell's long-standing significance in the Netherlands, Shell's J. G. C. Boot was the primary spokesperson. Esso's Coen Smit was at his side. Stewart led the presentation, making the primary case to de Pous and the other government representatives. Klosterman, Orlean, and Van den Berg followed with individual contributions.

Minister de Pous reacted favorably to the premium plan, which directed the Groningen gas to both householders and commercial consumers; but at the same time, he expressed considerable concern about the oil companies being the sole distributors of his country's natural resources. He pointed out that the State Gas Board, State Mines at Limburg, and other small municipal groups were already distributing low calorie gas and noted that he had no desire to cut them out of the process.

The minister also had his own concerns about what it was going to mean to have two international companies joining what had heretofore been a state-owned monopoly. Minister Pous played his cards very carefully, placing particular emphasis on a role for State Mines. This group was 100 percent state-owned but nevertheless acted primarily as a well-run commercial enterprise, relatively independent of the government. He felt State Mines was best qualified in size and expertise to review the team's proposal.

It was also de Pous's conviction that State Mines would balance, in a very important way, what Shell and Esso brought to the table. When Minister de Pous suggested that Shell and Esso meet with State Mines, it was abundantly clear that it was going to be State Mines that would make the recommendation as to how things would proceed.

Stewart knew this was not a suggestion; it was an imperative.

After de Pous and his group departed, it was time for everyone to loosen their ties, take off their suit coats, and sort out what had happened. Stewart was particularly encouraged by the minister's reaction. What most interested him was what did *not* happen. "They could have said, 'We'll do it ourselves,' but they didn't."

Stewart and the team regarded that restraint as a small stamp of acceptance for their carefully constructed presentation. They also recognized it was not going to be just State Mines coming to the table at the next meeting; it was the government itself. With just a month to discover how to traverse this new and potentially tricky terrain of blending commerce and government, Shell and Esso decided the best course of action was to revise the proposal. Since NAM was a production company, not a marketing company, it made the most sense to create a new company focused solely on marketing.

As de Pous felt State Mines should play a role, the new company would therefore be one-third Esso, one-third Shell, and one-third State Mines. There were additional financial and tax reasons this made sense as well. Because the government already had a 10 percent royalty, plus income taxes, on production profits, which they would levy against NAM, the oil companies chose not to offer State Mines a share of the production revenue.

For Stewart and Orlean, the month evaporated quickly. They were shuttling back and forth between The Hague, working with Van den Berg and Van der Post, preparing for the Dutch State Mines meeting, and visiting Hamburg to assist Löblich's team with the German studies.

Although there was no assurance of the producing concession or the possibility of exporting the gas, Löblich and the Hamburg team were intently constructing the case for natural gas for the German market. He was doing everything he could to keep his work as secret as possible, even from most of the Esso people.

Now transferred from his job as head of energy sales at Esso A. G., Löblich moved to a private office in a villa near the Four Seasons Hotel on the Alster River. Löblich recalled they had experts from the parent companies providing technical knowledge about the problems of gas distribution and transportation that they were still missing. They had no contact with the outside and worked very secretively. Löblich's detail-oriented mind fueled their search for answers.

"Knowing how attractive the sales for this practically sulfur-free fuel would be to the premium market Stewart had described, we immediately set out to identify just where the sales markets were, what size they would be, and what the price should look like," said Löblich. "I was in charge for those first ideas, but they soon began to grow.

"We had information coming in to us from several of our other departments." To assist in his work, Löblich had been assigned an assistant, Dr. Dobmeier, and a secretary. He had access to Esso's Dr. Elfert in Esso A. G.'s department of national economy and to Herr Jani in the department of market research. Through Jerry Laufs, an American on loan to the project from Jersey marketing in New York, Löblich had access to everything all the departments in New York had to offer.

Löblich described the magnitude of the team's complex task. "After I assumed this responsibility, one of the first things Doug asked us for was a preliminary study on the potential of gas sales as to regional future volumes and prices. Since there was no real natural gas business in Germany in those days, determining these possibilities became the great challenge for me. Only one week after Doug's briefing, Martin Orlean came to Hamburg to work with us."

In summary, their job was to find out the possible sales potential for natural gas for the entire country as well as for the regional possibilities in every town and district. They also needed the different possible prices for single areas of usage and the costs for transportation and distribution of the natural gas.

Löblich's group also made contacts with Ruhrgas and Thyssengas, just as Stewart had suggested, but always under the guise of selling them split naphtha and refinery gas and the possible availability of frozen liquefied gas from Esso's plant in Libya.

Through those discussions, Löblich was able to discern a high level of interest. "While these companies were very anxious to get natural gas, they had no idea of the potential Esso was already sure would be available. Stewart and Orlean were frequently with us throughout the whole of the effort, helping and guiding and making new suggestions."

While their countries were once military adversaries, over the course of their many encounters developing these studies, Stewart and Löblich shared not only their work but also their firsthand experience of war and its aftermath. Löblich was a graduate engineer who learned oil fueling in the '30s as a young midshipman in the German navy. He and his wife, Gisela, were married during the war, when he was a young naval officer. He ultimately rose to the level of engineering officer on the battleship Bl*ü*cher.

As the ship entered a Norwegian fjord, the Norwegians fired three torpedoes from shore, which sank the ship with direct hits on two of its three boiler rooms. Löblich, luckily, happened to be in the third boiler room and was rescued. Those very torpedoes had been installed for Norway by his own country in 1906, long before World War I. That they were still in sufficient working order to be employed to bring down an invader was a testament to his country's engineering excellence. This was an irony upon which Löblich was to reflect more than a few times in subsequent years.

After Löblich's escape from the sinking ship, he returned to active duty as an executive officer on a destroyer. For a very long time, Gisela did not know what the fate of her husband was. And Löblich had to live with the terrible fear of not knowing her fate when the news came to him of air strikes against cities across Germany. Particularly frightening to him was the news of the firebombing and destruction of their home city of Hamburg with such a colossal loss of civilian lives.

When hostilities concluded, Löblich was briefly a British prisoner of war. He was assigned, and courageously carried out, the dangerous task of postwar minesweeping cleanup so that harbors would once again be free for commercial and peacetime recreational traffic. His final responsibility was turning his ship over to the Russians, and then he returned to civilian life to help rebuild the economy of his country.

Over the years of the Dutch gas project, Stewart, Löblich, and their wives developed an enduring friendship that became transcontinental and had endured for all these decades. In 1999, Löblich and Gisela made a surprise visit to the Stewarts" fiftieth wedding anniversary, at which he extended the appreciation of the German people for all Stewart had done during the years of the Dutch gas project.

"About thirty-five years ago, Doug was on his way from New York to The Hague," said Löblich in his speech. "There was a big problem because the Dutch had all this natural gas in the ground. In 1963, there was no natural gas in Germany. With Doug, we started a study, but we had no idea how to sell natural gas. Doug and Martin Orlean came and helped us with that and also helped to convince the very big cokery gas people to give that business up and to convert to natural gas. Doug Stewart and his partner pushed us. Every time they came, they had new ideas. We were successful in Germany because of that steady pushing. Thirty-five years later, natural gas is 32 percent of the energy in Germany. We are enjoying this natural gas in Germany, and we thank you for this. We wish you and Jane all that is good in the next decade and that you are in good health and enjoying your family."

In 1960, all that lay in the future. Orlean and Stewart worked closely with the German team, passing on to them any useful information that was developed by the team in The Hague.

Orlean was particularly impressed with Löblich's efficiency. "Almost everything that was said in every meeting was taken down. Hans was fantastic when it came to documenting and filing things. He used to scare me. He was so efficient. Not like me or Doug."

Löblich really appreciated the cooperation and coordination of Stewart and Orlean and The Hague team. He remembered one particular problem for which the pragmatic Orlean had the perfect solution. "At one point, our group calculated the existing gas grids would fill up rapidly, and enormous expense would then be required to distribute gas to the households because of the very large loads, particularly during peak demand periods. We concluded the whole thing would be uneconomical until Martin visited us and explained that the problem could be inexpensively solved by overlaying the low-pressure grids with a few high-pressure lines feeding natural gas by regulators into key points."

Dutch State Mines

On April 6, Stewart, Orlean, and Smit were driven to the meeting with Dutch State Mines by Willem in the big Esso limousine, while Van den Berg went on his own in his brand-new yellow Volkswagen. He presented himself at the front door, arms laden with all the view graph slides and other data the teams had prepared for the meeting, only to find himself stopped cold by the States Mines doorman, who informed him there was an important meeting going on and just where did someone the "likes" of Jan think he was going. Jan's ever-present charm could be employed at any social level, and it didn't take long for him to convince the man that what he had in his arms justified his place at that very meeting table.

When the team finished its presentation, State Mines countered the team's enthusiasm by announcing that they had performed their own study. Much to Stewart and the team's dismay, State Mines's own study reached a conclusion similar to the original Shell study. State Mines expected to direct all efforts to heavy industry and power plants. State

Mines simply did not yet grasp the main contention of the team that the major opportunity was in the domestic household premium market. The members of the team did their best not to show disappointment. The result was certainly less than they had hoped for, but they were relieved the presentation had not been wholly rejected. State Mines agreed to review their suggestions and to have a second meeting in Rotterdam on April 27. Eventually, on the domestic issue, State Mines swung in the team's direction because of the Hilversum study, which had been right there from the beginning in the initial presentation to de Pous. It was the Hilversum study that helped establish price levels and became the foundation for everything to follow.

In his book *Subterranean Commonwealth*, Wolf Kielich refers to the Hilversum study and to the team of Stewart, Van der Post, Van den Berg, and Orlean as the Esso Four, particularly commending their tenacity. "The Esso Four did not allow themselves to be driven from the field. They intended to prove irrefutably that not only was their plan practicable but that economically, for distributors, it offered enormous possibilities."

Kielich also quoted Van den Berg explaining that the model the team used illustrated what would happen to a gas company with twenty thousand connections over a period of twenty years. "With this theoretical model, we were able to completely justify the theory of low consumer sales and reasonable company purchase prices leading to good profits for the gas company in the context of conditions in the Netherlands." Van den Berg summed up the final result. "It set the keynote for all further developments."

Unknown at the time was that shortly after that April 6 meeting, State Mines sent a representative over to the United States to visit with leading gas distributors there. That visit confirmed to State Mines that The Hague team's Hilversum study had a validity they could not deny. A large home heating market could be obtained in the Netherlands, similar to what they found in America.

Their recognition of that possibility became a highlight of the meeting on the twenty-seventh, but they brought something else to that meeting, which sent reverberations all the way to New York and London.

Dutch State Mines presented The Hague team with their new vision of how things should be done. They were now not only enthusiastic about the possibilities of the premium market and with the idea of sharing in the marketing revenue, but they also now had brand-new revenue demands. State Mines not only expected to participate in marketing revenue, but they also wanted one-third of the production revenue. Even more shocking, they demanded one-third of everything outside the border in export as well.

Shell's dignified Mr. Boot did not register his considerable dismay at this stunning turn of events. He quietly explained that these were serious issues that would have to be reviewed with the parent companies. Esso's Coen Smit advised the Dutch State Mines representatives that every consideration would be given to this new idea, but after the meeting, the team felt they had reached an impasse they could not get around.

The difficult task of conveying State Mines's dramatic shift in attitude to Jersey fell to Stewart. The one good thing about this trip back to New York was his being able to go back home to Jane and the children. This last trip had not been just weeks; it had been months. He had never been away from Jane and the family for such a long period.

In New York, Jersey was utterly unimpressed by the fact that State Mines had actually accepted a very crucial part of The Hague team's proposal, that is, that States Mines (in effect the Dutch government) was going along with the idea that Esso and Shell would participate in the domestic gas business as partners with them. Instead, the New York office was focusing on State Mines's request to participate in export marketing. Stewart was perplexed by Jersey's attitude. "They blew their top. None of the Jersey people had been present for our hard-won negotiations, but now they wanted to second-guess how our team had gotten there."

Jersey, of course, was looking at the State Mines negotiations through the prism of their concerns about the new demands by Middle East governments for a direct interest in both production and worldwide marketing. At that time, these countries were totally shut out of these profits by old contracts. The oil companies termed the desire of those governments to share in the profits of their natural wealth beyond their borders as the "sheik effect."

The formation of the infant Organization of the Petroleum Exporting Countries (OPEC) in Baghdad the previous September had heightened Esso's concerns about retaining control of those profit centers. It was not yet evident that the birth of OPEC heralded the day when the Middle East would cease making appeals. Although that event was just below the horizon, the oil companies did not foresee the day coming when the Middle East countries would just eliminate foreign oil companies from the equation by nationalizing the entire industry and appropriating all its assets.

The specter of that future had actually dawned years before in 1951 when the Majlis, the democratically elected Iranian Parliament, voted to nationalize Iran's oil industry, seizing control of the British-owned and-operated AIOC (Anglo-Iranian Oil company).[5]

Dr. Mohammad Mossadegh was appointed prime minister on April 28 of that year after the assassination of the previous prime minister. Mossadegh was powerful enough to enforce Iran's Nationalization Act until August 19, 1953, when he was arrested in a coup fostered by the intelligence agencies of Britain and the United States, and the Shah assumed power.

Nationalization reared its multifaceted head again in 1956, when Egypt's president Nasser nationalized the Suez Canal. Esso was not sitting idle during these crises of the '50s but had already launched a long-range secret study group looking at what nationalization would mean, particularly in Venezuela.

To get around the sheik effect, Shell had come up with an idea to grant the Dutch government additional participation in the producing profit by forming a partnership with Dutch State Mines, sharing in the production to the wellhead. NAM would be the operator and would sell

---

5 Mossadegh Conference: May 3 to May 6, 2001, Northwestern University, in Commemoration of the Fiftieth Anniversary of Dr. Mossadegh's Government (1951–1953) © 1995, 1999, 2004 Alaa K. Ashmawy.

the gas to a new domestic company, and NAM would sell surplus gas for export.

Smit and Stewart both realized that it would be politically necessary to go along with Shell's idea, but it was Stewart who had to sell this to Stott and the other executives in New York. Stott was especially incensed. His tirade about the "greedy Dutch government" was salted with what he regarded as the presumption of those "ungrateful Middle Eastern sheiks" because they were "trying to ram their way into" the international marketing side of the oil business.

As far as Stott was concerned, giving the Dutch a piece of the marketing pie, even just domestically, was a step that would set the stage for having to give the sheiks that very big piece of the Middle East pie they were asking for.

Stewart tried to help Stott understand what they were dealing with in the Netherlands. "I pointed out that it was not all bad to have State Mines in the production side of the business. Otherwise, there would always be government pressure to lower the wellhead price and move the profit from production into marketing. I explained we actually might not be losing any overall profit since the share given up to State Mines in production would be largely offset by the high commercial wellhead price, which would keep the gas steered into the premium market, where the profits would be so much higher. If the government were on both sides of the fence, they would be more inclined to favor the commercial wellhead price. The lower wellhead price would be competing with Stott's closed view of his precious fuel oil markets. He just didn't get it that natural gas was a new world, a whole new business, with revenue opportunities that had never before existed." Stewart was face-to-face with a corporate "generation gap." Stott represented old corporate thinking. He was largely feared by his subordinates, who found him to be stubborn and ruthless. The fuel oil business was his model, that is, big market share but not a lot of profit. Stewart represented the future, that is, brand-new business with the potential for vast company profit.

Differing with Stott was not without consequences. By presenting fresh ideas on pricing and new revenue possibilities, Upstream Stewart was giving Downstream Stott marketing advice. "I tried my best to get the older men to look into the future we were offering. I pointed out that this partnership the Dutch government was suggesting was far preferable to nationalization and could be looked on as sort of an extra tax that wouldn't encourage the Middle East sheiks."

His effort to raise the consciousness of Esso's old guard was successful. However, the response of Stewart's superiors to his report revealed that these men did not grasp how complicated and time-consuming the Dutch gas project was going to be. They actually believed it would all be brought to a close within a few months.

—Chapter 11—

Family Chronicles

The Dutch gas project was the biggest challenge of Stewart's career, and pursuing it had taken him away from Jane and his family. Jane's patience during those long absences was a source of strength, especially during this last separation of several months. But there was no substitute for Jane's daily presence, her engaging mind, and the environment she created for their life together.

When Stewart said he "didn't really know Jane until he married her," the phrase was more than his discovery of the qualities about her that made the two of them such a match for each other. Beyond Jane's practical nature, her qualities of leadership, organization, and flexibility, and the deep comradeship he had with her, illuminated Stewart's personal life in a way nothing else ever did.

Without Jane to come home to, life for Stewart just turned into a dull monotone. He wanted the miles between them to dissolve and to have Jane and the children with him. He knew he could not expect corporate to approve anything other than a visit from his family. He didn't even try. He simply requested, and the company agreed, for him to bring his family over "for the summer." He had no clue about how he would manage to keep them there beyond that. He was, however, as certain he would find a way to make that happen as he was that the Dutch gas negotiations would go the way he was predicting they would go.

That night, Stewart went home and delivered the happy news that Jane and the family could join him in the Netherlands for the summer. On the day they closed the door of their house in Connecticut, neither of them ever imagined that it would be four years before they would resume their lives in the United States.

As soon as friends of the Stewarts heard the news about the family's summer in the Netherlands, there was a rash of farewell events and surprise parties for the couple.

The speed with which the family was ready to leave was not a surprise to Stewart. "As always, Jane swung right into the task at hand, this time to uproot herself and the children from everything familiar. The adventure before us just seemed to spur her organizational skills to new heights."

The Stewart children had vivid memories of their ocean voyage and their years in Holland. The eldest son, Douglass Jr., a film editor in Los Angeles, recalled his reaction when he realized the family was going abroad. "I didn't know anything about Holland except for windmills, wooden shoes, and tulips, so I was pretty unsure of what I was headed for. At first, going to Europe just meant something like eleven different immunization injections, and by the time I got to the end of all that, this business of going overseas was no fun at all. My arms were sore for weeks."

Doug Stewart Sr. still marveled at his wife's calm. "In very short order, Jane and the children and I, along with our by now pregnant little dachshund, Trudy, were ready to leave. We closed the house, and off we went to Europe on the good ship Liberté."

Jane Ann, the Stewarts' only daughter, now an artist and production designer in the film industry, particularly remembered the departure of the Liberté. "Our friends from Connecticut came to the docks in New York to see us off. I remember they came on the ship and looked at our staterooms, and then there we were, standing up on the deck, looking down over the railing at them waving to us from the dock. When I think of it now, it seems sort of like being inside one of those wonderful old black-and-white movies from the '30s. It was very, very exciting to a six-year-old."

Her father remembered "exciting" as the order of the day aboard the Liberté. "The company sent us first class, which in those days meant formal wear for dinner. I thought this was living pretty high for an Okie from Muskogee."

Younger son Mark, now a pastor in Boise, Idaho, fondly recalled the shipboard experience. "We three kids had a room to ourselves, with our parents in a room adjoining. We stayed up late almost every night. When our parents went dancing was when the pillow fights broke out. I think my sister always won."

According to Jane Ann, the nights might not have been quite so late as they seemed to three small children. "The Liberté really meant liberty to us. As soon as our parents closed the door on us, all hell would break loose. That's when those pillow fights happened. I remember it seemed like a big deal that we ordered orange juice from room service at night— just because we could. I remember my mom and dad would come to our room in all their finery, Mom in a formal gown and Dad in his tuxedo, on their way to eat at the captain's table or in the grand ballroom."

Doug Jr. remembered the fabulous food and the staterooms. "It was a great adventure to have the opportunity to order steak and french fries in our cabin. And we got to try out our snorkels and fins in the saltwater pool. We eventually found out the North Sea of Holland was no place for skin diving, but practicing in the ship's pool when it was swaying was interesting."

> Mark also recalled those swimming pools. "One was fresh water, the other salt water. It was the most fun when the ship was rocking because it made huge waves. It was even kind of scary when that happened. I knew that if I fell overboard, I would be a goner. Little Trudy got a lot of attention. She was kept in a kennel with the other dogs, and we had to pet her through the bars and bring her goodies from the table."

Doug Jr. knew it was coming to an end before anyone else. "Near the end of the voyage, I remember going to the front of the boat and looking at the French shoreline coming closer. The magical voyage was about to end."

The first place the family stayed was in an old castle called the Kasteel oud Wassenaar, which had been converted to a hotel in the town of Wassenaar.

Doug Sr. found the castle a wonderful treat. "The gas business was looking like more fun all the time. An interesting thing was that three years later, the final arrangements for an agreement with the Dutch government were signed at this very place."

Real life started immediately for the family and signaled Stewart's intent that this was not going to be just a summer vacation with his family. "It was early spring, and we didn't want the children to miss a whole semester of school, so we enrolled them in the Dutch Montessori School."

The first morning, the children left for school in a chill April rain wearing their yellow American rain slickers. Doug Jr. found that this was a completely un-Dutch look and ran headlong into the language barrier. "Mostly, that school was an endurance test. Can you imagine trying to learn a totally new way of measuring (the metric system) and a new monetary system (guilders) in a language you didn't speak? Fortunately, there happened to be another American boy in the class who helped me with the work. I do recall learning one very important lesson in respect. You must let the teacher come through the door first before trying to pass your own way. Yikes! I was glad to be let out for summer that year."

Jane Ann's memories of the Montessori school were much happier. She was only about six and picked up the language very quickly. "The older kids helped us younger ones, and I got a lot of help. Back then, they liked Americans. I got invited to a lot of kids' houses. I didn't think school was hard because all of us were learning new things. I remember that, to me, this was all just going to be a temporary thing."

The Kasteel oud Wassenaar was pricey, and after a few weeks, Stewart sought other accommodations. Housing was still difficult to obtain in Holland because there had been very little construction since the war.

They found a summer rental in a little townhouse in the suburb of Voorburg, of which Jane Ann had fond memories. "That house was in front of a canal that was covered with green moss, and we tricked our little Trudy into thinking it was green grass. She wasn't very happy about the water."

Stewart thought they could hasten the breakdown of the language barrier with the purchase of some Dutch-English language records. "Later, I also acquired German and French language books and records, and although I gradually gained some knowledge of all of them, I would find myself in situations trying to speak Dutch with our German friends and German with the French. Jane started taking Dutch lessons right away and quickly got to speaking a little bit of Dutch so she could communicate with the vendors who came round to deliver various things we needed on a daily basis. One day one of them knocked on our door, and after a brief conversation in Dutch, Jane went upstairs to get our laundry for him while he went back out to bring in chickens. He was the butcher, not the launderer. She always loved to tell that story."

Daughter Jane Ann was now aware of a cultural difference she had no way to recognize as a child but which affected her in a very positive way. "My second-grade class back in Connecticut went to the Bronx Zoo, while my second-grade class in Holland went to Paris, a huge cultural gap of which I wasn't then really aware.

"We fully embraced Dutch life. I ice-skated almost all the way to school on the canals one year. That was really fun. Some kids still used wooden skates, just like Hans Brinker. And then there were still people who dressed on a daily basis in traditional Dutch dress."

Little Trudy finally gave birth to her pups. Stewart remembered they were fascinating for weeks and weeks. "The kids really took care of them, and our Dutch neighbors came by, and they loved them. We found homes for everyone."

Jane Ann's connection with the Dutch people she met was truly an affectionate one. "I never felt any criticism from the Dutch people. They made me feel as if I were very special. There weren't very many American kids."

Just as Stewart expected, the State Mines negotiations dragged on and on. As their summer lease neared its end, pressure mounted dramatically for him to locate permanent housing that would let him keep his family with him.

"As we sent the children off to summer camp, we were face-to-face with the fact that time was running out. Jane and I did not want to ever be apart again. I didn't know how I was going to swing it, but I was not going to send my family back to the U.S. We followed up every lead to no avail. By mid-August, the housing shortage looked more bleak than ever."

Early on, Jane had found her way to The Hague's American community, mostly in the suburb of Wassenaar. There were a women's club, an American church, and an American school. Jane's personality quickly attracted a circle of friends that included the U.S. ambassador to the Netherlands. His invitation to a reception one evening turned out to be a signal turning point for the Stewart family. During a conversation with the assistant U.S. consul, Stewart learned the consul was being transferred from Holland that very week. The consul was renting a house on the edge of Rijksdorp, a suburb of Wassenaar.

"When he said that as far as he knew, the house hadn't been rented, I asked for the landlord's name, excused myself as soon as it was polite, grabbed Jane, and we slipped out the door into a pouring rain to find that house," said Stewart. "There, in the side of a small hill, nestled in a grove of trees, was a three-storied thatched-roofed little villa. There were no lights on in the house, and we could see nothing inside, but in our desperate situation, we had to have it. By now, the rain had turned into a deluge. The windshield wipers were having trouble keeping up as we frantically searched for a telephone booth. Fortunately, we not only found one. We found one that worked. And luckily, the landlord spoke English. So standing there in the rain, on a phone, I made a deal for a four-year lease for a house we hadn't even been inside. Never mind that Jersey had sent me there for what they thought was going to be a three-month assignment. I knew in my bones what Jersey just didn't get. I estimated this project could take as long as a year or more."

He could not know that his prediction of a "year or more" would turn out to be very conservative. What Stewart did know, standing there in the dark and the rain that night, was that his days in the Netherlands were not going to be a dull monotone anymore. He was going to have Jane and his family right there with him, however many days this job was going to take.

The area of Rijksdorp, which means roughly "rich city," is located on sand dunes. It was actually just a very small village. Stewart's memory of the house was as fresh as a new photograph. "The house sat on five acres, on sort of a narrow-shaped lot, with the driveway and a little garage in a grove of trees below the house. You came through a gate from the road in front of the property and then walked up to the house from there. In a way, it wasn't that big a house, but with its thatched roof, it felt like a very quaint storybook kind of house."

The next week, when Stewart and Jane took possession of the house, they discovered a Dutch rental wasn't anything like renting in America. Here, it was up to the renter to furnish everything except the outside bricks, it seemed. There were no light fixtures, only dangling wires; no stove; no refrigerator; no drapes. They were even responsible for installing wallpaper and floor coverings.

"Since we'd come only for a summer visit, we had no furniture," said Stewart. "Fortunately, one of the couples Jane met through the American community actually had two households of furniture. They lent us some of theirs, but it was pretty sparse at first."

Jan van den Berg's wife, Ciny, particularly remembered Jane's resourcefulness. "She would take home some dingy black pot from a flea market, and the next time you saw it, it was transformed into a shiny silver tea service that looked as if it had just come from a very expensive store."

The children were still away at camp, so for about a week, Stewart put his Boy Scout skills to work and built wood fires in the backyard to heat breakfast coffee and toast for himself and Jane. "I went to all my negotiations smelling of wood smoke," he said. "I'm sure my colleagues were relieved when we bought an electric burner."

Jane Ann loved the house and remembered she had one of the rooms under the pointed roof. "I remember thinking it was so neat that I had a sink of my own, right in my room, which was great. I could brush my teeth right when I got up. It was very romantic, almost like living in a fairy tale."

Doug Jr. found remnants of what was not a fairy tale time in Holland. "The sand dune behind our house was rumored to have been a chosen spot for a German machine gun nest during World War II. The story was that our house had been the first house taken during the wartime occupation, when soldiers parachuted into those tulip fields. While playing there one day, my friend Chris Reardon and I found an old telephone wire coming out of the sand."

Stewart's youngest, Mark, and his friends played on that same sand dune, and he remembered that story too. "I played soldier on that sand dune, and once, my friend and I found some old machine gun shells that proved to me the story about the machine gun nest was true."

Stewart met the present owners of the house, Liz and Emiel van Veen, when he made a nostalgic visit in 2005. The Van Veens verified the story about the machine gun nests as well as some other events that took place around the house during the war. In May 1940, German airborne troops dropped around that quarter of Rijksdorp to take over nearby airports.

Emiel explained that the house was commandeered as a headquarters of some kind. "In 1942, the inhabitants of Rijksdorp were forced to evacuate because the Germans started building concrete pillboxes in the dunes as part of what they called the Atlantic Wall. This was meant to block or discourage any invasion from the Allies. Of course, the German military did not want any snoopers around, so people had to move out of their houses. Only two Dutchmen who sympathized with the Germans were allowed to stay. The quarter was firmly closed from Dutch people who lived there. They put a fence of barbed wire around water trenches and built wooden shelters all around Rijksdorp as part of that Atlantic Wall. On September 5, 1944, on what we call Dolle/Crazy-Dinsdag Tuesday, there was a wild rumor flying about that the Germans were about to flee because Allied troops were nearing Rotterdam. This rumor caused people in and around The Hague to go out jubilantly into the streets to celebrate. Unfortunately, it turned out not to be true yet. The occupiers took revenge by plundering all the houses of Rijksdorp. After the liberation, in May 1945, the houses in Rijksdorp were restored to their owners. Hereafter, Jhr. (a noble title) Quarles van Uffort, stepfather of Audrey Hepburn, and her mother lived in our house for many years."

Perhaps because she is an artist, Jane Ann had color-filled memories of their house and their life in Holland. "The breakfast room looked out over an endless patchwork made of every kind and color of tulip. We children thought the tulips were ours. We didn't know the little moat separating us from the flowers, about two feet wide, was something official, but we quickly found out the first time we stepped across that moat to pick those tulips. A stern man appeared out of nowhere to warn us those blooms were for looking only."

Jane's mother also had an experience with the tulips on the other side of the moat. She invited the wives of the team with whom Stewart was working to come one morning to see the tulips in all their glory.

Ciny van den Berg remembered the event. "Jane was very excited for us to see that field of flowers. There was Paul Miles's wife, Caroline, and Martin Orlean's wife, Sylvia, and myself. Jane prepared a lovely morning coffee for us, right in front of the windows that looked out on the tulips. But when she drew the curtains for us, we found that in the night, the tulips had all been harvested, and there was nothing left but earth and brown stubble."

Stewart remembered a happier moment he shared with his wife. "One day a white dove with a little black band around its neck showed up, and I caught the pretty little thing for her. We bought a big cage for it and put it right there in Jane's kitchen. We bought a mate for the bird at the market and brought him home to our little dove. They must have been happy as they had babies."

Over the several years the Stewarts lived in Holland, they had the opportunity to see most of the quaint towns and farms in the Netherlands and neighboring countries by car and by boat. In a newsy letter home to her sister, Jane Stewart described one of those vacations trips.

> *We took the children to Ghent, in Belgium, last weekend. It was the Queen's birthday and a national holiday too. There was a marvelous van Eyck panel in a church we wanted to see. It is called the "Adoration of the Lamb." It was really beautiful. We also visited the house where Louis took refuge when Napoleon returned for his 100 days. It is still completely furnished and has been beautifully preserved as a museum.*
>
> *The kids are just crazy about Belgian fried potatoes. In Holland, the little stands that sell them put mayonnaise on them (I found this hard to take). But in Belgium, they also put mayonnaise or pickled onions on mussels, which are like a red-orange oyster. It is the darndest combination you ever saw or tasted.*
>
> *The kids are really camp-bound this summer, to camps near Geissen, Germany, and they seem to be awfully good camps. And then we will pick them up the last of July there and take them to Arosa, Switzerland, for three weeks. It is a gorgeous place and a very good ski resort. They have everything, from horseback riding to skin diving. And all three are going, so Mark won't have to be lonesome. Two of the children in his room will be there too.*
>
> *Back at the ranch, Doug and I are going to drive on down to Italy, up thru Austria and wherever else we can get to in that time. I haven't left them at home with a babysitter overnight since we came here, and I did want them to see Pompeii and Rome, but Doug said they can come some time when they are bigger.*
>
> *There was a special showing at the American Embassy of Jackie's tour of the White House. I was invited too, and it was wonderful, wasn't it?*
>
> *Doug is off to Brussels today, then over to London and back Friday. Between the May Fellowship Day luncheon and*

the Mother-Daughter banquet, I will be busy. But we still hate for him to be gone from us.

Much love from all of us. Write soon.
Jane

Looking back, Stewart had no regrets. "I might have advanced my career further if I'd been willing to give up those family weekends and vacations, but I never did. I promised Jane weekends belonged to her and me and the kids. Now that all the kids are all grown and Jane has passed, I know we were right to put ourselves before the job. Jane went with me to many wonderful social events that were part of the job, and sharing those occasions with her is treasured memories for me."

Jane's Weston Connecticut friends gave her a farewell
party, and many came to the ship to say goodbye.

Aboard the Liberté, all the dinners were formal affairs.
Seated on the right are Jane and Doug.
Meanwhile, the children were having pillow fights in the stateroom.

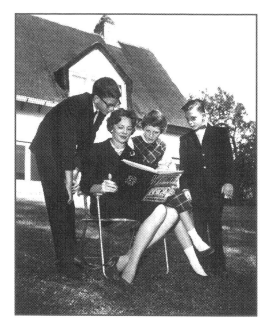

The Stewart family outside their home in
Rijksdorp, Wassenaar, Netherlands.
Left to right: Doug Jr., Jane, Jane Ann, and Mark Allan.

Jane Stewart as president presiding over a meeting of
the American Women's Club of the Hague.

—Chapter 12—

Brussels, Beyond, and Home Again!

The State Mines negotiations proceeded as slowly as Stewart predicted. A third meeting took place on May 15, with the Esso/Shell team voicing their strong objections to State participation in production and export. Two more meetings in June produced an aide-mémoire, which they presented to Minister de Pous on the twenty-third. This time they gave into State Mines's demand to participate in production while reserving the right for NAM to make export sales. The minister's reservations about the joint operations continued. It was apparent to Stewart that de Pous would not relent to any proposal that placed the government in a minority position.

"Minister de Pous appointed a committee headed by Prof. W. C. L. van der Grinten, who served as chairman, alongside H. Vos, a Labour Party member of the First Chamber, and Th. P. Tromp, an ex-minister of Public Works," said Stewart. "Months went by while they talked to politicians, town councils, gas works, State Mines, and others. We continued consultation with the ministry, but step by step, our original proposal was eroded, modified, and reshaped."

Meetings crawled through the month of August and were sure to continue deeper into the fall. Stewart was resolute in his conviction that negotiations would ultimately be resolved. Since all the early predictions about the vastness of the Groningen discovery had been surpassed, the Esso team did not slow down their export studies. There was not a flicker of doubt in Stewart's mind that all the nearby countries—Belgium, France, Austria, and even Britain across the Channel—would be eager for natural gas. Buoyed by the data in the Hilversum study and by what the studies in Germany were revealing, Belgium seemed the most natural place for the next round of studies.

On the way to Esso's Belgian headquarters, the train carried Stewart and Orlean through villages dating back to the Middle Ages. "The first large town was Delft, famous for its canals and cobalt blue trimmed pottery," said Stewart. "That industry was certainly going to want natural gas. We glided past low-lying fields of grazing cattle and thatched-roofed farms. Here and there were great stacks of hay and sometimes high dirt mounds to which both cattle and farmers could flee in times of flood."

Just beyond the Rhine River, between Holland and Belgium, the land is broad and flat. Across the border is Antwerp, with its large port. To the west lie Ghent and Brugge, whose gems of medieval architecture were bypassed by time when their access to the sea sanded up centuries ago. To the east is the industrial fortress town of Liege. South of Brussels is Charleroi, in the coal region. In the distance is Bastogne, the scene of World War II's Battle of the Bulge. The last time Stewart passed this way, he was leading a convoy following the liberation of Paris.

In November 1944, Lieutenant Stewart was sent on detached service in charge of forty men to convoy trucks and vehicles from the ports to St. Dizier, France, to establish another motor pool. In December, he returned to the east of Charleroi, where the Germans were advancing on Bastogne to launch their Battle of the Bulge offensive. Before him and his men lay the bitterest and most profoundly important battle for the Allied forces.

"We could hear the big guns, but then they stalled, the weather broke, and the skies cleared," recalled Stewart. "Overhead, at last, were waves of our bombers headed towards the front."

By Christmas, Stewart's company was near the village of Charleroi in time for the tide-turning Battle of the Bulge at Bastogne. They were assigned to dig in there to protect the village in the event the Germans were able to overrun Bastogne. The battle raged bitterly, with massive loss of life, before the Germans were finally driven to retreat.

In appreciation for the protection of the 944th company, village officials presented a Medal of Appreciation to Stewart and his men before they moved forward. The battlefields the company crossed were strewn with what appeared to be a massive, grotesque jigsaw puzzle.

"I took a convoy through Bastogne," said Stewart. "The city was rubble, and the surrounding fields were littered with blown-up German tanks that had run out of gas. Painted white to camouflage them in snow, they now loomed out in sharp relief against the thawing ground. One field was a sea of abandoned bicycles the Germans had used in their original advance. Trees that had shaded the countryside for centuries were now but shattered husks. By the time we passed through, the human remains of the carnage, both military and civilian, had been taken away. The fallen horses, rotting in the sun beside their fallen wagons, were mute evidence that the Germans were in much worse shape than we were as far as equipment goes. I am sure their soldiers suffered in the bitter cold and snow, as did our men. Soldiers have to sleep on the ground or find a barn or a haystack, and there were few of those to be found in the Ardennes Woods."

In 1944, Stewart's company continued moving through Limburg, in the Netherlands, and then deeper into Germany. Following the frontline troops, their convoys passed trucks going to the rear full of emaciated, skeleton-like men staring blankly at them. "At first, we thought that they were prisoners of war because of their striped, tattered clothes, but then we realized from their shaved heads that these shattered people had just been rescued from concentration camps. We had only heard rumors about what the first troops had found in those places, but now we were looking into the ravaged faces of survivors, the magnitude of whose ordeals we would only know much later. We waved and cheered them as they passed by, but they were too weak and traumatized to return our salutes. They could only stare back numbly."

From Charleroi, they passed through Gembloux in Belgium, where the French and British had fought their first battle of the war before the soldiers who survived were driven to the beaches of Dunkirk. Stewart and one of those young French soldiers were destined to meet in a peaceful pursuit that would involve that very same territory.

On May 10, 1940, in the Liege region of Belgium near Gembloux, a young French soldier named Yves Monod was in the Discovery Regiment of the Eighth Battalion of the French army when its first contact with the German Army took place in a battle in the Liege region of Belgium. Although they and the British forces who joined them were victorious, a bigger battle began on the twelfth near Gembloux. The Germans followed up with such awesome airpower nearly 400,000 men were forced to withdraw to the beaches of Dunkirk, facing the North Sea. The biggest navy ships could not get near enough to the beach for rescue, so in one of the most heroic and daring rescues of the war, nearly 900 ordinary English citizens responded to an appeal and set out in stormy seas in every kind of personal vessel capable of crossing the English Channel. Altogether, 338,226 troops were evacuated over several days in this way.

On May 30, Yves's regiment embarked on an English destroyer for Dover under very difficult conditions. Six days later, they were returning through Bournemouth, re-embarking to Plymouth on a pack boat, knowing they were on their way back to combat. Just as they were to leave port, they were heartened by the sound of the "Marseillaise" ringing out across the harbor, courtesy of the Plymouth Army orchestra. In a valiant but vain attempt to slow the enemy advance, Yves and part of his regiment engaged them at Saumu on the edge of La Loire. The regiment's struggle continued until June 27, when the Armistice of 1940 was signed between France and Germany.

Capt. Francis Stewart and 2ⁿᵈ Lt. Douglass Stewart met in Wales, UK, just before the Invasion of Normandy. They both landed on Omaha Beach on July 3, 1943.

Left to right: Captain Cameron, Lt. Douglass Stewart, and two sergeants in Normandy beachhead in July 1943.

Stewart's company, the 944 Ordinance Motor Vehicle
Distribution Company, was stationed in Charleroi, Belgium,
during the December 1944 "Battle of the Bulge."
The company received a Commemorative Medal from
the town for its defense. Here, Stewart, on the left, led
a platoon receiving the medal at the Town Hall.

As Stewart and Orlean stepped off the train into the Brussels of 1961, there was no remnant of the war left, save its memorials to those whose lives were claimed in its conflict. The two men found themselves in the midst of a city abounding in commercial success.

The Grand Place was only a block from their hotel. The meeting wasn't until one o'clock, so Stewart took advantage of the time for a bit of exploration. Rounding a corner, he took a step back into time. Before him were the magnificent seventeenth-century Guild Halls dating from the time that Belgium was the center of Europe's wool and linen weaving industry. Sadly, their gold trimmed facades were fouled with the residue of centuries of soot from coal burned to warm the city's homes and fuel its industries. "I thought then that if we could only get clean burning natural gas into Belgium, perhaps we could help clean up the city," said Stewart. "If you have been to the Grand Place lately, you will know we succeeded, with, of course, the help of an army of building washers."

That afternoon, Stewart and Orlean met with the Belgian Esso board and several of their managers and economists. They made essentially the same presentation they had made in Germany and garnered valuable information to take back to the team in The Hague.

"We learned that in Belgium, Distrigaz was the one large intercity gas distribution company," said Stewart. "They connected a number of smaller independent gas distribution companies and municipalities. The largest independent company was Imperial Continental, located in the Antwerp area."

Imperial Continental was the epitome of this country's "old guard." They had been one of the earliest gas companies in Europe, beginning in the early 1800s, when gas was first used for street illumination. Surprisingly, Imperial was not actually a Belgian company; it was British-owned, with its stock openly sold on the London stock market. Stewart wondered whether it might be feasible to just buy up the stock of the company and own it, but that idea had to be discarded because of the complexity of such a transaction.

The most significant and powerful element of the Belgian old guard was not a coal or steel company or even a gas company. It was, instead, one of the largest financial houses in Brussels. The Société Générale is a bank that dates back to the fourth of May 1864, the date of the authorization decree signed by Napoleon III and the month in which the company started to hire employees and establish offices.

The bank's ambitions were reflected in its original articles of association, when it took the form, very unusual at the time, of a limited company, a "société anonyme." By 1870, the bank had fifteen branches in Paris and thirty-two in the French provinces. It set up a permanent office in London in 1871. From the beginning, the sign above the entrance to the offices carried the engraved, enameled glass inscription "Société Générale"—favoring the development of trade and industry in France.

Since that motto matched Stewart's own intentions, it seemed to bode well for his mission there. Many of the other small Belgian distribution companies, as well as the much larger Distrigaz, were all controlled financially, one way or another, by the Société.

Home heating was more advanced in Belgium than in Holland, but coal still dominated heating oil. Industries of all types, particularly steel and coal mines, were mainly scattered along the Meuse River, running roughly north and south through the center of the country. Esso Belgium had about 20 percent of the oil markets in Belgium and a large refinery in Antwerp. The low-BTU town gas distributed in Belgium came largely from steel cokery plants and from municipal gas works. There was no natural gas.

Stewart was gratified when Esso Belgium followed Esso Germany's lead and agreed to begin studies for a future gas business and an analysis of the market potential along the same lines of the studies being done in Hamburg. Two economists and a lawyer were assigned to the task. To entrenched Belgian industry, Esso would have been viewed as a "new kid on the block." Stewart knew there was no way to be certain Belgium would take seriously a study done by "upstart Esso." At least in Belgium, the new gas business would be in private hands.

From Belgium, the next stop was Paris. On his way there with Orlean, Stewart recalled his first visit there, seventeen years earlier. Then he had been at the head of an army convoy a few days after Paris had been liberated in 1944.

"My assignment was to establish a motor pool in the Bois de Vincennes. We had no trouble finding Paris, but we arrived at night knowing only that the park was to the east of the city. We all just slept on the sidewalk and figured we'd find that park in the morning. We woke up surrounded by a crowd of civilians chattering away at us in French, obviously very happy to see us. The locals let us use their facilities, and then they brought us wine and bread and told us where to find that park where we were to keep our trucks. As we moved through the streets, crowds of well-wishers surged around us. The guys were kissing all the girls, flags were waving—it was an unforgettable scene. The troops who had done all the fighting had been through first, but they had to keep moving, so we were the lucky ones, getting the cheers and attention."

On that triumphant day, Yves Monod, who had married his wife, Solange, after returning from combat, was on a bicycle trying to find milk for his newborn baby daughter with no idea that among the troops camped in that park was a young American lieutenant who would one day be his business colleague.

By 1961, what a change had taken place.

"We were just foot traffic," said Stewart. "There were autos everywhere. It was foggy and raining this time, and no one paused on their busy way to give Martin and me a second look.

"The George V Hotel's vast gilded plush red interior was impressive. From the restaurant wafted the garlicky odor of its famous food—it wasn't going to be half-bad looking for gas markets in France."

The gas business in France, new or old, was the province of a long-established government-controlled monopoly. Given that circumstance, the question for Stewart was whether Esso France could be convinced to undertake a study at all.

The Esso building overlooked the city from a hill two miles north of the Champs Elysées. After a brief introduction to the board, Stewart was surprised to find that the meeting was not going to take place in the office but was to be conducted over lunch in a penthouse dining room at a large white linen-draped table complete with flowers, wineglasses, and gold-rimmed plates.

"I was impressed, but somehow the portrait of John D. came to mind, and I wondered if he was scowling down on our expensive lunch. With typical American bravado, I launched into my by now well-rehearsed Dutch gas story and ventured the remark that it was possible the gas just might reach all the way to Paris and that we would like to be selling the gas in France directly from our own pipelines.

"Serge Sheer, the president of Esso France, was sitting at my right. He interrupted my spiel by reaching over, plucking my hard roll from my butter plate, and placing it on the white tablecloth in front of my dinner plate. 'In France,' he said, 'it's customary to put your bread on the tablecloth.'"

Was he being helpful to a brash young American, or was he, in his Gallic way, telling Stewart there was a lot to learn about France? Stewart hadn't noticed before that "on the table" was exactly where everyone else had placed their bread. There would be much more for him to learn about France in the many days to come.

Over trout amandine and Pouilly-Fuissé white wine, Stewart learned there was natural gas production in the south of the country near Lacq, and there was already a sizable gas network south of Paris. The government had established Gaz de France as a virtual monopoly to distribute natural gas. While it did look like there could be a large market for Dutch gas in France, the chances for Esso to participate in direct marketing and pipeline transportation seemed fairly unlikely. The Esso affiliates in Germany and Belgium had responded quickly to the idea of studies as a way to discern their own future financial possibilities, but Stewart had to take a different tack with the Paris affiliate because their primary target was the light industry, where Esso France had a large share of its oil market in France.

"I was able to convince them to initiate a study exploring the legal aspects of what would be involved with a private enterprise engaging with a government monopoly in France. They also agreed to undertake a study looking into the possible natural gas markets that could develop from the import of Dutch gas. They assigned one economist and a lawyer to the task."

Though that decision seemed to be the end of the day's business, no one left the table. Cognac and cigars had to be savored before Stewart and Orlean were free to bid their French colleagues goodbye, promising to keep them informed. Stewart remembered they barely made their flight back to London, where their next appointment was with Esso UK.

In London, Stewart and Orlean would once again be in the position of having to convince an Esso affiliate there was value in doing a study when the gas business was in the hands of a monopoly, namely, the British Gas Council. In their discussion during the flight to London, this was a concern to Orlean, but Stewart was eager to get there.

"When we landed, nothing had changed from our previous meeting with Shell," said Stewart. "Smog from coal fires still filled the air, soiling the buildings and parks. As we rode in from Heathrow, I looked up at all those rooftops sprouting thousands of smoking chimneys and felt a surge of excitement. This was an enormous potential premium market, if only we could get England to reach for it."

The now famous North Sea oil and gas discoveries had not yet been discovered. Although they had had an enormous impact on the quality of life throughout the country, at the time of Stewart and Orlean's visit, the only source for natural gas in England was LNG (liquefied natural gas), brought in by ship from Libya or Algeria at high cost and available only in small volumes. Esso UK believed that the government monopoly would be the only customer for Dutch gas.

The UK led Europe's Industrial Revolution in the 1800s and also in the production of available coal and gaseous by-products of steel and coke ovens. Low-BTU town gas had first been used for illumination and cooking over one hundred years earlier. By 1960, the country was interconnected with gas grids, gas manufacturing plants, and except for very rural areas, all houses were served by gas mains.

Even so, high-grade anthracite coal and coke were the preferred fuels for homeowners' stoves. Because those fuels were so expensive, diesel oil and kerosene were making rapid inroads into the home heating markets.

Town gas was used for heating the more affluent areas, but this was mostly consumed for hot water heating and cooking. The Gas Council was aggressively trying to expand their source of town gas by constructing reforming plants to crack LP gas and light oils into low-BTU town gas. Despite the high cost, the council was actively negotiating to import liquid natural gas from Algeria and from Esso in Libya.

Before the council would consider the enormous task of converting gas grids and homes to the high BTU gas that would come from the Netherlands, they first would have to be assured of a large, long-term, safe supply. They would have to be convinced that imported Dutch gas would not involve the high cost of shipping it by sea. They would also need to be assured of the feasibility of conversion and of the value of premium market potential.

Stewart knew the answers to those questions would be found by initiating studies that would reveal them. "We assured Esso UK the supply was there if the UK would pay a gas price sufficient to make an undersea pipeline economical and to make a contract more attractive than other European purchasers. No gas pipeline of the size we were contemplating had ever been laid at the depths of the North Sea crossing, but Jersey's pipeline engineers believed the technology could be developed."

Now that there were four Esso affiliates in addition to Esso Nederland studying the potential for natural gas, Stewart could see that the team needed some expertise in pipelining. He asked to have a pipeline expert join him and Orlean on The Hague team, and Paul Miles from the New York office was assigned to the task.

Primarily because he had been dispatched by the board to Europe first, and because of the forcefulness of his ideas and personality, Stewart had functioned as the leader without having been officially designated in that role. For the first time, because of Stewart's ideas regarding the UK study, that leadership role was challenged. As far as Stewart was concerned, the North Sea pipeline was not only needed, but it was also going to happen. Even though Esso UK agreed to establish a gas study group, Miles made it immediately clear he did not share Stewart's vision about that pipeline. As far as Miles was concerned, the pipeline was not only not needed, but it was also not going to happen. Orlean agreed. The two of them simply did not understand Stewart's strategy in initiating the study.

The primary issue for Stewart in the UK was not about importing natural gas, nor it was even about that pipeline. "Although I privately felt the study might not turn the tide in the UK, I firmly believed we had to present a solid front to every European gas distributor, demonstrating in every case that we were intent on entering the gas business. We could not, in these early negotiations, back off from a single country without weakening our position with the others. Miles never grasped the fundamental soundness of this strategy. He was not only a continuing thorn in my side. He became an obstruction to what I saw as a need to be absolutely consistent across the board."

Miles and Orlean were not only united in their opinion of the pipeline, but they were also equally adamant in their conviction that it was useless to think about entering the gas business in the UK because of the Gas Council's monopoly.

Stewart was not going to be dissuaded by internal dissension from tackling the technical and economic challenges of exporting Dutch gas from the Netherlands to anywhere in Europe and certainly not to the UK. He and Orlean had a number of arguments about various tactics.

Getting Miles and Orlean to move decisively into the pipeline study became a tug-of-war. Possibly because of Orlean conveying his reservations back to Jersey, corporate advisors from New York suddenly appeared on the scene to look into the team's progress. Stewart dubbed these fellows "Mutt and Jeff." "These two spent their nights carousing and frequently bragged about their nocturnal adventures. Mutt was a little guy, a mild-looking, clean-cut sort of fellow, except when he got drunk and turned pugnacious. He seemed to have always been in a scrap of some kind, showing up the next day with a black eye or a puffed lip. Probably one of the reasons these two were so frequently in our hair was because they got away from home base and had the freedom to explore the carnal pleasures of Amsterdam."

Mutt and Jeff reported negatively on things Stewart regarded as progress; for example, the fact that the team was pushing ahead on so many fronts.

"Miles and Orlean often met with Mutt and Jeff on their own, likely to pass on their own ideas, which they probably hoped would be carried back to Jersey, along with their complaints about my ideas and about the way I was pushing them," said Stewart.

"Although Jersey never seemed to do anything to hinder my progress, the negativity this behavior injected into the situation sometimes made it more difficult to sell my ideas in New York."

Stewart wanted to keep the freedom of activity for the team on a day-to-day basis, but it was becoming something of a strain trying to figure out how to keep New York informed but not give them enough information to impede the elasticity of the team's negotiations. Certainly, Miles and Orlean were filling in the blanks for Mutt and Jeff every time they descended on the team. Eventually, Stewart replaced Miles, but he never considered replacing Orlean.

"Martin was often an effective counterbalance to my overenthusiasm. He was a shrewd economist and deserves much credit for the success of the study teams." While the Esso team was preoccupied with kicking off export studies with affiliates, Smit of Dutch Esso and Boot of Dutch Shell continued their interaction with Minister de Pous, who was having struggles of his own.

Impasse Resolved

Minister de Pous was recognizing that the whole natural gas project could become a very hot potato publicly, particularly with the opposition Labor Party. He also may have been getting objections from other Dutch entities, such as the State Gas Board and some of the municipal distribution companies. The committee he had appointed earlier, now known as the Van der Grinten Committee, with L. G. Wansink serving as secretary, quickly began holding hearings.

The oil companies now recognized that nothing short of State Mine's participation in production and marketing would break that impasse. They arrived at a point where they were able to agree to a one-third share of production and marketing for State Mines. Because of the "sheik effect," they had to remain steadfast on their point that export must be excluded. The government remained just as steadfast in its demand for 50 percent of the export revenue.

In December, the Van der Grinten Committee sent a secret report to de Pous that included the following passage: "The oil companies have made it very clear that for their position, vis-à-vis other countries, they find it extremely important that participation by State Mines in the winning sector, acceptable in itself, be masked in a form so as to not endanger them. This request can be met if the concession is formally granted to NAM and NAM brings the concession into a partnership with the State Mines."[6]

In a meeting on June 26 among de Pous, Wansink, Verkade, Dutch State Mines, Shell, and Esso, both sides were intransigent, but that deadlock evaporated in just twenty-four hours.

Shell's Lykle Schepers, who was in charge of natural gas for Shell, had been responsible for setting up the first meeting in which Shell executives got on board. He was once again the deciding factor, this time in moving through the impasse.

On June 27, Schepers and Minister de Pous came face-to-face in an intriguing meeting, now dubbed "the horse trading session," which had far-reaching consequences.

In his article "*Striking Bonanza*," Prof. Arne Kaijser described the outcome:

> *Lykle Schepers was de Pous' major counterpart on the industry side and was the main representative of the NAM partners. He was one of the most influential industrialists in the country. On one occasion, negotiations got stuck and Pous invited Schepers to his office for a tête-à-tête. The minister*

---

6   Subterranean Commonwealth by Wolfe Kielich.

used the ultimate threat: he told Schepers that if NAM did not agree to his proposal, the state would refuse them the concession for the Groningen field and give them a ⬜once and for all⬜ compensation package instead. Schepers responded by telling de Pous, in that event, the refineries and petrochemical plants in the Rotterdam harbor would not be expanded further. Confronted with their mutual dependence on one another, they recognized open conflict would be disastrous. They just had to find common ground.

That common ground was revealed when Minister de Pous submitted his report, along with his proposals for the government's share of marketing and production revenue. There would be a marketing and transportation company to be named Gasunie. A total of 40 percent of Gasunie would be owned by State Mines, 10 percent by the Dutch government, and 25 percent each by Shell and Esso. This new company would purchase all the natural gas from NAM and would sell the gas domestically and also in export via NAM.

The profits of production would be shared in a separate partnership called the Maatschappij ("Maatschappij" means "company"). A total of 40 percent of this would be owned by State Mines, 30 percent by Esso, and 30 percent by Shell. Because the government also had a 10 percent royalty, in effect, this was a 50 percent participation by the state in the production. When income taxes were added, the government would receive approximately 70 percent of the revenue. NAM would be the exploration and production operator.

According to another article by Prof. Arne Kaijser, *"From Slochteren to Wassenaar: The Creation of a Natural Gas Regime in the Netherlands, 1960-1963,"* "On July 11th, 1962, the important bill, 'Nota inzake het aardgas,' was presented to Parliament. On October 4th, the bill was discussed in the Second Chamber. The moment of truth came when the Nederlander representative of the PvdA (the Social Democratic party) gave his speech."

Now all de Pous's careful consensus building came to fruition. A minimum of debate occurred after the Nederlander's quiet and firm endorsement of de Pous's efforts: "We are, in all honesty, compelled to say that the minister has had an open eye to our objections. He has truly informed Parliament we cannot blame the minister for not achieving everything during the negotiations. In the same way, we don't blame the other party after the phase of negotiations, now dawns the period of cooperation. A fresh wind will start to blow through the somewhat sleepy gas world. The community can only profit from it."

A gas memorandum was agreed to in the Second Chamber without dissension. Shell, Esso, and State Mines could now begin in earnest to plan the establishment of the new company and to develop details for pipelines, in anticipation of ultimate approval for the production concession by the Dutch Parliament. The minister suggested that the new company, which came to be known as Gasunie, and the producing Maatschappij be coordinated by a steering committee of five designated delegates—one from each oil company, two from State Mines, and one from the government.

Until this point, Stewart's group in The Hague and the Esso study teams in other countries were the only players actively exploring export prospects. Now, however, a new player in the Dutch gas scenario, named Johan Bernard Schepers, was about to stride onto the Dutch gas stage—all the way from Casablanca.

—Chapter 13—

The Dutchman from Casablanca

The telegram from Royal Dutch Shell arrived in Casablanca just as Schepers and his wife, Louise, were about to receive guests. He had, by then, traveled across the globe for Shell in one leadership role after another. He and his family had been stationed in London, Spain, Indonesia, Algeria, and Canada. This time they were sending him home—to Holland.

When Holland was invaded by Germany in 1940, Schepers and his family were living in the small town of Voorburg. Known as Krik since his boyhood, he was just entering his teenage years. His father, Jan Dirk, an officer in the Dutch army, was deported to a German prison camp, so Krik became the man of the family. During the years of occupation, food supplies became more and more sparse, and he was able to supplement the family's meager food rations by riding on his bicycle to an area of farms around Zoetermeer, which was about an hour and a half away.

His family's biggest fear was that the Nazis would discover that although he was only seventeen, he had already graduated from high school. Under the German occupation, upon graduation, all boys were subject to deportation to Germany either as forced labor or to be impressed into the German army. Safe for a while because he looked younger, Krik and a friend got involved in the Dutch resistance, carrying messages and observing certain people's movements.

Another friend of Krik had a job working as a secretary in a local German administration office. Part of her job included getting various documents signed, and she was able to get a signature on a document that permitted Krik to be out after the eight-o'-clock curfew, enabling him more leeway in what he was doing for the resistance.

When his closest friend was arrested in the fall of 1944, there was a good chance the police would be looking for Krik as well, so others in the resistance helped him to hide in the Voorburg hospital.

When the Allies were able to liberate the southern part of the Netherlands, this resulted in the occupation growing more brutal in the rest of the country, accelerating still more harshly after the success of a national railway strike. The strike was called for by the exiled Dutch government to stop the transport of citizens to forced labor and to concentration camps and also to aid further Allied liberation attempts.

There was an aborted attempt to liberate the Netherlands in September 1944, an event depicted in the film *A Bridge Too Far*. Many Allied ground troops, paratroopers, and Dutch civilians lost their lives in a battle near Arnhem. Other Dutch civilians risked their lives to harbor those few British and American paratroopers who escaped. As punishment for both the railway strike and the liberation attempt, the Germans embargoed all food transports to the Western Netherlands. By November, the embargo was partially rescinded, but an exceedingly harsh winter set in, compounding the problems of food transportation. The situation in the hospital where Krik was hiding became so desperate patients were starving to death. Because of the recent embargo on food transportation, there were good supplies of food in the north from the fall harvest, but there was no means by which they could be distributed to all the provinces.

Krik had family on farms near Groningen, and this was where the High Food Commission was. He proposed to the hospital administrators that he set out on his own to find a way to bring food back for the patients. Although they looked upon the chances of success for this slender, intense teenager as slim, the administrators gave Krik letters of requisition for the commission and letters to hospitals along the way requesting that he be given lodging.

The friend of Krik who worked in the administration office also had family in Groningen, and he agreed to take her along. He borrowed the motorbike of a doctor he knew, but they only got as far as Utrecht before the Germans confiscated it.

Because five years of German is required in Dutch schools, Krik spoke the language flawlessly, and with the German papers he had, he was able to get his friend and himself on a military transport heading north. This was an exceedingly dangerous thing to do because the only trains traveling in Holland were German transports, and the Allies bombed them every chance they got. Therefore, the trains could only travel a few hours each night, and it took days for the two teenagers to get to their destination.

In Groningen, Krik's friend set off to join her family, while Krik headed for the Food Commission. Standing on a street corner, he was alarmed when a German officer approached him, but he turned out only to be seeking directions. Because of Krik's familiarity with Groningen, he was able to help the man, who expressed surprise at Krik's courteous demeanor and his very proper German. (The one small act of defiance Dutch people could exercise during the occupation was to pretend not to understand German.) The officer went on his way, none the wiser about Krik's bold intentions.

Officials at the High Food Commission were eager to give him all the supplies the letters from the hospital requested, but there was one very big problem. The only means of transporting the precious cargo of food was by boat. Undaunted, Krik went to the harbor and found it filled with German boats doing nothing. Selecting one that looked large enough for his cargo but not large enough to attract attention, he climbed on board. Waving his German papers and speaking in perfect German, he asked the officer, in the most urgent terms, if he would take on the job. However, instead of telling him the food was destined for the civilian hospital in Voorburg, Krik said that it was headed for a German military hospital. Convinced he was helping his fellow countrymen, the captain agreed, provided Krik got a transport order from the presiding German marine officer.

Ignoring the danger he would face if his subterfuge was discovered, Krik nevertheless set off to find the marine office. To his surprise, that marine officer turned out to be the very officer Krik had helped on the street. Once again, using the German word for a military hospital, he presented his German authorization papers, to which the officer gave but a cursory glance. Spending a little more time on the list of supplies stamped with the seal of the Food Commission, the officer ordered the preparation of the necessary transport order. Sitting quietly, Krik dared not betray his very real anxiety over whether some last-minute glitch would reveal his true identity and mission. While waiting, he engaged in a casual conversation with the officer as if his life was not at risk. However, Krik knew he would not really breathe easily until he was back in Voorburg.

With the transport order in his hand, he headed back to the boat, where the crew readied the ship for its cargo.

During daylight hours, ships on canals were also shot at by the Allies, so Krik's ship moved only at night from Groningen to Friesland, arriving at the town of Lemmer. Before they could cross the Ysselmeer, the boat had to wait for a convoy to form. If the military personnel swarming about decided to board the ship to verify his destination, his precious cargo might not reach Voorburg and the people who needed it so desperately. In such an event, Krik would never see Voorburg again either. When the ship was finally permitted to pass, Krik let himself breathe a little easier.

During the rest of the journey, the captain became friendly with Krik and confessed that he knew the war was nearly over. He just wanted to get home and was hoping that he and his crew of three could get a good meal at the hospital at the end of the trip. Krik decided to tell him the truth. There was no military hospital. The captain made no attempt to interrupt Krik's mission. Instead, he asked if Krik could help him and his crew find some civilian clothes so they could disappear at the end of the trip and find their way back home. Krik readily agreed.

In Voorburg, Krik was as good as his word. While the crew hid below, he managed to find the necessary clothes and brought them back, along with some food for the crew, who then helped unload the ship for the hospital. As he watched the ship sail off toward Amsterdam, never to be seen again, Krik took his first deep breath in a very long time.

It was December now, and the winter of hunger in Holland would claim thousands more lives before liberation came in May. The supplies Krik brought saved many lives in the Voorburg hospital but also made him a target for the German authorities, so he was hidden by friends in the loft of a garage until liberation day. When his father was released from his long captivity, Krik was there as the whole family welcomed him home.

After the war, and still a teenager, Schepers left home once again, this time for officers' training in England. He served his country in Indonesia, returning to Amsterdam in 1949, where he entered the business world with Shell. His resourcefulness and his ability to recognize opportunity were born in the Dutch resistance and developed as assets that became well honed in the years that followed.

Krik's wife-to-be, Louise, was a pharmaceutical student in 1949. It took but three months of courtship for him to convince her to marry him, but two obstacles immediately conspired to separate the lovers. Shell transferred Krik to their offices in England, and Louise's parents expected her to complete her studies.

Louise's father was a physician, and her mother a pharmacist. In those days, medications were not conveniently dispensed from corner drugstores or supermarkets by pharmaceutical giants. They were handcrafted for specific conditions to the specifications of the physician. Her mother had mastered the craft and worked side by side with Louise's father. It was a vocation in which they expected Louise to follow. Although she completed her studies, she did not enter the newly emerging field of professional pharmacist.

When Krik returned from London a year later, he and Louise were married in Amsterdam. The young couple first lived in Epsom in the Netherlands, where their daughter, Louise, was born. A year later, in Haarlem, their first son, Jan Dirk, was born on June 24, 1953.

Louise and Krik Schepers at London Ball 1962 after he was transferred from Morocco to join the Shell Dutch gas negotiations.

In early 1945, while the Netherlands was occupied by the Germans, the teenaged Schepers talked the Germans into giving him a boatload of hospital supplies, and then he bluffed them into helping him barge the badly needed supplies to a civilian hospital near The Hague.

Shortly afterward, Krik was transferred to Madrid, and Louise and the two children joined him there in August.

According to Louise, "We were hardly settled in Madrid when Shell needed Krik in Tangier, to be the general manager of the tiny Shell company there. It was then an enclave, internationally governed. Morocco was still unspoiled and folkloric. It was a bit of a culture shock when we arrived, but life was very pleasant. There were lots of expatriates from France, England, Holland, and Spain. We lived five minutes from the beach, so with the kids, this was ideal.

"Our second son, Willem, was born in Tangiers on February 18, 1955. We were transferred to Canada for a year then returned to Morocco in 1956, but this time to Casablanca for about six years, until we were called to The Hague in 1962."

Just prior to receiving the telegram in 1962, the Schepers had been discussing the possibility of requesting that Shell transfer them back to Holland for their daughter to have her high school years where her parents had been educated. But before they had made up their minds, the decision was made for them. When he arrived in The Hague, Schepers did not find things quite as he had expected.

"I thought I would be getting some kind of marching orders as to what my duties would be in this new job, but when I asked J. C. Boot, who was the head of everything, what those might be, he said, 'I haven't got a clue. Why don't you write down what you think you should get as marching orders?'"

Schepers's uncle Lykle was the Shell executive who had already been so effective in Dutch gas negotiations. Schepers had long ago established his own unique position within the company wherever he was, and this time was no exception. Since the corporation provided no job description, he had to define it for himself. He started out by stating what he didn't want to do.

"The first thing I wrote was that I wasn't going to be away from home more than three nights a week so that I could keep the family life together. I declared that I thought the job could be run that way."

With not a jot of concern, Boot just said to Schepers, "That's okay with me."

With duties unnamed, it felt at first a little like trying to navigate the foggy autobahn wearing dark glasses. "In this crazy job, I was given a little room near the managing director's office, where they used to have the office for the assistant secretary of the board. It was therefore a very old, dark-paneled room. I was sitting there on my own, not quite knowing what being number 5 in the cast of managers was supposed to mean. I do remember asking for a secretary, and they sent one. She sat before me for her interview and commented, 'This is a nice office. But what is your job?' I said, 'I don't know.'"

Over at Esso's offices in The Hague, Stewart heard the first rumor that Shell had appointed their own coordinator for the Dutch natural gas business. There was no way for Stewart to tell if this appointment was the result of Shell having gotten wind of Esso's export studies or whether it was simply an assignment to serve as a sort of counterweight to Stewart's position with the Esso team.

"I didn't know whether Schepers would be what I'd come to recognize as the classic, initially reserved Dutch business personality or a widely traveled, more open international businessman," said Stewart. "On the day he first walked into our office, Martin, Jan, and I were busy planning our next approach to negotiations in the export countries."

Stewart looked up from his work to see a tall, lean Lincolnesque figure with a mane of dark blond hair filling his doorway. Schepers greeted him in fluent English with a slight Dutch accent. Stewart came to recognize that those indelible blue eyes fronted a wily, resourceful mind. Schepers's ready smile and jesting manner belied a driving ambition and a fierce competitiveness, not unlike Stewart's own. Stewart liked him at once. "It was immediately, 'Call me Krik.' I was taken with his affable manner and ready intelligence, just liked him right away. But he was a Shell man. It was obviously prudent to hold back most of what we were already doing in the potential export countries."

At the same time Schepers was engaging in his "So what do you do at Esso?" handshake questions, those incisive blue eyes were taking in the flow charts Esso had on the wall illustrating the various Esso study groups Stewart and the team had launched about potential markets in other countries.

"While Schepers and I talked, he wandered around the big barnlike room where we had our desks," said Stewart. "On the wall was a calendar crammed with trip dates and places to which Martin and I were constantly traveling in pursuit of our export studies."

Schepers's first comment left no doubt he'd grasped the purpose of those charts. "I see you are going to Germany and Belgium frequently. Think they could use any gas there?"

Stewart responded casually, "I made some noncommittal remark that we were studying the possibility and changed the subject. I learned later that after Schepers's visit, he galvanized Shell into action. Schepers was not going to let Esso take the lead if Dutch gas was going to be exported."

"Stewart's charts set off my alarm bells clanging in no uncertain terms that Shell was temporarily outmanned," said Schepers. "I could see before me the evidence that Esso already had technical and economics people at work on studies in other countries. I could see they were far enough ahead of us that they might very well go forward without us unless we jumped in. I was not about to have this American and his Esso team diminish Shell. I took what I had discerned on that wall, went back to my own offices, and had Shell quickly set up a study team of our own in The Hague. We made a number of visits to Germany and Belgium. In quick time, I was satisfied. Shell would not be outdone by Esso when the time came to compete for gas business in those countries."

Shell's research team was deeply interested in the way natural gas had become a household fuel in the United States, so Schepers and a colleague named Vi Vizzard from Shell's London office went together to the States to get a firsthand look at how the process worked.

Schepers recalled his concern that Esso was already ahead of his firm. "We tried to take shortcuts to get at whatever useful information we could find about the practical uses of natural gas. I had our office organize trips to various utility companies in the U.S. Vizzard was so English, always with a handkerchief up his sleeve and very proper. We toured and met the utility people during the week. Then each day we'd write about what we'd learned. We had the weekends off, and Shell encouraged us to go to whatever other cities we wanted to see in America. Once, we went to Las Vegas. We didn't gamble, just wanted to see what this entertainment mecca was about. Shell had always arranged our hotels for us, but on the night we arrived there, it was after 7:00 p.m. The porter carried our luggage up to the desk, where the reservations clerk said, 'Sorry, you didn't show up. The reservation has been sold.' We didn't have a room because the office hadn't guaranteed it. 'Don't worry,' the clerk said, 'next door they'll have a room.'

"Now next door was about five yards away, but the porter wouldn't carry our bags to the adjacent hotel. This did seem a bit inhospitable to us, but we carried them far enough that the porter in the other hotel agreed to help. It turned out they were on different, rival union rolls. And here was this Englishman with his handkerchief up his sleeve, expecting much more proper deportment. Poor staid and serious Vizzard lost his handkerchief in the revolving door and got tipped topsy-turvy inside the turning mechanism and got quite silly trying to recapture it.

"We also went to Los Angeles one weekend. We were booked into a hotel, and everybody else had a car, but for some reason, we didn't. We hadn't a clue about where anything was or where to go, so we ventured out to a bus and told the driver we wanted a ticket to the end of the line. When we got there, it was not just the end of the line. It was land's end. We had come to the ocean in Santa Monica, with its very long pier upon which, to our surprise, sat a whole roller coaster. We elected not to experience that, but we enjoyed the view and the food served in little paper boats."

The Esso groups in the other countries, urged on by the team in The Hague, made real progress in delineating the export opportunities for markets and pipeline investments. Stewart knew by now that Shell had undertaken its own studies into those very issues, and he began to question his own earlier thoughts about Esso going it alone beyond the Dutch border.

Now that the government and the oil companies were close to agreement that the gas would be sold domestically and in export through NAM, the idea of separately marketing Esso's share of the gas without Shell no longer seemed realistic. It was, of course, equally unrealistic to imagine that Esso could transport the gas on its own to other countries without the approval of the Dutch government. They would be looking to protect their valuable resource and optimize its value. Shell certainly wasn't going to turn over their share of the gas to Esso anywhere.

Schepers was, by now, becoming a regular visitor to the Esso offices, and he was openly welcomed by Stewart. "Krik had began to drop in frequently to chat and have lunch. He was the kind of man who would have intuitively sensed any manipulative intention. Once lost, the trust of a man like this, which is so necessary to successful negotiation, could never have been reclaimed."

Stewart was no longer dealing with a faceless rival corporation. He was, instead, in frequent contact with a man whose good sense and intelligence were certain to be examining the very same problems with which he and his team were wrestling. Stewart determined the best course of action was to be direct. "It was apparent to both of us that it was utterly impractical not to combine the resources of both our study teams regarding market information. With the approval of our lawyers and head offices, Krik and I moved into adjacent offices in the KLM building and worked together to coordinate the efforts of the combined Esso/Shell study teams in Germany and Brussels. We hadn't even tried to solve how or which of our companies would actually be exporting the gas."

Schepers's regard for Stewart continued to grow. "As a business partner, and as a friend, Doug was so completely reliable it made working with him so pleasant and easy. I did not have to waste time thinking, 'How could he double-cross me?'"

Schepers likened the success of their working relationship to that of a successful marriage. "It is often said that a sense of humor keeps marriage relations healthy, but the same applies to a business relationship. I enjoyed very many moments of his good and excellent sense of humor. The three years working with Doug were the best of my working life."

The success of both their work and their personal relationship was rooted in the integrity and commitment that each of them brought not only to their work life but also to a friendship that lasted for forty years.

Stewart, to this day, credited the personal regard he and Schepers had for each other with a big part of their success. "One of the reasons we were so successful in the export negotiations in Germany, Belgium, and France had to do with the degree of trust we developed in each other."

Family life was central to both men. Stewart and Schepers made a commitment to each other in the first days of their association that weekends belonged to the family. They would travel only three days a week. This was an agreement they managed to maintain throughout the years they worked together.

For Stewart, the fresh opportunity to focus on export with Schepers was made more difficult by the fact that he was still supervising all the study teams not only in Hamburg and The Hague but also those in Belgium, France, and the UK. In addition, he was assisting Smit with the Dutch negotiations, which showed no sign of resolution in the near future.

"All of these responsibilities kept pulling me away from the export preparations, which was where I wanted to be," said Stewart. "I knew that when the export effort really kicked in, a different kind of travel schedule would also be demanded. I was not willing to sacrifice my family life in this way, so I made a management decision to go to New York, explain the growing work load, and to make clear my need for additional personnel."

As Stewart prepared his presentation for Jersey regarding his need for additional manpower, he stopped to write a report for Milbrath detailing his conclusions about sales of "interruptible gas" and the useful effect its sales would have on pipeline investments. "Every time I talked to NAM, the drilling success continued. The gas reserves continued to grow. I could see that export would be a big part of the gas demand and that Jersey would have enormous profit potential if we could succeed in our efforts. In order to economically build the pipelines for these new markets, it was apparent to me that there would be economic and political pressure to expand the gas sales into lower-priced industrial markets. It was also obvious to me that sales of 'interruptible gas' could be what would optimize the pipeline investments without having to take year-round sales into those lower-priced markets."

The sale of "interruptible gas" capitalizes on the difference between the low volume of gas sold during the summer periods and the high volume sold during the winter. The investment required for pipelines requires that the lines be sufficient for carrying the demands of the peak winter months. In effect, this means that the transportation costs to supply winter demands bears the whole cost. There is an opportunity to amortize this cost when sales in the premium household market are low. Instead of investing in storage facilities for the gas during these low demand periods, the gas could, in those periods, be sold to the industrial market for short, interruptible periods during which those companies would realize considerable savings by turning off their coal- or oil-fired boilers and bringing in natural gas.

Stewart had some concerns that the concept might not be appealing to Bill Stott because Stott would lose some of his summer fuel oil sales, which he regarded as his particular baby. Nevertheless, he sent off his report on interruptible gas to Milbrath, confident it would be circulated appropriately. He went back to his primary concern, his presentation about his need for more personnel.

Stewart hadn't yet received a response from Jersey about the interruptible gas report when he had an unexpected visit from Mutt and Jeff. "Naturally, I brought them up to date on the current status of everything, and in the course of our conversation, I also shared with them my conclusions regarding the ever-increasing gas reserve estimates and my ideas about the feasibility of sales for interruptible gas."

Stewart's suggestions about interruptible gas were about to unspool a fresh round of corporate red tape as well as another eruption of the corporate generation gap, unexpectedly shifting his career in a different and very dramatic direction.

—Chapter 14—

Stewart Interrupted

S hortly after the visit from Mutt and Jeff, Stewart got an urgent call from New York asking him to return there as soon as possible. The urgency of this request didn't register with him as much as the opportunity it offered to quickly get a hearing on his petition for increased staffing.

"I went to New York prepared to lay out my case for more staff in the strongest terms possible," said Stewart. "I was going to make them understand that our workload was growing exponentially in the exact proportion to our growing prospects. I already knew just which people I wanted to pull out of various Jersey offices to fill the emerging responsibilities so that I could free myself to concentrate on export. I wanted to spend more time on the export effort because that was where I knew I could be most effective."

On Stewart's arrival in New York, he set about interviewing some of the people he knew he wanted to have in The Hague. He was suddenly confronted with an unexpected demand from Bill Stott.

"He was insisting that I make a full presentation on interruptible gas, something I had not come prepared to do. I had only written the report on it because I felt we needed to give some thought to the effect it could have on the premium market concept and pipeline economics, not with any thought of promoting it in some way."

In hindsight, Stott's demand for this presentation was a red flag Stewart didn't recognize. He assumed it had been triggered by the interruptible gas report or that Mutt and Jeff had passed the ideas on to Stott with their usual negative interpretation.

Stewart had the facts for utilizing interruptible gas and its benefits firmly in mind, so he quickly prepared some view graphs showing the size of the gas reserves alongside a forecast of the probable Dutch market, illustrating the large volumes that would be available for export. He still intended the main focus of his presentation to emphasize the project's immediate need for increased staff. "I began by explaining our staffing needs and presented my appraisal of the marketing outlook for Dutch gas in export countries. I then went on to present the information about interruptible gas, illustrating how the fluctuation in demand for the winter, as compared with the summer, would affect the investment for pipelines. This visualized for the group how the sales of interruptible gas would level off the demand and improve the overall economics. To my absolute amazement, Stott interrupted me, loudly and vividly."

"We're not going to go along with that," said Stott.

It was as if Stott hadn't listened at all to the information, which clearly demonstrated how sales of interruptible gas worked to Esso's benefit. There was no acknowledgment at all of the Dutch gas project's need for more people. Instead, Stott launched into one of his trademark tirades.

"Yet again, my ideas got me into hot water with Stott. It was as if he'd come to the meeting with his mind already made up. I thought Bob Milbrath could have spoken out because I'd sent the report to his attention, and I knew he certainly understood the concept, but obviously, he wasn't about to push Stott in front of twenty people. Stott was a son of a bitch, General Patton sort of a guy. It's a wonder Stott didn't fire me right there."

Actually, Stott couldn't peremptorily fire Stewart. The Dutch gas project had originally been budgeted out of Jersey's production department in New York and had recently been transferred out of Jersey's marketing department. The year before, on March 10, 1961, Bob

Milbrath had been elected president and executive committee chairman of the Esso Export Corporation, Esso's international marketing affiliate. Export efforts were part of Esso's international framework. This made Milbrath's interest in, and support for, Stewart and the Dutch gas project more formal and was actually in effect at this time.

Once the meeting broke up, Stewart was determined to find out why Milbrath hadn't spoken up. "After the meeting, I went straight to Milbrath, wanting an explanation for why Stott acted as if he were dealing with new information. Milbrath expressed his dismay that I hadn't prepared Stott in advance of my arrival. He asked if I'd forgotten how Stott regarded fuel oil sales as his baby. Bob thought I should have predicted Stott's reaction and gotten the information to the department in advance. I reminded Milbrath that, after all, he was right here in New York. If he had bothered to read my report, or at least look at the charts, which I most certainly did send, he could have interceded with Stott himself. Before I could finish my sentence, Milbrath held up his hand. We practically turned on a dime and, without another word, went straight to the fellow who was responsible for receiving my reports and letters and passing them on."

Although the interruptible gas report was there all right, along with everything else Stewart had been sending, none of it had moved beyond the man's desk. There wasn't even an office circulation stamp on any of it. Was this fellow just a human weak link who attached no significance to what was happening with "that project over there" in the Netherlands? Or had the fellow possibly been directed to sit on all of Stewart's information because Stewart was upstream and any information from him was not regarded as related to marketing?

In the discussion that followed, Stewart and Milbrath reflected on the meeting and mutually agreed it wouldn't have made any difference if Stott had seen that preliminary interruptible gas report. The immediacy of Stott's outburst clearly indicated he had made up his mind to reject the idea before the meeting ever began.

Since Stott's outburst deflected attention from the project's need for additional staffing, it may have been as deliberate a choice as Stott's rejection of the interruptible gas idea. The increased number of people and the generation of additional activity might have transformed Stewart's freehanded, but hitherto undesignated, leadership into a more formal appointment. But more importantly, the outburst might have been triggered by Stott's recognition that Upstream Stewart was again treading into his downstream marketing territory.

"Stott didn't like to have people around who didn't toe his line," said Stewart. "And he particularly disliked anybody who had the temerity to offer bold ideas that hadn't originated with him. Stott seemed to have taken my ideas as a personal affront as if I, personally, was stalking his oil markets."

Eventually, when those pipelines became a reality and exported Dutch gas had spread to the most densely populated areas of Europe, the validity of Stewart's predictions about interruptible gas was proven many times over. By 1976, Ruhrgas, the biggest gas company in Germany, made reference to the significance of interruptible gas contracts on page 12 of its annual report for that year: "The gas industry must conclude Interruptible Gas contracts under which natural gas is supplied to power plants during periods of low demand and deliveries are stopped when natural gas demand is high. *If this option were not available, the gas industry would be unable to maintain secure supplies to the residential, commercial and industrial customers.*"

But in 1962, it was Stott's shortsighted view that prevailed. Not long after his blowup, Jersey issued a general corporate policy memo notifying all concerned that the company would not condone interruptible gas as part of any marketing strategy for Dutch gas. Only premium pricing would be considered.

Stewart had no doubt that the memo was directed at him personally. "In spite of the fact that I had originated the premium price strategy from the start, someone, most likely Stott, had been able to convince the hierarchy at Jersey that they might not be able to trust me to maintain my own idea of premium price strategy. The memo indicated I might have started selling gas into the lower-priced markets. That was not what I was proposing, and certainly, Stott knew that."

Although Stewart had no formal title in the beginning, he certainly was chosen for his expertise and background. Over time, those qualities, coupled with his personality and drive, had brought the upstream natural gas project right to the place Stewart predicted in his first full presentation to the Jersey board. In another management climate, the combination of Stewart's expertise in engineering and economics, along with his negotiating talents and inspired marketing ideas, would have been recognized as a unique and valuable combination of upstream and downstream activity. But this was not another management climate; this was Jersey 1960.

The Dutch gas project was part of Esso's international framework, but Stott engineered a curious restructuring that brought it under the marketing department's influence. Stewart's request for additional personnel was filled with men of Stott's own choosing. Don Cox, an American and a downstream man trusted by Bill Stott, was already in Europe as the vice president of Esso A. G. in Germany. Cox was transferred to The Hague and appointed as the coordinator for the Dutch gas project. Coen Smit, as president of Esso Nederland, would remain the chief contact with Dutch Shell and the government. Bill Ganskopp, brought over from one of Jersey's U.S. affiliates, was named project manager for domestic Dutch gas affairs. He would be responsible for working on the day-to-day negotiations with Smit and for planning with a joint Esso/Shell/State Mines committee preparing for a possible domestic natural gas company (later to become Gasunie).

Although Stewart would no longer be the undesignated, freehanded person in charge of the entire project on a day-to-day basis, he was appointed project manager for Export, which was exactly the place where Stewart wanted to focus his energy. He would technically report to Cox, who had no experience in this new natural gas arena. If Stott's intention was to put Stewart in his place, he had actually just handed him what he wanted more than anything else. "I had asked for help because the Dutch program was becoming detailed and technical. I wanted more than anything to be able to focus on the export possibilities. I hadn't anticipated this broad management shift, but being project manager for Export freed me from those daily committee details, giving me the freedom to be in the thick of making export happen. I loved the challenge of negotiating with other people and was definitely intrigued by the opportunities for travel, which export activity was certain to carry with it."

Whatever Stott's intention, it was brushed away like a speck of lint on Stewart's jacket. He never looked back. To facilitate the work of the Esso/Shell export project teams, Stewart and Schepers had already moved into the KLM building. Both of them began bringing in the people each considered most valuable.

While in New York, Stewart had already interviewed and chosen the people he knew were best equipped to deal with the challenges of export. "I found a way to ease the negative Paul Miles back to New York and replaced him with Millard Clegg, a pipeline expert from Humble Oil. I knew his considerable capabilities from my own days at Humble. Millard was really knowledgeable about natural gas and its technological requirements because of the success we'd had developing the King Ranch recycling plant."

Clegg recalled how he got the job. "Doug interviewed me and another candidate for this job, both at the same time, which was a little unsettling, but the job turned out to be mine. I was told I was needed urgently. I agreed to take the job for just one year, provided my wife and family would be with me. In September of '62, when I got there, I reported to the old Esso kirk offices. Doug hadn't yet returned from wherever he was, and nobody could tell me who I was supposed to work for. I was put in an office with a fellow who had the idea that I was working for him. This seemed to last a long time before Doug got back to set him straight. Doug quickly advised this fellow that working for him was not what I'd been brought over there for. About that time, we moved into the KLM building with a group of Shell people."

Clegg also remembered that one of Shell's chief engineers was a Dutchman named Van Leerdom, who spoke several languages. "He facilitated a good many things for me because of his linguistic abilities. He told me his father had been a language teacher in the Dutch colony in

Indonesia during the war and had been imprisoned there by the Japanese, along with many other Dutch citizens, for the entire duration of the war."

Stewart remembered the story he'd heard from the Shell geologist on his way to Oldenzaal, and he and Clegg wondered if the imprisoned teacher might have been Van Leerdom's father.

It had been a mystery to Stewart how Clegg was able to come up with answers for which he'd always had to wait for days to get from Miles because they had no computers. Clegg explained the ingenious system he devised to deliver those figures. "We made up a bunch of alignment charts that let us take certain items, such as volumes, and make an estimate that gave us a point on the curve. Once we'd plotted the points of all these myriad elements, we could come up with an optimum cost to do something. We'd have a line for one case, a line for another. Then all we had to do was go to this alignment chart, go across for volume, and it would give us the optimum tariff for that particular condition, and we could predict the cost in a few seconds."

Clegg recalled a good deal of travel with Stewart during his year with the Dutch gas project. There were various locations in Germany, Belgium, France, and the UK. "The problems I dealt with often had to do with assessing the market potential in a particular city or country in order to forecast possible volume growth. Among the challenges, we had all the different monetary systems and the units and construction practices in each country."

Dorothy Clegg, Millard's wife, recounted that the winter of '62 and '63 had been reported as Holland's coldest winter in 183 years. "One night there was this heavy, heavy, heavy fog. On our way home, the fog actually froze, and you could hear all this ice clattering to the ground. Then it was suddenly just as clear as a bell. It was absolutely fantastic. The winter was so cold they set up the service stations out on the Zuiderzee, and people would drive out there to fill up. I guess they figured out it had finally thawed out when cars began to fall in the water. Actually, we had a hellacious year in Holland that most folks who get transferred to foreign duty probably don't have. We had to move house twice and had four children to organize to and from their different schools. Once, our little boy fell out of the third-story window. And we were burglarized twice. As if that wasn't enough, the house caught on fire when a neighbor, whose house shared a chimney with ours, decided to light a fire, not knowing storks had built a nest on top of the chimney. And to top it all off, I broke my leg that year!"

Doctors in Holland made house calls then, and on one visit, her doctor pointed out an intriguing surprise right there in Dorothy's dining room.

"Our house had once served as the Israeli Embassy and was furnished," she recalled. "In the dining room was this huge china cabinet, the bottom of which I used as a liquor cabinet. The doctor stared at it for a minute then walked to it and said, 'Let me show you something. Behind it, there is a sliding door.' When he pulled it back, there was an open space we never knew was there. The doctor had been part of the Dutch resistance, and that little space had been used to hide British and American airmen who had parachuted into Holland in the Battle of Arnhem. We had no idea our house was a part of Dutch history."

Millard Clegg was a big help to Stewart in planning the export pipelines, but before Europe's energy revolution could flow beyond the borders of Holland, American antitrust legislation and the Standard Oil Consent Decree were barriers that held it in check, just as the seawall at Scheveningen holds back the North Sea. At a well-known restaurant above that very seawall, Stewart and Schepers would try to find a solution that respected the barriers and permitted the free flow of Dutch gas into the rest of Europe.

—Chapter 15—

The "Uitsmijter" Solution

As the months passed, approval from the Dutch government for a domestic and export program drew nearer. And with every day that passed, Stewart became more concerned with what the organizational structure for the export plan was going to be.

"Before Krik came on board, and when Orlean and I made our first trips to the other countries, I proceeded as if it were possible for Esso to build its own pipelines and sell its half of the gas at the border. But now that our two companies were jointly negotiating with the Dutch government and we were jointly conducting export studies, it was obvious export sales could not be done separately. No matter what scenario we dreamed up, the lawyers sent it back. Antitrust legislation absolutely prohibited Shell and Esso from marketing jointly." The Jersey lawyers finally turned up a single piece of new information. Although antitrust legislation dictated that Esso and Shell could not market together, the consent decree permitted them to share pipelines. This new nugget of information from the lawyers began to nudge at something in the back of Stewart's mind, which he, at first, couldn't quite bring to form. One morning, he suggested to Schepers they travel out to Scheveningen for lunch at a restaurant named *The Sienpost*, which overlooked the North Sea. Since sienpost means "lighthouse" in Dutch, this may have been a dash of serendipity.

"Krik and I were scratching our heads as to how we could get around the legal and political problems which were slowing us down," said Stewart. "We both ordered the typical Dutch special of the day—an 'uitsmijter'—consisting of two fried eggs, sunny-side up, on an open-faced steak sandwich. When the waiter placed our order on the table, something clicked."

That unformed "something" in the back of Stewart's mind jumped at him right off the plate. There it was, the answer for moving Dutch gas from the shared study stage to actual export.

"Krik, there it is!" said Stewart excitedly. "Why not form two separate companies? One will market the gas at the Dutch border, and the other company will transport the gas from the Dutch border to consumers in the export countries for a fee."

This eliminated the legal questions that would emerge in joint marketing. Joint participation in pipeline transportation was already an acceptable and common practice.

"So, Krik," Stewart continued, "you'll be president of a NAM subsary. You'll sell it."

"What'll we call the darn thing?" asked Schepers.

"You decide, Krik. It's your company."

"We shall keep it simple. NAM Gas Export, with Shell as the operator."

"Okay. Then I'll be president of the pipeline company, fifty-fifty for Shell and Esso, with Esso the operator. What'll we call this one?"

Schepers added a Dutch designation. "Doug, you, my friend, shall be general manager of Internationale Gas Transport Maatschappij."

"Maatschappij? I can't even spell it."

"Maatschappij is the Dutch word for company. We'll use the acronym IGTM."

In the middle of two very broad grins, Stewart saw a new obstacle. "Neither one of our offices is going to go for us making our own selves head of anything."

"You're the one with the fantasy. You figure out how to make it to happen," said Schepers.

"You could tell Shell that Esso proposed the two companies, and I'll tell Jersey that Shell proposed it. Let's see what they do."

Each of them fired off those cables. Stewart recalled that for several days, there was no reaction from either side. "In those days, because of the time difference and the difficult phone connections, I was reluctant to telephone, and anyway, I didn't want to be questioned at length about Shell's 'proposal.' Suddenly, there it was. Ms. Krullars, Mr. Smit's secretary, called and said there was a cable for me from New York. I rushed over from our office in the KLM building to read the cable: 'Shell's proposal for NAM Gas Export and Internationale Gas Transport Maatschappij has been reviewed here and approved. Please contact Shell for arrangements.' Bursting with excitement, I raced back to the KLM building and popped into Krik's office, holding the cable behind me, with a grin on my face a mile wide."

"And what are you up to?" asked Schepers. "The size of that grin is not for nothing."

Stewart bowed deeply and announced, "I am here to officially inform you that Shell's proposal to form the two companies has been approved by Jersey."

"It has? Let me get on to headquarters and see what their reaction to my cable is." Stewart waited while Schepers contacted his people. "After a long conversation in Dutch over the phone, of which I understood not one word, he turned around with a big smile and said, 'Ongelofelijk!' The lawyers have to do the details, but you and I are in business, my friend.' He had to explain to me that the odd Dutch word meant 'unbelievable' and went on to explain that not only did his office approve. They were enthusiastic about Jersey's proposal. I thought we ought to head right over to the t'Jagertie Club for a conference. Krik declined."

"No, no. We wait until it's on paper."

Some publications have described the formation of NAM Gas Export and Gasunie without making it clear how and when NAM Gas Export originated. The tentative agreements with State Mines and de Pous had reached a solution that a new company (Gasunie) would deliver and transport the gas domestically throughout the Netherlands to industries, municipalities, and Dutch householders. Although it was understood NAM would sell the gas in export, how, or by what means, was not spelled out. Perhaps because of that early reference, NAM Gas Export has been reported to have existed from those earliest days when, in fact, it did not. It was not until April 8, 1963, that a BPM/Jersey participation agreement gave birth to NAM Gas Export and created IGTM. Esso's Cox and Shell's Vale were appointed as advisors to Stewart and Schepers. On June 21, IGTM was formally incorporated, with Douglass Stewart as general manager. J. P. Schepers was appointed general manager of NAM Gas Export, a newly formed subsidiary of NAM (the original exploration and producing company).

April 8 was the day IGTM and NAM Gas Export were officially "on paper," and on that day, Schepers and Stewart took their team to celebrate at the t'Jagertie Club.

At first, Stewart didn't give much thought to how corporate was going to regard the two of them. "We just wanted to be free to forge ahead, more or less unfettered. When we walked in to negotiate, we wanted to walk in with the kind of power the gas companies in other countries would recognize and respect."

Over time, the two of them came to realize they'd actually gotten something they hadn't asked for, something that turned out to have a value far exceeding what they did ask for. Named as general managers of these two new companies, Stewart found that he and Schepers were accorded the corporate courtesies and independence from their own parent companies that management policy dictated for heads of affiliates.

"We were regarded by management and gas distribution companies alike as executives empowered to negotiate deals," said Stewart. "Ultimately, of course, everything went to corporate headquarters and to the Dutch government. But we were not received simply as employees who would have to get back to corporate for approval. It was not Esso and Shell at those bargaining tables where the deals were initiated and hammered out. It was NAM Gas Export and IGTM. That perception was invaluable. It was Krik and I who would be doing the back-and-forth negotiating until we got those deals to the place where there was something real for corporate and the government to take a look at."

The creation of IGTM as a distinct affiliate of the parent company did something particularly important for Stewart. While organizationally attached to Esso, he was able to slip the corporate bonds of Esso's upstream/downstream dichotomy.

The next day, after the little celebration at t'Jagertie Club, Schepers and Stewart met with their team to plan their strategy. Schepers opened the meeting. "The first thing we have to do is to get ourselves some decent offices. We need to create an image that we are up to competing with big boys like Ruhrgas." Schepers turned to Donald Maclean, a young Englishman he had brought into the project from within Shell. "Donald, can you find us some really first-class offices?"

The enterprising attitude for which Schepers had recruited him was immediately evident because Maclean announced he'd already located them. "I've been thinking about this ever since you guys started talking. There's a really great building on Smidswater, just around the block from the American Embassy. It's been sitting on that canal for three hundred years. It's got a great facade. The landlord says we can do over the whole interior however we want. It has three floors and should be more than adequate to handle our whole group and then some."

Not surprisingly, it was Orlean who jumped in first. "That'll cost a lot of money. What makes you think our companies will go for that?

And not surprisingly, Stewart had the answer. "They've already set up an unlimited expense account. There's no budget spelled out for this particular operation. We can surely justify that we need the image, so let's do it. Once we start it, there's no turning back. Krik and I'll take the lumps if they start complaining."

Schepers had just one thing to add. "Maclean, set it up."

They moved quickly to renovate the lovely old building at Smidswater 23. It sat on a charming tree-lined street on the brim of a stone-banked canal, just across the street from the house where Mata Hari, the famous World War I spy, had once lived. Stewart called on Millard Clegg to put his engineering talents to use in the gutting and reconstruction of the offices.

Clegg recalled that the redesign was not only a big job, but it also had an ASAP deadline. "On the ground floor, we had the clerks. The main offices on the second floor had these dramatic tall ceilings. Stewart had the one big lush corner office. He had a huge desk, flat-out intended for show. Schepers took the slightly smaller one, but it was actually the more important one from a working standpoint. There, we built in a combination conference table/booth around which so much strategy was planned. The only real executive perk Stewart and Schepers wanted was their own private restroom, which was kind of a big deal then. Maclean, with his impeccable taste, brought in the latest in Dutch modern mahogany furnishings, grass cloth walls, and sheer see-through drapes. As intended, Stewart's office was where visitors were received. Not only were the customers impressed, but when Esso's Smit and Shell's Boot heard about all this lushness, they also came to inspect, demanding to know where the budget approval for all this was."

According to Clegg, the nonchalant response was vintage Stewart. "So what were they going to do, tear it all out?"

There did come a time when the project received more oversight, but this basically amounted to nothing more than a rearrangement of bookkeeping. Stewart admitted Smidswater was not the typical "by the book" office, and neither were any of the others that were set up in the export countries. "When we started IGTM and NAM Gas Export, Jersey and Shell financed our expenses through some sort of a giant expense account that was later reconciled. But all the while, Krik and I had pretty much of a free hand to set up some very beautiful headquarters at Smidswater and in the other countries. We got a little bit of flack from Shell, who put up the expense account for Germany. They said our offices in Frankfurt were too elaborate and they had to return some furniture, but we maintained we had to demonstrate we were a going big outfit. As far as I was concerned, there's no doubt it really did pay off when the German or Belgian gas companies visited those offices." As Stewart predicted, none of it was torn out. It all stayed in place without being altered and produced the desired effect many times over.

Now that Stewart and Schepers had their own building, they called on their parent companies to staff the new organizations with technical and legal experts. From Esso, Stewart recruited Jack Windham, a pipeline engineer from Texas, to replace Millard Clegg, whose one-year stint would end in September, and Jerry Laufs, an American economist from the Esso A. G. German staff. Shell assigned a brilliantly able Dutch lawyer, Joop Hoogland, and also sent their Teo Hondius to handle public relations matters. A short time later, Stewart tapped a savvy young engineer/economist named Paul Mortimer to work with him at IGTM. Mortimer was, at that time, developing a report for the Jersey investment advisory committee regarding large capital expenditures. Fluent in Dutch, and originally from South Africa, he was a Rhodes scholar; had studied politics, philosophy, and economics at Oxford; gone to Harvard Business School for his MBA; and had joined Jersey in 1962.

Mortimer had a lively recall of the first time he encountered Stewart in 1963. "When I met Stewart, I was an analyst for Jersey's coordination and petroleum economics department in New York. I was doing a long-range world energy study and was asked if I would help push some numbers for this flamboyant character, a certain Doug Stewart. Part of what I had been working on was the economics of Nigerian and Algerian liquefied natural gas going into Europe. So I guess they thought I was a good person to contact. I went over to the Esso International building to introduce myself and spent two or three days with Stewart. I didn't understand a thing he was talking about because he was talking in a kind of shorthand, which I really was having trouble following. But at the end of the two or three days, we produced some economic analysis, which he used in a presentation he was to make. About two or three weeks later, I was asked if I would consider a position with a company called IGTM in The Hague. I started working there as an analyst, reporting to the head of their economics group."

Mortimer had ample opportunity to gain insights into the team of Stewart/Schepers in the years before he himself assumed the presidency of IGTM in 1968. "Exxon, at that time, was considered the best-run company in the world by *Fortune Magazine*. Internally, however, it was run by layers of committees, gathering input from all quarters when making major decisions. Ostensibly, the purpose of all these committees was intended to ensure that every department had input into every decision. It was, however, a cumbersome system for new ventures, which required initiative and action. Fortunately for the company, there were inevitably strong individuals with the ability to push things through. It was extremely fortunate for both Esso and Shell that they each happened to have these two men who both had that kind of initiative to bring to the Dutch gas project. Both these companies were actually stuck in a sort of vacuum at the very beginning of the project. The only guy who had, as Doug says, any idea of what this was all about, or could be all about, was the geologist who discovered it. Everybody else was wondering what the hell to do with it until Stewart came along with his ideas about premium marketing, initiating economic studies, and pipelining, and also the idea of exporting the gas to the countries bordering the Netherlands and beyond.

"Schepers was also a very positive and forceful character, a very lively man who made decisions, got on with it, and lived with his mistakes. He was, however, at the same time quite political and sensitive to the politics of the companies and of the government. The reason he could get away with so much was because he knew just how far he could go."

Stewart and Schepers were, by now, moving as far and as fast as they could go, even while Smidswater was under construction. At a meeting with Stewart and Orlean, Schepers's immediate concern was dealing with the intentions of their own Esso and Shell affiliates in Germany.

"Those offices were sure to want to take over negotiations, just because they're already there," said Schepers. "Especially Scheffer. He's Shell's managing director in Germany and imagines himself a titan in influence. I can already see the look on his face when we tell him, 'It's not you running the new business in Germany. It's going to be our two new companies selling Dutch gas and doing the negotiations.'"

Orlean's excited interruption was properly pertinent. "Our study team is in the Shell offices right now. How do you propose getting them out from under Scheffer's thumb when they're already there?"

Stewart's answer was succinct. "Geography, Martin. We move our office right out of Hamburg and down to Frankfurt, beyond Ruhrgas, so we're out where some of the southern gas companies already have an association. This also puts us beyond Thyssengas and is a very, very long way from Scheffer's heavy hand." Schepers liked that right away, but Orlean couldn't resist another query. "Oh, come on. You guys may get yourselves out of Scheffer's way, but you've got the same situation with affiliates in the other countries. What about De Housse in Belgium and Monod in Paris?" Schepers knew both men personally. "Martin, in the first place, those are two men who have a unique situation to maintain in their own countries. They're already on our side. Besides, we'll just put them in new offices too."

Interference from local affiliates could have been a problem that might have severely hamstrung Stewart's and Schepers's negotiating flexibility. They made it clear to Orlean they were going to establish Dutch gas as a separate entity, under their control, and they were going to accomplish that with geographically separate offices in every single country.

Orlean posed one last challenge. "Have either of you any idea whatsoever what that kind of setup is going to cost?"

Stewart was running out of patience. "Jeez, Martin, if we're going to have to batter our way into this new business, we have to look like we mean business. You think Ruhrgas is going to take us seriously if they find this operation in some two-bit place?" Schepers didn't wait for any more dialogue. "All right, Maclean, here's another real estate task. Get down to Frankfurt and set that up. Doug and I are off to give Scheffer the bad news."

When Schepers and Stewart arrived in Hamburg, they were welcomed at the airport by Scheffer's personal chauffeur in his private limousine.

"Just as Krik expected, Scheffer was all prepared to tell us how to do our jobs," said Stewart. "He, of course, did know about the new export effort. The study team was right there in his own office. Over lunch, he proposed that all of our future activities be channeled through his office right there in Hamburg. This would have made him the one to coordinate everything in Germany. Krik did rather enjoy explaining, quite politely as I remember, that we were now two companies operating independently from our parent oil companies. When we told Scheffer we would be opening our own brand-new offices in Frankfurt, not Hamburg, the wine dried up, the limousine disappeared, and we had to take a taxi to the airport."

Over time, other attempts by other management from both Shell and Esso in the Netherlands and in Germany were made to undermine the independence of NAM Gas Export and IGTM and to wrest the export activity away from Schepers and Stewart. One of the first, and strangest, came not just from one of their corporate parents but also, in a way, from both.

Shell and Esso had a fifty-fifty exploration/producing company named Brigitta in Hanover, Germany, similar to the NAM exploration company they had established in the Netherlands. As with NAM, Shell was also the operator of this company. Brigitta had several small producing fields in Northwest Germany. On May 14, 1962, the Dutch and German governments signed a supplement to the Ems-Dollard Treaty defining the line of demarcation between the two countries in the water. Brigitta drilled a well on the German side, just across from the Groningen discovery, and found gas in the Rotliegendes sand. It turned out that part of the Groningen gas reservoir extended into the bay of the Ems River, where Brigitta had a producing concession. Even though NAM Gas Export and IGTM were also fifty-fifty Shell Esso affiliates specifically formed for the express purpose of marketing and transporting Dutch gas to Germany, Brigitta formed its own marketing and gas transportation group to sell "their" gas within Germany. If Brigitta's plans in Germany were to go forward, they would be in direct competition with Stewart and Schepers' efforts. To find out just what the company was up to, they made an appointment with Brigitta's general manager, Paul von Forgash.

Stewart was certain the gentleman would be equally curious about what he and Schepers were doing. "Early on, Schepers and I went to visit Brigitta. Initially, we had a very nice reception, in which Von Forgash explained about the couple or three 'small discoveries' of gas Brigitta had. He told us they were 'interested' in our ideas."

During what began as a very cordial lunch, Stewart and Schepers shared with Von Forgash their ideas and plans for developing the premium market and its potential for opening a huge home heating market that had never before existed in Germany. Von Forgash was definitely enthusiastic about these new possibilities but was only concerned with a much narrower plan to create their own small network to connect local towns to Brigitta's own natural gas wells. His intention was for Brigitta to purchase additional Dutch gas supplies, thus opening the door for Brigitta to thereafter act as marketer and distributor in their area of Germany.

Stewart knew Schepers's response by heart. "Krik straightaway reiterated the exact same position we'd given to Shell's Scheffer, who'd proposed essentially the exact same move in his effort to take over all export activity in Germany. Krik made it very clear to Von Forgash that NAM Gas Export was to be the exclusive marketer of Dutch gas in his country, and it would be IGTM transporting that gas in an Esso pipeline system."

Not unexpectedly, Von Forgash's reaction echoed Scheffer's. Having been prepared for this reaction by their earlier meeting with Scheffer, Stewart and Schepers did not have to walk home. They'd already arranged in advance for their return transportation.

"Schepers and I kind of got crosswise with Brigitta over that. They flat out didn't want us in there, and things very quickly got to the point where they wouldn't talk to us."

Meanwhile, Ruhrgas was pursuing its own agenda and, in 1963, negotiated a contract with Brigitta for natural gas supplies in the area of Westphalia. Part of the gas Brigitta sold to Ruhrgas included gas they were pulling out of the Groningen field from the wells they had drilled under the Ems River on the German side.

Ruhrgas also purchased refinery gas from Shell and Esso in Northern Germany.

These additional supplies were not sufficient or flexible enough to enable Ruhrgas to achieve their goal of seriously entering the home heating market, which was exactly what Stewart and Schepers's activities would one day enable them to do.

Although Brigitta's efforts in Germany were small and regional, they conducted their business as if unaware that NAM, just across the river in the Netherlands, was a fifty-fifty Shell and Esso company, exactly as they were. Cooperating with Stewart and Schepers on Dutch gas could have led to something far more significant for Brigitta than the small contract they made with Ruhrgas. This does pose the question of whether one corporate hand knew what the other corporate hand was doing.

By now, Stewart knew exactly what he and Schepers were doing. "We were strongly committed to representing the interests of the Dutch people and NAM. In a way, Krik and I pulled away from the oil companies and became a kind of international combine, sort of an arm functioning for the interest of the Dutch people."

In doing so, both men knew they were taking a gigantic gamble. Stewart felt both of them put their jobs, and their very careers, on the line to achieve that objective. "At that moment, we had no consumers to buy the gas. There were no pipelines. Construction would require an outlay of hundreds of millions of 1960 dollars and a still unpredictable amount of construction time. I was dead certain this was all going to happen. I think I became a bit arrogant, and maybe I could have been more politic with some of the Esso people who could not or would not see what I saw so clearly."

The two men were absolutely determined not to be pinned to the Dutch border. The genius of Stewart's idea to present NAM Gas Export and IGTM as two independent entities quickly proved itself in practice as well as theory in many varied circumstances. Because he and Schepers were now assured of independence in activity and decision-making, they were able to maintain the continuity of intention Stewart had declared was necessary in the early negotiations with the UK and France. He and Schepers were now free to advise every prospect in every country beyond the Dutch border that there were going to be Esso/Shell pipelines from the Dutch border into Germany, Belgium, and France. To demonstrate to the German gas companies in very specific terms that they were not just talking about a German pipeline system, they quickly opened an office in Vienna. The parent companies validated what they were doing by complying with Schepers and Stewart's request for personnel for all the other new offices they began to open. In addition to those in Frankfurt and Vienna, Stewart and Schepers established a broad network of operations, beginning with Brussels, London, and Paris and moving those already existing study groups into new quarters, generating new studies wherever they were needed. These study groups were headed by senior executives recruited from the marketing and economics departments of both Shell and Esso. In Paris were Yves Monod from Shell and René Cozzi from Esso; in London, Gordon Usmar from Esso and Phil Corbett from Shell; in Brussels, Jacques de Housse from Esso; in Frankfurt, Gerd Sottorf from Shell and Hans Löblich from Esso; and in Austria, Raymond Kandler from Esso. Later, an office was even established in Switzerland with a Shell engineer named Nahmani, with whom Schepers had worked in Morocco. Into each of these offices, Stewart and Schepers brought aboard marketing experts, pipeline engineers, gas conversion specialists, economists, attorneys, and public relations personnel. Within a few months, the two men were no longer just supervising a study group in a few cities, but they were also now presiding over a full-blown marketing and pipeline organization operating all across Europe.

Stewart's career had expanded in direct proportion to the effectiveness of the studies he'd initiated, first in Texas and then in The Hague. The addition of these specialists in all these offices meant the studies he wanted could be expanded in scope, right along with his career. "In each of the countries, we asked the staff to look into the rights of the local gas companies. Did they have monopolies in their areas as they claimed? Were there any pipelines already there? How could we obtain easements for our own lines? Who owned these companies? Who and what was the management in each case? And we asked for anything else which would help us compete with these companies or even how to buy into them."

Dr. Liesen explained how Ruhrgas did not take particular note of all these offices opening. "This was seen by us as a kind of marketing measure preparing the way for natural gas deliveries to Germany. We knew Shell and Esso had not even the right to get the gas out of the ground. They had yet to convince the government that working with them was in their best interest. Moreover, Shell and Esso would have to agree the size of the market warranted the massive investment needed to transport the gas. There was not even an agreement about what entity would be granted the right to transport it. The bright possibilities for these markets all hinged on to what company and when would the Dutch government grant the concession."

The detailed planning of the study teams revealed what could be accomplished and also recommended potential pricing and pipeline routes once that producing concession was granted.

Stewart knew they were ready. "We knew what we would do if the concession came through. We were ready to hit the ground running if we got it. And by god, we did!" On May 30, 1963, the long-awaited concession was granted. They were in business.

After the documents were signed in the Kasteel Oud Wassenaar setting up the Gasunie and clearing the way for the States Mines, Shell and Essor Maatschap, the parties celebrated with champagne. Left to right: NAM director P. M. Bongaerts; Douglass Stewart, general manager IGTM; and Coen Smit, general manager Esso Nederland.

Stewart and Clegg in front of the NAM Gas Export/ IGTM offices at Smidswater 23, The Hague.

Stewart at the Smidswater canal 1963.

Stewart and Schepers in Stewart's office at Smidswater 23. The Shell head office was shocked at the "elaborate offices" of NAM Gas Export and IGTM. Stewart replied, "What are they going to do, tear it down?" Ruhrgas and Thyssengas were impressed and were convinced that Shell and Esso were determined to get in the gas business.

*As part of the arrangements for the new Dutch gas venture,
a committee composed of two States Mines executives, a
representative from the government, and an executive from
each of Shell and Esso was established to supervise the Gasunie,
the gas sales, and the NAM producing Maatschaap.*

*Above: J. P. M. Bongaerts, director of NAM, chats
with J. C. Boot, general manager, Shell Nederland, and
Coen Smit, general manager, Esso Nederland.*

*Below: Delegated supervisors W. E. Van Os, States Mines, L. G.
Wansink, Ministry of Economic Affairs, stroll with P. A. Zoetmulder,
newly appointed general managing director of Gasunie.*

NAM Gas Export and IGTM established "study offices"
in London, Brussels, Paris, Frankfurt, and Vienna.

Above: Gordon Usmar (Esso), Douglass Stewart, and Vi Vizard (Shell
head office gas department) at NAM Gas Export/IGTM London office.

Left: Jack Windham, vice president, IGTM pipeline department, discussed
proposed pipeline routes with Paul Mortimer, IGTM economist.

The NAM Gas Export/IGTM offices were set up in the Rue Washington, Paris. Here, George de Gelas, economist (Shell); Yves Monod, manager (Shell); and Rene Cozzi, economist (Esso) discussed strategy for the coming negotiations with Gaz de France.

Below right: Capt. Yves Monod in the French army before the Germans invaded Belgium. Monod received the War Cross and the Legion of Honor medal.

Captain Monod was with the French army group that were evacuated to the UK at Dunkurk. He returned to France to fight again until the French surrender.

Chapter 16

Stonewalled! Battered in Belgium, Foiled in France, Undenkbar in Germany

With the official signing of the documents forming Gasunie, the NAM/Maatschappij arrangements and the granting of the Groningen concessions, the development of the Dutch gas industry began in earnest. For almost a year, planning had been under way for the future gas pipeline construction and transportation as well as for the marketing operations of Gasunie and its coordination committee, composed of Shell, Esso, State Mines, and SGB people. NAM, likewise, was far advanced with engineering and drilling programs.

The fact that the export teams hit the ground running was a testament to the preparation and negotiating strengths of Stewart and Schepers. First, in the singular trust each held for the other and, second, in the distinct and separate skills each brought to the bargaining table. Schepers's diplomatic and linguistic capabilities were matched by Stewart's engineering know-how and his unfailing stream of marketing ideas.

Schepers and Stewart also had something else going for them. People who were there recount, in quite vivid terms, that when these two tall, strikingly handsome men walked into a meeting, they certainly walked in with the full weight of their international corporate structure. They also brought into the room an air of authenticity and authority that was strongly reinforced by the acumen, pragmatism, and knowledge of both men. Although the domestic Dutch efforts moved rapidly with the natural gas program, the initial contacts by IGTM and NAM Gas Export immediately ran into opposition from the gas distributors in the other countries. These companies had their own very independent ideas about what they were going to do with natural gas.

Belgium

Belgium was chosen as their first target because Belgium had, early on, signaled a high interest in Dutch gas. Recognizing an opportunity, Stewart and Schepers quickly initiated profiles of the country's potential needs, which enabled them to walk into their first Belgian meeting with a prediction in their pockets about those needs.

Stewart recalled their request for a meeting was quickly agreed to and set in the offices of Imperial Continental in Antwerp. "Schepers and I entered the conference room to find an enormous oval conference table where the representatives of nearly every municipal gas company, as well as Imperial Continental and Distrigaz, were represented, sitting two or three deep. The air was already heavy with stale cigar smoke. Half-empty soft drink and mineral water bottles gave evidence that a lot of heavy discussion—or plotting—had been going on for some time before we were ushered in. Things began quietly. We exchanged pleasantries."

Stewart's introduction as managing director of IGTM drew a number of puzzled questions about what it was and how IGTM related to Dutch gas. The spokesman for Imperial Continental opened the serious discussions. "We've waited a long time to obtain natural gas from the Netherlands. We read from the papers that NAM Gas Export is to sell the gas for export, and we have been doing our own homework as to our requirements. We are prepared to purchase as much as three hundred thousand cubic meters per year at the Dutch border, provided the border price is sufficiently low enough."

Stewart and Schepers did a quick mental calculation. What Imperial was talking about was only a small percentage of the volume the study group had already calculated Belgium could use in premium markets after conversion. Schepers responded with a statement so audacious his hosts were stunned into silence. "Our companies are not planning to sell the gas at the Dutch border into your transportation line. What we're planning is a brand-new pipeline through Belgium to Paris. We'll deliver gas directly to industry and municipalities at the plant and city gates in Belgium along the way."

The initial silence was swiftly followed by a swelling roar of disbelief and denial, which the Stewart-Schepers magnetism did not dispel.

"We've been here since 1809," said one of the representatives. "We were the first gas company in this country. We are the gas pipeliners here, not Shell and Esso."

The Belgians would not discuss the proposed alternative plan, period. They would consider nothing less than buying gas at the Dutch border and transporting the gas in their own lines. The meeting was over.

Stewart remembered that he and Schepers were ushered out almost abruptly. They headed for the nearest bar, hardly able to wait to compare notes.

Remembering what Stewart had told him about the earlier research revealing that shares of Imperial Continental were for sale on the stock market, Schepers's wry sense of humor saw a way the meeting might have had a very different outcome. "It would have gone a lot better today if we had just bought that whole Imperial bunch right off the stock market when we first found out they were on it."

Stewart agreed. "Can you just see the face of that bird from Imperial if we could have interrupted his pompous spiel and told him, 'Sit down, fella. You're working for the two of us now'?"

The big question, of course, was really how to find a way to raise the Belgians' sights, and appetites, for larger volumes.

"Krik, throwing us out does not square with what they said when we walked in," said Stewart. "We know they're in a hurry for Dutch gas, and from what they said today, they have no idea of how much gas they really can use."

"Doug, our legal studies tell us there's no way Belgium can hold back a pipeline to Paris. Think of the flare-up in France if Belgium's gas companies even tried to deny natural gas to the French people."

"I say we get the word out to the major Belgian industries about the possibility of direct supply right to their plants," said Stewart. Schepers thought Jacque de Housse, their Belgian manager, was just the right candidate to start spreading that word. "Every one of those Belgian plants is connected to a major Belgian financial house. It won't take long for word to get back to the men at today's meeting that we meant what we said in there today."

Stewart leaped ahead. "No matter how much these Belgians act as if they have a monopoly, the lawyers tell us they do not. If we get that contract with Gaz de France, we'll sic De Gaulle on 'em if they even make a move to try to stop our pipeline."

France

Yves Monod, the Shell man in the Paris office, first met Schepers when he had been in charge of the French staff overseas. Monod had just returned from serving three years as the president of Shell Chile. He had let Schepers know he could set up a meeting with Gaz de France whenever he and Stewart were ready.

Monod related how appealing he found Stewart and Schepers's direct approach. "I so well remember how Stewart and Schepers were both so pleasant to work with, even though they were so very different. They were representing then a whole new business which had not before existed. They would have liked to sell their Dutch gas, at least to begin with, to the industries where Esso and Shell were already selling fuel oil, even though this meant Shell and Esso would be losing those oil customers. I was already certain, at the same time, Gaz de France would be telling them, 'We have liquid gas from North Africa, and we can do without you, Shell and Esso, thank you very much.'"

Undaunted by the possibility of that very French response, Schepers asked Monod to make the appointment. Just as Monod promised, he arranged for Stewart and Schepers to meet with Monsieur J. Couture, energy general secretary of the French government. They explained to Couture that NAM Gas Export had approximately five billion cubic meters of natural gas per year to sell to France and that they wished to transport the gas into France through IGTM. Mr. Couture advised them that all French negotiations for those things had to be held with Khun de Chizelle, general manager of Gaz de France. Because Gaz de France was, in fact, a legal monopoly in France, Stewart and Schepers's strategy was to present their case to Chizelle by first talking about those very Esso and Shell customers to whom they were already selling petroleum products. If they could get the "camel's head in the tent" on the premium industrial gas market, they could then later make the case for the premium residential market.

At the very first meeting with Chizelle, Stewart made the presentation. "Our two companies wish to lay a pipeline to Paris and sell gas to industries in the French industrial belt of Northern France."

As expected, Chizelle reminded them of the Gaz de France monopoly, not only on the sale of gas but on gas transportation and marketing as well. He assured them Gaz de France would only consider purchasing gas at the Dutch border. The study team's lawyers had done their homework; Schepers was able to surprise Chizelle. "According to our legal investigation of French law and the charter of Gaz de France under the Armengaud Law of August 2, 1949, a joint marketing/pipeline system is legal if Gaz de France agrees and participates.

"And why would we agree to that?" asked Chizelle.

This was Stewart's opening. He laid out for Chizelle the vast, presently untapped premium residential market that could open to Gaz de France if such a joint marketing/pipeline system for importing Dutch gas could be developed.

The Frenchman replied, "We'll just buy more gas at the Dutch border."

Schepers's response was quiet and direct. "Monsieur, by then, there may not be that much Dutch gas available to France. We're already exploring sales to Germany and Belgium. If we make a deal with you here, you will be assured of an adequate long-term supply for the French premium market. *If* we can make a deal here, of course."

The meeting concluded with Stewart proposing that Gaz de France sit down with the NAM/IGTM study team and jointly study the possible French markets for natural gas. Chizelle made it clear he did not think much would come of the effort. "I don't know how useful that could be because our experts already know our own markets, and we certainly don't need your help building pipelines."

Schepers and Stewart left Paris that day recognizing they'd have a tough fight before them if they were to successfully enter the French business. Schepers made his usual ironic comment. "Well, at least we're getting well versed in rejection."

"Krik, it's not over until it's over," replied Stewart. "At least the idea of a joint study is on the table, and as long we can keep getting them to agree to meetings, we'll keep making our case."

Germany

By 1963, the stage was set for the arrival of natural gas in Germany. The Ruhr valley, with its vast industrial complex and concentrated population, was a primary target on Stewart and Schepers's radar. Even though Löblich's research had shown the demand for gas in Germany had grown very rapidly in recent years, they expected negotiations to be tough.

The gas industry in Germany had been in existence for 135 years, primarily dispensing gas manufactured from coal. In 1826, the Imperial Continental Gas Association started Germany's first public gas system in Hanover and also set up gas systems in Belgium around the same time. Thereafter, gas systems were built in towns all over Germany, and by 1885, there were over seven hundred separate gas works. By 1926, two main gas distribution companies dominated the Ruhr area, Thyssen Gas and Ruhr Gas. Then there were only about 200 kilometers of pipelines, but by 1943, this had expanded to a total of 1,636 kilometers, a system that included two large sulfur removal plants and sixty-one plants that manufactured gas from coal (coke gas) for distribution primarily to industries, with some sales to households for heating and cooking.

At the end of World War II, only three coking plants and one compressor station had survived the war and were still working. Working through the rubble of the bombed-out cities and the tangle of twisted pipelines, Ruhrgas accomplished a near-impossible task and restored the entire system in only two years. Just as they had been in 1926, Ruhrgas and Thyssengas were still the largest gas distribution companies in 1963, when IGTM and NAM Gas Export began their export effort. Both Ruhrgas and Thyssengas were facing supply shortages and had actually begun to look for additional gas supplies from German refineries, from German exploration companies and to acquire liquid natural gas from Algeria. Löblich's team discovered that the two giants were only thinking of adding those supplies to the demand for low-calorie gas. They were not thinking of the looming home heating market. Most certainly, they were not considering that Esso and Shell would come crowding into their cozy domain. Stewart and Schepers tried repeatedly to meet with each company separately, but the two giants held fast to their pact of togetherness and insisted there be only a joint meeting in Essen at the Ruhrgas offices.

Hans Löblich recounted their progress. "Our Studiengruppe Erdgas team in Frankfurt went through very tough preparations for this meeting. Stewart, particularly, pushed us in almost weekly meetings to deliver the needed data as quickly as possible, better yet, 'yesterday.' Because of their attractive personal appearances, the luxurious offices which Stewart and Schepers had in The Hague, with voluminous carpets, expensive exotic cars, and their charming secretaries, Wanda and Mary, we originally started out calling the two of them our Gold Dust Boys. On the other hand, because the two of them showed up in Frankfurt almost daily with new ideas, resulting in ever more work for our small group, before long, we started calling them our Terrible Twins. Nevertheless, they always commanded our full cooperation as well as our confidence and our sympathy. Ultimately, we were finally successful. The impressive development of natural gas in Germany will always be connected with Douglass Stewart."

Stewart already knew from his first encounter in Germany that breaching the barrier presented by the entrenched industrialists, particularly the coal interests, would present many difficulties.

"Our first meeting with Ruhrgas and Thyssengas took place on May 16, 1963," recalled Löblich. "Maclean and I, along with Schepers and Stewart, met with executives from both the gas companies. These included Dr. Schelberger, managing director of Ruhrgas, Dr. Liesen, later to become managing director of Ruhrgas, several other executives from Ruhrgas and Thyssengas, and Mr. Swart of the Bank voor Handel en Scheepvaart, a bank owned by Baron Thyssen."

Stewart remembered that after an enormous lunch, which included the first seagull eggs he had ever eaten, they got down to business. Since the meeting was held in German, Schepers presented their case.

According to Löblich, "The negotiation on the NAM Gas Export/IGTM side was by our 'Terrible Twins.' Schepers explained the authority of their two companies to sell the gas in export. He pointed out they would never sell at the Dutch border without participating in the gas business in Germany. He explained that Esso and Shell had made that mistake in the United States and didn't propose to repeat it in Europe. He advised them that the oil companies were planning a pipeline through the Ruhr to Bavaria. They expected to sell to industry and domestic gas customers off that pipeline only on the basis of Dutch border prices and transportation costs."

Schepers went on to explain how the gas markets would greatly expand with high BTU distribution and that the oil companies would have to participate in the increase.

Schelberger of Ruhrgas responded with uncharacteristic volubility. "Undenkbar (unthinkable)! Shell and Esso shall never market gas in our own territory."

Without acknowledging Schelberger's not unexpected attitude, Schepers quietly replied to the outburst by proposing three phases of discussion: First, they would jointly study the market for high-BTU natural gas, without touching on the specific border price. Second, they would negotiate about pipelines. Third, "We shall have a great fight if we can't agree." The only point on which all did agree that day was that Schepers was right about his third point. With that, the meeting was over.

In less than a week, the first step toward the predicted "great fight" was taken. The Germans demonstrated their determination to call the shots by filing a plan with the local governmental authorities for their own pipeline over the very same route Shell and Esso had just proposed.

Dr. Liesen explained the Ruhrgas rationale for taking that action. "In the legal situation existing then, such a pipeline·had to be approved by the German supervisory authority. Notification of plans for such a Ruhrgas pipeline would automatically result in a need for negotiations between Esso/Shell and Ruhrgas because, following notification of Ruhrgas's own pipeline, Esso/Shell could no longer expect approval of its pipeline project to the exclusion of Ruhrgas. Instead, it now had to be assumed that the supervisory authority would urge the two parties to reach a compromise, to build together."

At that time, however, Stewart and Schepers could not have known the Ruhrgas application for the pipeline was a way to force them to rethink their independent attitude. Instead, with "Undenkbar" echoing in their ears, the Terrible Twins took Löblich to dinner, hoping for some native insights on how to move the "undenkbar" attitude from outrage to assent.

Löblich pointed out the obvious. "That the first contacts made were with Ruhrgas and Thyssengas alone was totally incomprehensible for us. Even though our research documented that Germany was ready for natural gas, there was no direct connection to the final consumer, as Esso and Shell had had with marketing fuel oil."

Löblich felt the two of them had gone into the meeting justifiably full of confidence about the opportunity they were presenting to the two giants, but they also attempted to leap over the tremendous power of the individual executive personalities as well as the prestige and power of their companies.

Perhaps, most of all, the Terrible Twins had failed to address the serious technical problems these companies were going to have with conversion as well as the very big pipeline investment that would emerge as they moved into the natural gas business. Schepers reminded Löblich they'd never gotten far enough into the meeting to address the technical problems.

Löblich went on to explain they would have to find a means to deal with the legally existing German gas market monopolies in both the present and in the hoped-for future. There were concession contracts between districts in which the gas companies in those districts owned the exclusive rights for marketing gas, whether cokery or natural. The existing grid gas companies had long-term, exclusive contracts with their partner communities and corresponding management monopolies.

Stewart and Schepers recognized the basic wisdom of Löblich's counsel. Even though the desire of Ruhrgas and Thyssengas for new sources of gas, especially natural gas, was known, the Terrible Twins would never get to the ultimate consumers without the cooperation of the two giants.

Löblich laid out a plan to subtly cultivate individuals within the gas companies by forming a new neutral gas business association. He suggested that while he and the Frankfurt team worked on this possibility, Stewart and Schepers could, at the same time, approach the smaller southern gas distributors, who had formed an association of their own, in an attempt to combat the efforts of Ruhrgas and Thyssengas to expand into their region.

The first time Stewart and Schepers visited this group, they were greeted politely. Although the companies welcomed the idea of natural gas, they were forthright in their position. They wanted no part of the oil companies delivering gas directly to industry in their area.

Stewart was undaunted. "We hadn't expected to obtain agreement on our first meetings in Germany, but we had planted the seeds in the minds of these small gas distributors about the huge opportunities waiting with natural gas. We were intent on fighting our way into Germany and to participate in gas transmission. And it was clear to us, on their part, they intended to keep us out." These negotiations would get much more difficult before they got better. And so did the way Jersey was looking at the export efforts of Stewart and Schepers.

On one of his periodic tours of European operations for Jersey, Bob Milbrath made an unexpected personal visit to Smidswater. He was impressed with the offices but was very candid about their so far less than successful export activities. "To summarize what you two are telling me, it appears that in the UK, their gas councils have a monopoly and are not likely to welcome Shell and Esso in their business. Gaz de France in Paris feels the same way. You've been thrown out of Belgium. The German gas companies told you it is 'unthinkable' you can possibly do anything for them they can't do for themselves. And to prove it, they've filed permits with their government for the very pipeline routes you propose we build. Will one of you please tell me something that'll make Jersey feel good about keeping all this going?"

Schepers intervened. "Mr. Milbrath, every time we go out there, we're armed with facts and figures from our study teams that nobody else has. These gas companies may not want to be in business with us yet, but over and over, they ask for the information we've assembled about the profit possibilities. There's nowhere else for them to get that information."

Stewart interrupted, "Bob, the promise of those profits that we're putting before them is so vast they can't be ignored indefinitely. Right now, we know more about the potential than they do, and more than anything, we've got the gas we know they need. There are so many players in this thing. If we can get even one of these dominos to fall, they're all going down."

Milbrath shot back. "If? You're telling me that a great, big, enthusiastic Doug Stewart 'if' is the only thing I can take back to Jersey?"

Schepers posed a very different and very Dutch point of view. "Mr. Milbrath, I appreciate how you Americans like to see things happen overnight, but here in Europe, things happen a lot slower. In Holland, it takes a lot of weather to get the bulbs in the field to the tulips on the table. You might want to reflect on a story we like to tell here about the young bull and the old bull. When winter comes, cattle are taken from their grazing fields to the farmers' barns to protect them from the bitter cold. In spring, the cows are transported back on small barges to the fields first, followed by the bulls. After being penned up in that barn all winter, so near to the cows but yet so far away, the bulls' anticipation noticeably rises as they come to the landing. The young bull says to the old one, 'Let's leap over that barrier and grab ourselves a few.' The old bull says to the young one, 'Let's take our time and have 'em all.'

"We mean to have them all, Mr. Milbrath. That's what you can take back to New York."

—Chapter 17—

Success Breeds Control

When the Terrible Twins advised Löblich and Maclean about the lack of response from the small southern distributors with whom they'd been meeting, Maclean's agile intelligence leaped to a new possibility. Because of all the research the Frankfurt team had already done, Maclean focused his attention on a small and well-placed, well-organized gas distributor fortuitously located in the Weser Ems area of Northwestern Germany, just across the bay from the Groningen field. Perhaps, thought Maclean, a personal visit to that manager would pay off. If properly approached, he believed the manager just might respond to the possibility of Dutch gas so close by that it could be easily transported to his particular customers.

On his own initiative, Maclean visited this manager and found, to his delight, that not only was the company seeking natural gas but that they would also be more than happy to join with NAM Gas Export and IGTM to finance pipelines and sell the gas in their area. Maclean obtained a letter of intent from them and gleefully returned to the effusive appreciation of the team.

Löblich remembered Maclean as "one smart cookie," and Stewart recounted the significance of Maclean's achievement. "Maclean had done it. This agreement for participation in pipeline financing was our first breakthrough into the gas business outside the Netherlands. We all celebrated at our favorite hangout, the t'Jagertie Club, right around the corner from Smidswater."

The celebration was short-lived, however. For the first time, Stewart and Schepers felt the corporate reins begin to tighten. The success of Maclean's initiative with the Weser Ems distributor was the first small pebble dropped into a little pond of success. It did not, unfortunately, make the ripples the teams expected. Instead of corporate acknowledgment for their first real progress, the Weser Ems deal turned instead into the threat of a huge administrative wave that was sweeping toward the freedom of operation Stewart and Schepers had been enjoying. They never saw it coming.

"We had never been wholly independent because we did make periodic progress reports to the Gasunie delegated supervisory committee (at this time composed of Van Os and Bogers from State Mines, Wansink from the Dutch government, Boot from Shell, and Smit from Esso) and also to our own corporate advisors, Cox and Vale. As long as we reported only progress, we had a free rein. But the first time we reported actual success with the Weser Ems deal, we were confronted for the first time with attempts to restrain us."

Shortly after Stewart reported the Weser Ems deal to Smit and Cox, he received a phone call from Smit asking to see him at the Esso kirk. Smit said he wanted to update Stewart and Cox on a meeting that he and Shell's J. C. Boot had just had with the Gasunie supervisory committee. Boot and Smit were the point men for the oil companies with that committee. Boot and Smit had long been part of the business and political life of The Hague. Because of that, they were respected by the committee.

On the morning Stewart left Smidswater for the meeting with Smit and Cox, he was in high good humor, expecting some acknowledgment about the good news from Weser Ems. When he arrived, Ganskopp had been invited to sit in on the meeting. Smit began by telling them about a new agreement he and Boot had made with the committee some days before. Smit spoke in a manner so matter-of-fact it betrayed an utter innocence about the gravity of its consequences. Stewart was astounded to be told that, henceforth, before proceeding to any negotiation meeting in any country, he and Schepers would have to personally report to the designated delegates to obtain, in advance, approval for whatever they intended to do in that negotiation.

Perhaps it was Smit's and Boot's connections in the business community or their acute awareness of the political climate that influenced them to agree to this. However it came about, none of the other men in the room registered any recognition of how seriously this agreement would impact day-to-day negotiations. Stewart's first thought was to find a way to explain in simple terms the serious ramifications of the decision. "If Krik and I had to get approval for every step we needed to take before we took it, we would be stifled before we got out the door. We needed to be able to respond quickly to the widely differing situations that emerged unexpectedly and which differed so dramatically from country to country."

To Stewart's particular amazement, Cox just sat there, assenting to the decision. Perhaps, as a newcomer to The Hague, he was bowing to the wisdom of those with long experience in Dutch politics. Yet Stewart could not understand how Cox, with his European business experience and his responsibility as the Esso advisor for the export project itself, had not immediately grasped the international implications.

The kind of government control to which Boot and Smit had just agreed would give to the Dutch exactly what the Arab countries were asking for and would certainly serve as ammunition for those countries to advance the ambitions they had for their own natural resources.

Stewart was aghast. "This was the very thing Jersey had been trying to avoid. Neither Boot nor Smit seemed to have recognized their agreement with the government committee members was setting loose the sheik effect on our whole effort. And Cox just sat there nodding in agreement."

Stewart's mind was racing over what might have triggered enough concern to set this problem in motion. Although the government had agreed State Mines would not participate in the gas business beyond the Dutch border, had the Weser Ems deal confronted the government representatives on the supervisory committee with a possibility they'd never apparently thought of before? Did they fear this Weser Ems pipeline deal meant the oil companies were going to make exorbitant profits with the Dutch natural gas once it went beyond their borders? Since the Gasunie delegated supervisory committee would see every contract before it was signed, Stewart realized this agreement might not be about either of those things. Perhaps this was not just about having control of the negotiations but of having control of Schepers and himself.

If this was the case, the question was, had the idea originated with the delegates themselves, or had the idea been borne right there in Esso's office with people who had no grasp of what actually took place at a negotiation table for a business that did not previously exist? There was no short course on freewheeling negotiations for an unknown market to which Stewart could refer Cox and Smit because he and Schepers were the instruments of its development.

Stewart briefly struggled for a way to explain the problems that had been set in motion. Suddenly, he was overwhelmed with anger at the absurdity of not only what had been agreed to by Boot and Smit but also that the agreement had actually been made without so much as an attempt at discussion with him and Schepers. Stewart impulsively stormed out of the office. "Perhaps I was a little arrogant, and I was impulsive. I'm not exactly sure why my blood boiled. Certainly, part of it was that Schepers and I were under extreme pressure with so many different negotiations up in the air. We were traveling and negotiating three and four days a week, keeping all those study teams up to date, applying pressure on them to give us what we needed to keep the negotiations on track."

Stewart headed straight to Smidswater.

Schepers was just as outraged at what Shell's J. C. Boot had done, but his reaction was even sharper. "Doug, this isn't just about putting the sheik effect in neon lights for the Middle East. This hamstrings us in red tape every step of the way. Every damn thing we need to do will be delayed in a committee second-guessing it."

Negotiations that were, at that very moment, inching their way through the complex government and corporate interaction of each country could be slowed to a near halt. Even today, Stewart still bristles at the obstacle that had just been thrown into the midst of what he and Schepers were doing. "We'd already been in situations where we needed to exercise our authority as corporate affiliates and to be able, at times, to agree or disagree on the spot. And on the spot was so often the order of the day. Krik and I were fully aware of the enormous responsibility we carried every time we had to make those kinds of decisions. We knew the success we had had to this point was a direct result of our very ability to respond that way. By now, we'd had a taste of the efficiency our independence gave us. We'd had the excitement of taking the risks. Either our companies were going to support our actions or they weren't."

Both men fired off cables to their respective home offices. Schepers went over Boot's head to Boot's superior, Dennis Vale, who was the Shell supervisor for the export project in London. Stewart wired directly to Milbrath, who was Cox and Smit's superior. Almost immediately, Vale cabled back from London, advising Schepers that he unequivocally supported Schepers's position. There was no question in Vale's mind that export efforts would be severely hampered.

Having cooled down a little, Stewart went back to the Esso office to talk to Cox and Smit, who, by then, had in front of them a copy of Stewart's cable. "They were, of course, upset that I had gone over their heads. In talking it over, I acknowledged I had been a little hasty but pointed out that unless some kind of compromise could be worked out with that committee, they were exposing Jersey to renewed demands in the Middle East. I thought, at least they could understand that. There was no point in addressing whether or not there was some internal effort afoot to control me and Schepers."

Stewart subsequently sent another cable to New York asking Milbrath to ignore his first one. But of course, the question the cable posed about the sheik effect could not be ignored. Within twenty-four hours, one of Milbrath's assistants was on his way to The Hague.

Stewart had a clear recall of that meeting. "We all sat down together and worked out a compromise. It would not be in Jersey's interest to have the government telling us what to do in other countries. However, the government's need to be informed had to be recognized and respected. Smit was directed to go back to the committee and to reach a compromise."

At Shell in London, Vale remained firm against compromise, but corporate interests above him prevailed, and the order came back for Boot to compromise as well.

Looking back, Stewart now recognized there really was a huge issue that the Weser Ems deal forced the designated delegates committee to confront. "The oil companies would have to commit to a huge cash outlay for pipelines in the export countries. The Dutch government and their newly formed Gasunie, instead of simply serving the needs of its own people, was now face-to-face with the reality that it was about to commit the resources of its people beyond their borders. It's one thing to say we're going to do this and another altogether to actually be doing it. It's tantamount to agreeing on a marriage but being faced with signing the prenuptial contract."

Ultimately, Smit and Boot's diplomatic and adroit presentation resulted in the supervisory committee agreeing to modify their original demand for direct supervision. The delegates would be satisfied to receive periodic reports from Schepers and Stewart and would therefore be informed about, but would not be controlling, the day-to-day activities of what the export team was doing. They would, of course, retain the right of final approval.

Stewart was relieved. "After this flare-up, my previously cordial relationship with Smit was considerably cooler. Until this happened, he had looked upon me as a subordinate, and so had Cox. But my independence had now been established, and everyone around us knew it. Cox once asked me why I had gone around him, and I never really answered. There was no way to take back what was there in black and white in my first cable."

Schepers and Stewart were ever after scrupulous in their dealings with the committee about what was going on in all their negotiations. However, they did not send up signal flares about what might be brewing or on the way.

"Once a month, we met with this Gasunie committee in a castle just across the Rhine in the Southern Netherlands," said Stewart. "We would spend the day meeting with them and explaining what we were doing. Although once I had to explain to Mr. Wansink, de Pous's representative, that the exact purpose of IGTM was to simply serve as a vehicle by which the oil companies could enter the pipelines business in the export countries, they never really told us what to do. They just wanted to be apprised, which was entirely appropriate. We were selling the gas in which their country and their government had such a big stake."

Stewart now acknowledged that there were times he and Schepers delayed reporting some details here and there, and at times, they even delayed information about things that were more than just details. "In the end, of course, the Dutch government had the right of final approval on every single sales contract and would have to consent to any final arrangements made with distributors for any amount of gas we ever committed to before anything actually happened. The final result of any negotiation was right there before them."

Given the government's substantial 75 percent share of any export sales Schepers and Stewart arranged, there was no financial benefit that could have accrued to either Shell or Jersey because of the timing of their reports.

Stewart explained any delay in reporting simply enabled them to maintain their initiative in the exceedingly slow-moving export negotiations. "To be able to respond to the unexpected was all Schepers and I ever wanted. I know we earned the committee's trust because everything we accomplished has, over time, proven to be truly in the interest of the Dutch people. The committee, in turn, earned our respect. They maintained their early agreement with us that the Dutch State would not participate beyond the Dutch border, and Gasunie would confine itself to domestic activities. The initiative for the export markets would remain in the hands of Shell and Esso, subject to the delegates' supervision."

Wisely, Gasunie had spared itself not only the financial burden of building the pipelines needed to transport the natural gas beyond its borders, but also because of that decision, they were also spared the many political complications of trying to construct them across other borders into other countries.

Stewart and Schepers now shifted into second gear for their ascent to the peak of the export mountain.

The NAM Gas Export/IGTM study group office was established in Frankfurt so as to be beyond the Ruhrgas and Thyssengas distribution networks and also to remove it from the close influence or the Shell and Esso German affiliates in Hamburg.

Hans Löblich (Esso), the initial manager of the Frankfurt office, helped Shell and Esso break into Germany by starting a joint study with the Dusseldor Gas Works for the advantages of natural gas.

Above left: Naval engineer Lieutenant Löblich escaped from the sinking of the battleship Bismarck.

Above right: Löblich in Frankfurt office.

Donald McLean, assistant manager, Frankfurt.

McLean secured the first commitment for Dutch gas and an agreement for Shell and Esso to participate in the gas business in Germany with his Weser Ems letter of intent.

Chapter 18

Ascending the Export Mountain

I n a very short time, Löblich's new strategy of creating a "neutral focus" for the German companies was in place. He and his team invited these companies, and an older association of German gas and water works called VDGW, to meetings of a new organization called the Group for Studies of Natural Gas in the IGTM/NAM Gas Export offices in the city center of Frankfurt on Meisengasse Street.

The purpose of the group was to facilitate an understanding with the local companies as to the advantages of natural gas. Shell transferred Maclean to other responsibilities, and Gerd Sottorf became the project manager for the new organization, with Löblich as the deputy project manager. They were gratified when Ruhrgas responded to one of the group's early invitations.

Dr. Liesen, former chairman of Ruhrgas, recalled wondering why Ruhrgas should have to go to the Frankfurt office and said they were informed "it was too much trouble" to transport the large new overhead projector. Of course, getting Ruhrgas into their own office was a matter of strategy the team wanted to accomplish one way or another.

Löblich was elated at the prospect of having them there. "They responded to our invitation and showed up at Meisengasse. I was very proud to finally be able to present our revolutionary study forecasting the natural gas business in Germany. We tried to impress our guests with our office, now done in great style by Maclean, and with the installation of our new overhead projector and last, though not least, with our numbers and diagrams. Part of the study was a proposal for creating a new company, with the name of RUNCO, to sell the natural gas. It was proposed that Ruhrgas itself would sell cokery gas into the area close to the numerous cokeries in the area of the Ruhrgebiet. In those days, I could not imagine cokery gas would come to a complete end. Cokeries were then of such vital importance for the huge steel industry in the Ruhrgebiet."

Löblich recalled some disappointment on his side because there were those from Ruhrgas who appeared to be bored. "Especially Dr. Wunsch, the great technical director of Ruhrgas. He was seated in our best piece of furniture, a 1,500 Deutschmark classic easy chair, in which he leaned back and seemed as if he would prefer to have a little nap. Of course, this was his tactic. I heard later that at least Dr. Liesen, who was then a young assistant in Ruhrgas, was very impressed. By the way, we had to give back this wonderful easy chair after Shell decided the Frankfurt offices were much too elaborate."

Meanwhile, the Frankfurt team organized a second meeting with the smaller German distributors. Instead of bringing a new group together for the purpose of making a sales pitch, the Frankfurt team offered instead a purely technical lecture in their air-conditioned offices. Since air-conditioning was not a common amenity, they were sure, if nothing else, the invitation would be seen as a respite from the furnace Frankfurt was that summer.

This program would deal simply with the technical problems in changing from city gas to natural gas, and invitations went to all members of the existing VDGW association and to selected individuals in related businesses. All were invited to bring interested experts.

NAM Gas Export and IGTM hired Mr. Carroll Kroeger from Stone & Webster to report about his long experience in the USA. But the smartest thing on that day's agenda was the speaker who was an executive with the city works of Bielefeld, a German city that already subscribed to natural gas from the Emsland area and had already been through the process of conversion. He described how Bielefeld had already experienced all the changes the other cities would have to undergo.

Löblich recalled the event as a big success. "The VDGW brought more experts than we counted on, and we had to get extra tables and chairs. Kroeger gave his clear, impressive lecture in English, and I translated, which gave the guests some time to take notes. We told ourselves to remember this day—July 4, 1963. It was Independence Day in the USA. In Germany, it was the day our gas economy heard about the changes to natural gas for the very first time. We had set a time fuse, and now we waited for the reaction of grid gas companies."

Löblich quickly moved to make a connection with German government officials to make certain they were informed about every development for this emerging energy market. According to Löblich, the government welcomed the new source of energy, but in his dialogue with them, they made references to the unavoidable issue of the many area monopolies and existing technical rules of the existing energy economy.

"While the federal government was, of course, happy about new competition in the energy market, the communities already on the gas grid had full knowledge of their strength and acted very arrogantly in the beginning," said Löblich. "We wanted to get as close as possible to the final buyer and to have full control over the whole business, so we started with Saarferngas (grid gas from Saarland) and Salzgittergas (gas from Salzgitter), which eventually led to dialogue with all the relevant groups."

Although business events were moving satisfactorily, the distance between Frankfurt and Hamburg made Löblich absent from his family for long periods. He recounted the various ways he kept himself personally occupied during those absences. "I was still living in a lodging house, and I took walks during the day with a copy of Shakespeare's *Julius Caesar* in my hand. I went over Antonius's speech, taking turns in German and English. I also memorized the proverbs and sentences that Gisela had had to write down in her time at the Bach School. I also played the organ in church, although I considered myself very amateurish. I am still wondering today that I had permission to play at all. I later got serious about my playing and was able to study properly with Klaus

Mayers, the organist in the Johannis church in Hamburg. I still play an hour a day today to keep my brain cells alert. In those Frankfurt days, though, with my family back in Hamburg, I filled those lonely hours by making music with others at Dr. Kniepp's place. I played the piano, and the doctor sang. For diversion, I studied hypnotism."

Because of the distance and the pressure of work, Löblich was absent for his wedding anniversary, in July, and hoped the telegram he sent would soften Gisela's disappointment. When their daughters were out of school, better family time was possible for the Löblich family. On the positive side, for two of those summers, he and Gisela were able to take the family to the beach at Vejers in Denmark while continuing to search for a suitable family apartment.

On weekends, Löblich was driving all the way back to Hamburg, a five-hour drive, to spend time with his family as well as to report to the Esso A. G. board on progress in Frankfurt. He tried to find an apartment from the very beginning of his assignment in Frankfurt because it was so wearing to be away from his family. But finding suitable housing in those days was very difficult. Finally, separation from his family was resolved.

"In the fall of '63, I found a first-class bungalow in Koenigstein, on Friedrich Bender Street, which I was able to rent," said Löblich. "The moving allowance from Esso was more than generous. I remember it as lavish. The house was located just above the town on the hillside in an area of new construction. From the street, you entered the first floor's big hall, where we put the grand piano. All of the rooms had exits to the terrace, which dominated the whole front of the house. The interior designer Boettcher, who had decorated another apartment for us, took over once again, to our full satisfaction.

"Thanks to the constant eagerness of their tutor, Moni and Gabi very soon caught up. Even though the girls were the only Protestant children in the school, they were accepted at Ursulinen, a very well-known Catholic convent school, and both sides got along very well. The girls took their confirmation lessons in the bustling Protestant rectory from Pastor Von Heil, who was always concerned that the nuns would 'poach' the children. After very intensive study and effort, both girls were confirmed on the same day. We had a very big celebration with the whole family."

A French Plateau

In Paris, Gaz de France's general manager, Khun de Chizelle, had been thinking more about the possibility of joint studies. He contacted Monod to tell him that he was ready to sit down with the joint NAM Gas Export/IGTM team of economists to study gas conversion and premium markets. Also on the agenda would be the possibility of establishing a joint company for the purpose of transporting and selling natural gas to public distributions at city gates and to large industrial customers.

Yves Monod related an amusing experience that happened in one of many meetings that followed that initial exploration. "Stewart and Schepers were both there. I was having trouble with my back and had been on holiday in Spain, where the roads were very bad, and my back was hurting me very much. Just as Gaz de France made their proposal for something new, I had a very sharp pain and cried out, 'Merde!' It made those people absolutely furious because they thought my outburst was a comment on their proposal. They thought I was behaving very well until I made that remark. Histoire! I did hasten to explain it was really my back, though, and that my remark had nothing to do with their proposal."

French negotiations proceeded, and hope emerged for an aide-mémoire that might lead to a natural gas contract for as much as five billion cubic meters of natural gas per year and a joint transportation and marketing company with a Shell and Esso shareholding of 50 percent.

The French negotiations simmered on in the heat of Paris. Ironing out the details of such an agreement was likely to take the remainder of the summer and into early fall. While this was brewing, Stewart and Schepers received a call from René de Brouwer, director general of Distrigaz.

"De Brouwer wanted to know if Schepers and I would come to Brussels to meet with him and Le Chevalier Albar Thys, a member of the Distrigaz administration," said Stewart

Belgium Assent

The day of the meeting, Stewart and Schepers took the train to Brussels to give them a quiet arena in which to discuss what they thought the purpose of a meeting initiated by Distrigaz was going to be. Stewart's concerns had to do with what the reaction of Jersey's lawyers would be. He wondered whether the Distrigaz proposal, if executed, would somehow expose Esso to the antitrust problems that NAM Gas Export and IGTM had been created to avoid.

Schepers's concerns had to do with how to get the proposal, whatever it was going to be, through the political intricacies of the government committees. It would not be just getting the Belgian government to agree to the involvement of two international oil companies in their domestic affairs. It also meant that two whole countries and their separate political committees would have to arrive, in a timely fashion, at a mutually beneficial agreement about a brand-new business that, technically and literally, did not yet exist.

Despite their questions, the Terrible Twins knew this meeting also had the potential to be an export breakthrough of major proportions. It would, of course, only be a breakthrough if the resolution of all these complexities led to actual signatures on completed contracts. Stewart, as ever, was certain that every difficulty would be overcome.

On arriving in Brussels, Schepers and Stewart met with Jacques de Housse, their study team manager, hoping Jacques had intercepted some hint of what Distrigaz was up to in proposing this unexpected meeting. Housse hadn't a clue or even any speculation.

Stewart recalled the Distrigaz offices as impressively located on a broad boulevard in Downtown Brussels. "We were ushered into a vast mahogany-paneled waiting room, through a secretary's office and into another large room, where we met Mssrs. De Brouwer and Le Chevalier Thys."

Over the always strong Belgian coffee and cigars, the serious talks began. Although Stewart and Schepers had been more or less dismissed from the last Belgian meeting in Antwerp, Schepers began characteristically mincing no words. He reiterated exactly what they'd been dismissed for at the last Brussels meeting. "Gentlemen, it remains the intent of IGTM to build the pipelines from the Dutch border to the municipal gates of the cities in Belgium. NAM Gas Export will sell the gas from the Dutch border to the Belgian cities, with each city then distributing the gas to the premium market householders. IGTM will transport the Dutch gas through separate connections directly to Belgian industry."

Schepers took a breath and waited for their reaction. Stewart was careful not to telegraph even a hint of the thought crossing his mind that this repetition of their earlier position might just result in the two of them being ushered out again. However, there was not a furrowed brow or frown in sight.

They were looking, instead, into the broad grin of Le Chevalier Thys, who offered an unexpected counter proposal. "Distrigaz has now come to see that in Belgium, there are many opportunities to be explored in this new gas business. Why don't we all just become partners in the whole enterprise?"

They were proposing that Esso and Shell take a 50 percent shareholding in Distrigaz, and then Distrigaz itself could buy the gas at the Dutch border. Thys also had ideas about those pipelines. "We'll construct the new pipelines together. We'll operate the natural gas system throughout Belgium together, and together, we transport this gas to France."

The Terrible Twins looked at each other, not betraying for a second their mutual recognition that this was not only a good solution, but it was also an offer they couldn't refuse.

Without a single nod to the originality of the Distrigaz proposal, Schepers simply extended a crisp and courteous response. "This is certainly not what our two companies have been exploring, but you can be assured we will give your proposal serious consideration, and we will get back to you."

Stewart remembered that they were beside themselves with barely bottled-up enthusiasm as they bid their polite farewells. "We could hardly contain ourselves from bolting from the room. Outside, we spotted a neat-appearing bar right across the boulevard and popped in to call Jacques de Housse and fill him in. Oddly, though, it was the middle of the afternoon. There was no one in the place. Instead of the usual large bar that always dominated a place like this, there were only secluded booths all along the left wall, with just a small bar in the rear. There was no such thing as a cell phone with which we could immediately share our enthusiasm with Jacques, so Krik headed to a telephone booth in the hall behind the bar. I took one of the deep leather booths and ordered two glasses of white wine."

Schepers came back to the table unable to stop laughing. "Doug, do you know where we are?"

"In a bar waiting for Jacques?"

"Jacques says this place is infamous. This is a trysting emporium, where married men meet their mistresses for the afternoon. The reason there's nobody in here is that they're all over there. See that door next to the phone booth? It leads to a little hotel next door."

Stewart interrupted the hilarity with an uncharacteristic negative. "What if that's an omen, Krik? Suppose Distrigaz treats us like a mistress, and we never get to the altar?"

His query changed the mood, and they began to wonder if there was a hidden agenda on the part of Distrigaz. There was also the inevitable question of whether antitrust legislation would be a factor if IGTM really were to take shares in Distrigas. With his unfailing optimism ever at the ready, Stewart was certain a way would be found for it all to work out. But his enthusiasm about the future with Distrigaz was muted by questions not in his power to answer. By fall, other questions and other events not in their power to control loomed in the path of the Terrible Twins.

French Slippage

Already buoyed with the progress in Belgium, Stewart and Schepers received good news from Paris. The agreement with Gaz de France was at last proceeding in a positive direction.

The anticipatory mood was darkened, however, in November by a phone call from the Shell attorney Joop Hoogland, who, with his wife, Louki, had become part of the Stewart's social circle. "Your royalty has been shot."

The news of the Kennedy assassination came only in bits and pieces at first, for there was no CNN or instant news source from the States. The Dutch people shared the mourning of the United States by sending a delegation to the funeral and with solemn and dignified commemoration in their churches. It was a strange experience for the Stewarts, and indeed for all Americans overseas at that time, to have something so indelible happening in their own country yet have no connection with the immediacy of the event because they were half a world away.

Despite the enormity of Kennedy's assassination, daily life and work quickly reasserted itself over the Americans in Holland. Only days later, on November 27, negotiations with Gaz de France arrived at the formal aide-mémoire. The announcement declared that arrangements for setting up a joint company among Gaz de France, Esso, and Shell had been arrived at for the sale and transport of Dutch gas to French cities and to the large industrial companies.

According to Stewart, "The aide-mémoire was the result of many, many months of hard negotiations. What we had been able to bring about was a letter of intent whereby Shell and Esso would participate fifty-fifty in a pipeline from the Belgian border to Paris, with joint marketing to industry in Northern France."

That night, in Paris, Stewart and Schepers gave their wives new charm bracelets with a gold Napoleon coin as the first charm. Stewart and Schepers returned triumphantly to The Hague to share the good news with the rest of the team. Only weeks later, on December 13, 1963, Monod called the office in Smidswater to tell them about an article that had appeared that day in Le Monde.

The issues raised by the article concerned the negotiations for importing Dutch gas from the Groningen field. In 1946, Gaz de France had been given a monopoly. There was an exception to this monopoly called the Armengaud Law, to which Schepers had referred in an earlier meeting. This exception was for businesses in which the majority of the capital came from public sources. The article accused IGTM of leaning on this law to claim for Shell and Esso a minority position in the business of transport as well as sales. The article also questioned how the price of the natural gas was to be determined. According to Le Monde, it was considered undeniable that the exploitation of these new resources from Groningen would translate into a raise in the price of energy. Shell and Esso were, after all, producers and refiners of gasoline and oil, and since, at times, natural gas would compete with oil, it would mean the oil companies would have the power to control the price of two different sources of energy. The article went to great lengths to emphasize that France had satisfactory alternatives to Groningen gas, not only from Algeria but from Libya as well. The public and political fallout that resulted from this article drastically altered everything with the Gaz de France agreement.

Within a few days, Chizelle was on the phone with panic in his voice. He was on his way to the The Hague. What he brought to Smidswater was as abrupt and unexpected as a snapped shoestring.

"President de Gaulle does not and will not support the aide-mémoire," announced Chizelle.

Like a cascade of dominos, the months of effort and planning, the negotiations and renegotiations simply tumbled in one upon another. The entire deal was scrapped. Heads rolled at Gaz de France. In the opinion of Hans Löblich, "If Doug and Schepers had been lesser men, they might have buckled."

They did not, and Mrs. Stewart and Mrs. Schepers did not return their gold Napoleon charms. Their husbands doggedly labored to restore what France had seemingly discarded so casually. If Gaz de France was not to allow Shell and Esso participation in the natural gas business there, Stewart and Schepers felt it would be unwise to proceed with just a gas contract that could jeopardize their negotiation position in Belgium and Germany. He suggested to Monod that their position might benefit if they adopted Russia's tactics with Napoleon. "We will just keep falling back and falling back until Gaz de France gives in for fear that we will sell all the gas to other countries, and there won't be any left for them."

In the Netherlands, Gasunie hit the ground running once the concession and other government approvals had been granted. They wasted no time in moving ahead to arrange domestic distribution and conversion programs. Because of their advanced planning and discussions with the local gas distributors, governmental authorities, and potential customers, Gasunie was able to begin laying trunk lines in early 1964. By the end of the year, a trunk line extended from Groningen to Geleen Limburg in the southernmost part of the country. Gasunie had to approach one hundred thousand landowners and tenants to obtain rights to lay their pipelines. They also began the task of converting almost five million appliances from town gas to natural gas. Though they were making good progress starting to convert the entire Netherlands on a task, that would take almost five more years.

Meanwhile, the export effort was facing roadblocks at every turn. Yves Monod explained that negotiations continued for nearly a full year before they arrived at a solution called an association en participation. In this arrangement, Shell and Esso would not participate in transportation, but it was agreed they would share in the profits.

On October 15, 1964, Monod met with Monsieur Alby and other Gaz de France executives. "The results of Gaz De France studies were presented concerning the most favorable way to distribute natural gas in Northern France. This meeting confirmed that Gaz de France urgently needed new supplies of natural gas. They were prepared to sustain the new 'association' idea against the government but only in an association where the NAM Gas Export/IGTM share was limited. Gaz de France continued to insistently demand a gas border price indication."

A week later, on the twenty-second, at a meeting among Stewart, Schepers, Monod, Bernard, Alby, and Bijard, the results of the meeting of the fifteenth were spelled out in English.

By November, things seemed on solid ground. Mr. Alby, now the Gaz de France deputy general manager, gave Schepers a confirmation of the "association en participation." Unbelievably, a brand-new detour appeared out of nowhere, and this extremely hard-won agreement was also abruptly canceled.

Within a few months, Stewart and Schepers succeeded in launching another round of studies between Gaz de France and NAM/IGTM. This time the group was to conduct an economics and market survey. They would also examine the technical, legal, fiscal, and financing issues. Esso France and Shell France provided temporary additional manpower and experts, including Esso's Monsieur Antoine, their legal manager. Shell provided their economics advisor, Monsieur Bouriez, and their legal advisor, Monsieur de Vauplane. Thereafter, the group met as necessary to resolve the following matters: a draft of gas sale contract at the border; a draft of the statutes of the "association en participation"; a pipeline project distributing natural gas in the North, Northeast, and Paris areas; and a statement of the total cost.

These studies became the foundation for the realization of the long-awaited pipeline.

"In spite of the diligence of the Esso/Shell teams, it was France who employed Russia's tactics against them," recalled Monod. "No one today is certain by what manner of influence this came about, but ultimately, a determination was made to set aside the Esso/Shell team's efforts at maintaining consistency in negotiation terms to which the team had adhered in the other countries. France was rewarded with their long-sought-for ideal. The sale price of natural gas to France was set at the Dutch/Belgian border. It was not until February 24, 1966, long after arrangements in Belgium and Germany had been finalized by NAM Gas Export and IGTM, that a contract with Gaz de France was, at long last, finally signed in Groningen.

"The now completed pipelines running from the Netherlands to France are today a symbol of peace that runs across the very regions which suffered for centuries in the conflicts of many wars, such as the Battle of Waterloo during the reign of Napoleon, la Somme during World War I, and finally, in May 1940, on the Belgian-French border, in the Battle of Gembloux, in which I took part in the Eighth Battalion of the French army. That's how history goes."

As a postscript, in June 2005, Gaz de France became a partially private company, 20 percent of which is presently quoted on the Bourse, the Paris stock exchange, a situation no one in the 1960s would have imagined.

Distrigaz

Getting Distrigaz to that contract "altar" required negotiations that lasted from 1963 until 1965 before arriving at a final consummation.

Stewart recalled some of the prenuptial steps on their way up the aisle. "First, we had to get permission from the parent companies that it would be acceptable for IGTM to take a 50 percent shareholding in Distrigaz and for NAM Gas Export to make a contract to sell Dutch gas at the Belgian border. We also needed to inform the supervisory committee of the designated delegates of these possibilities so they could give us the green light to proceed."

NAM Gas Export got that green light from the committee to negotiate a sales contract with Distrigaz. The delegates were informed that IGTM planned to arrange or the purchase of half the shares of Distrigaz for Shell and Esso. On May 5, 1964, a 50 percent participation agreement with IGTM was signed with Distrigaz in Brussels, and a letter of intent to deliver 150 billion cubic meters over a twenty-year period, with up to three billion per year, was also signed separately by Distrigaz and NAM Gas Export.

On May 12, NAM Gas Export held a press conference for the Dutch press about the Distrigaz agreement.

On that very same evening, just as the Dutch newspapers were informing their readers of the good news, the Belgian newspapers were trumpeting the news that its government was rejecting the deal. The Belgian government was suddenly demanding a one-third share of Distrigaz. Apparently, the Belgian politicians had looked across the border and seen that the Dutch government had a share of the gas business in that country, and they wanted to join the bandwagon. Now Stewart and Schepers and their future partners, the Distrigas executives, had another negotiation on their plate. During the years of the export project, the Schepers lived in Warmond, near The Hague, on the shore of the Kager Lakes. Schepers had a smallish sailboat called de rigeur, big enough for six people. Sailing with family and friends was a genuine pleasure for him and his wife.

According to his wife, Louise, Schepers never brought home worries about his work, but whenever he took that boat out on the lake alone, she knew there was something he was trying to work through. Schepers might have taken a turn or two in his sailboat over that unexpected demand by the Belgian government, but it was not in his nature, or Stewart's, to do anything except get back to the table and vigorously try to find a solution to this setback.

While Stewart and his family were away on vacation in 1964, an event occurred that sent Schepers to the lake, pondering whether their superiors in The Hague were trying, like many others, to take over control of the export effort or simply acting out of sheer ineptitude. One afternoon, Schepers got a call from Herr Thys of Distrigaz advising him that Cox had shown up with Kruizinga at the Distrigaz office in Brussels, attempting to speed up the Belgian negotiations.

According to Schepers, "These two had no insight whatsoever into the way things worked in Belgian negotiations, particularly with the entrenched companies. I guess the two of them somehow imagined they could just step onto the scene and bring it to the finish. Thys said that when he pressed them as to whether they were authorized to close the deal, they had to confess that they were only advisors to me and Doug."

Paul Mortimer described what was beginning to happen at Esso. "At that time, people inside the business were very happy and very complimentary with the way things were going. But the Esso and Shell people on the sidelines were constantly out to get Stewart because office politics are funny things. People get very jealous when somebody has a lot of influence over a new and exciting situation in which they're not involved. The whole world wants to insinuate themselves into those situations in order to share in the glory, so the situation becomes extremely political. For example, Stewart and Schepers were these two clever guys who'd realized they couldn't make a proposal to Esso and Shell until each one's own company approved it, so they each sent off the proposal saying it was what the other company had prepared. These two got the job done. But unfortunately, those clever things get known, and no matter that they were effective, the people at the local office start worrying if maybe this is what they're doing all the time."

Schepers did not know the origins of the attempted incursion into his and Stewart's activities, but he had no doubts about the result. "I don't know if Boot and Smit were behind this little foray into the export negotiation world, but needless to say, the failure of Cox and Kruizinga's visit to Distrigaz didn't improve the already cool relationships that Doug and I had with Boot and Smit. At least none of them ever again tried to interfere with NAM Gas Export or IGTM negotiations anywhere else."

The Distrigaz situation was not resolved until October 15. On that date, Distrigaz informed NAM Gas Export and IGTM that a compromise could be reached with the Belgian government. The government would take a one-third share in Distrigaz, and for this, Distrigaz would be granted a monopoly in transportation and distribution of natural gas. In view of the forthcoming elections in Belgium, it was necessary that they obtain a commitment from NAM Gas Export and IGTM on this arrangement and for a contract to be signed. Schepers reviewed the situation with the designated delegates and received approval to proceed.

—Chapter 19—

Scaling the German Summit

J ust like Ruhrgas in Germany, the directors of the small grid gas companies were convinced their firmly entrenched positions of power would mean they would be dictating the rules for "their" Dutch gas. Löblich and Mclean in the Frankfurt office had other ideas. The first step in preparing the gas distributors for the facts of life on what those rules were really going to be took place on July 4, 1963, with the first invitation to the grid gas directors to meet with the Shell/Esso group for "studies of natural gas" in the Frankfurt office.

To also facilitate the education of Ruhrgas, Löblich organized another carefully prepared event about the future of the natural gas business. "We again invited the boards of the biggest grid gas companies to visit our office in Frankfurt. They possessed a kind of arrogance because of how long they'd been in business. We were no less so because of our power as a supplier. But we were ahead because we knew what they did not. We knew how to make this new business work.

"In preparing for this meeting, we racked our brains with questions, for example, what would be the role of the Ruhr Gas Company, with its huge amounts of coking plant gas? This gas basically was the reserve for the entire German gas economy up until now. That was a big question for everybody. The poker game of gambling over the future of the natural gas business in Germany had begun."

The two giants, Ruhrgas and Thyssengas, were the keys to bringing Dutch gas to all of Germany.

Löblich recalled that both firms were very stubborn, and negotiations were prolonged. "It must have been very difficult for the owners of the grid gas companies, these Kohlbarons ('Barons of Carbon'), to give parts of their lucrative proprietary rights to their arch enemies, the oil companies."

These two giants were formidable as a united force, but Löblich and the team reasoned that if it were possible to put a wedge between the two, it would accelerate matters. They identified three cities in the Ruhr area receiving up to 50 percent of their gas from one or both: Düsseldorf, Cologne, and Duisburg.

The city gas works of Dusseldorf were supplied fifty-fifty by Thyssengas and Ruhrgas. The manager of the Dusseldorf gas works, Dr. Schenk, just happened to be an old acquaintance of Löblich, so Löblich made a bold move. He and the Dusseldorf manager were actually willing to go behind Thyssengas's back to launch a joint study of the conversion of Dusseldorf to natural gas, but to Löblich's great surprise, Thyssengas decided to participate—without Ruhrgas.

"I called Dr. Schenk and warmed him up to the idea of doing an economy study for a switch of the city to natural gas. He was interested at once. When Thyssengas agreed to participate in the study, we put people from both sides into one team to perform this study in a determined manner and without secrets from one another. A big help for us was that we had Jack Trachsel from Portland, Oregon, who was lent to us from the gas works over there, and he was able to bring all of his experience into our work."

The Dusseldorf study began in December of 1963. Löblich traveled to the town of Hamborn once a week to assist the Thyssengas planning department in establishing it. In the Frankfurt office, Löblich and his team were engaged in the difficult task of convincing the grid gas companies of Germany that sealing contracts with their communities for the changeover to natural gas could be profitable.

Löblich remained convinced today that the single most effective tool they employed in taking down what he described as the "biased opinions" of the directors of those German gas works was an all-expenses-paid trip for them to the United States. "We flew them one by one to Portland, Oregon, to show them how the natural gas business could work. In Portland, we would all stay at a hotel for about one week, and our guest directors had the opportunity to observe all areas of the natural gas business there. The most impressive days were those where they were able to join the U.S. gas sales managers on their sales trips or to witness the way in which complaints were settled, which was not a common practice in Germany."

The biggest surprise for the German visitors was learning that it was the task of the American salespeople to push every last household they contacted into changing from heating oil to natural gas rather than, as was the custom in Germany, to wait for the consumer to come to them. On such visits to prospects, Löblich felt they learned much about the normal American household and were quite surprised that some housewives seemed to be dying to tell the visitors about their worries.

"To us, everything about the households seemed very simple: the furnishings, the wooden houses with no basements," said Löblich. These kinds of houses did not conform to our very strict German construction rules. For example, the American households were allowed to store heating oil in simple sheet metal tanks in their yards. In these moments, we felt ourselves to be predominant."

Löblich recounted some other things that surprised the German visitors in the effectiveness of the American gas companies, particularly with regard to consumer communication. "There were many telephone saleswomen who sat row after row behind each other in a big room answering telephone calls in case of an emergency or complaint. The information was immediately printed out in first draft and put on a belt that ran through the rows and led to the next room, where the field representative responsible would receive the information and be able to respond immediately."

Löblich also remembered that the German visitors found the requirements for the Oregon sales representatives quite unusual for the demands it placed upon the men. "The system of constantly impelling the sales representative out into the field made us feel very odd. There was a board on the wall on which they wrote down the daily success of each and every one. Every month, they had a prize-giving ceremony honoring the best salesperson of the month or of the year. The prizes were so attractive, such as a vacation in Hawaii. All the salesmen seemed to be in the best mood. They dressed well, they were all young, and had to be, to our eye, under great big pressure. For our guests, these things and a lot more were a revelation. The change of their opinions came about, in large part, through these eye-opening trips."

The obvious high level of success of this American sales process was just what Löblich and the team wanted them to see. "For our guests, that was like a revolution in thinking. It was through this change of their opinions that it was possible for us to build success for the natural gas business in Germany."

While Löblich and his team were successfully changing the thinking of the gas company executives, the presentation of the Dusseldorf study brought to Thyssengas the enlightenment for which Löblich had hoped. The study showed a potential for the use of four billion cubic meters of natural gas per year for the next twenty-five years. Results also showed extreme economic advantages for the city works if they would agree to a fast switch, which certainly gave considerably more drive to the negotiations.

The Dusseldorf gas works eagerly took to the idea of converting to natural gas as quickly as possible. Armed with the information revealed by the studies, the city of Dusseldorf began to put pressure on both Ruhrgas and Thyssengas to provide its residents with natural gas as soon as possible. The slow pace of negotiations during these months was wearing on everyone, but an unexpected breakthrough moved everything forward dramatically.

Schepers vividly remembered a surprising call he received at the Smidswater office. "Herr Swart, a director for Bank voor Handel nen

Scheepvaart, the Netherlands bank owned by Heine Thyssen, who also owned Thyssengas, invited Doug and me to go to lunch all the way down to Maastricht. I knew he wasn't asking us to go that distance just to break bread."

On their way to Maastricht, Stewart and Schepers discussed strategy.

"The tough line had worked well in Belgium," said Stewart. "Krik decided we'd try it again on Mr. Swart. We got the surprise of our lives. It was Belgium all over again."

Before Schepers could speak a word, he recalled that Mr. Swart spoke up. "He told us that Baron Thyssen said that if he got the right price, he would sell half of his company to Shell and Esso, which would then purchase gas at the Dutch border. As Swart was only a representative of Baron Thyssen, he was not prepared to discuss any of the details. If we thought Shell and Esso were interested, he recommended that Doug and I arrange to meet with company officials at Thyssengas offices in Germany."

Stewart and Schepers stopped at a roadside tavern to take stock of what had just transpired. Schepers was certain the offer from Thyssen was a direct result of their colorful "Undenkbar!" meeting. "His own executives must have related to him the challenge we put on the table in that meeting when we expounded upon the enormous potential of natural gas in Germany. Heine Thyssen was an astute businessman who may have more quickly grasped the personal profit potential for himself, whereas the coal barons of the Ruhr were only looking at what was going to happen to their coal markets."

In Stewart's opinion, the offer to sell half his company might also have been influenced by a divorce settlement Thyssen's third wife was then demanding. "Our success may just have owed a lot to Baron Thyssen's divorce proceedings with model Fiona Campbell. According to gossip, she got $26 million in a settlement, which was just about the amount Esso/Shell paid for half of Thyssengas. One of the surprises we got when we finally closed that deal was that not only had we bought half of Thyssen's company, but Esso and Shell also found themselves with a half interest in a palatial yacht on the Rhine as well as an interest in the artificial insemination business because Thyssengas owned a large herd of fine dairy cattle."

On that day in Maastricht, however, none of those details had yet been revealed, and at the moment, Schepers was much more interested in speculating on what a deal with Thyssengas was going to do to negotiations with Ruhrgas. "I thought that if we made this deal with Thyssen, it would not only put a sword in the side of Ruhrgas. It would provoke all the other players to want to get their Dutch gas now. They would not miss this opportunity to slow down, the way Ruhrgas dominates their industry."

The Terrible Twins lost no time in arranging the meeting with Thyssengas. An agreement was quickly reached to launch a new series of studies with them, this time for the much bigger task of examining all the Thyssengas distribution areas.

Löblich designed the study. "To arrive at whatever the value of Thyssengas might be, and also to pinpoint the natural gas requirements for customers in all the Thyssengas distribution areas, we would have to compute the potential volumes of natural gas that would be needed to form the basis for a long-term contract. We scheduled new joint studies with the planning department of Thyssengas, which took many weeks."

After an extended period of tough negotiations with Thyssengas management over the value of Thyssengas shares, a meeting was set in the Thyssengas offices on July 27, 1964. IGTM and the Bank voor Handel en Scheepvaart in Rotterdam arranged for 50 percent Shell/Esso participation in Thyssengas.

On the day of the meeting, Schepers, Stewart, Orlean, Windham, and Attorney Hoogland were ushered into a ballroom-like reception room where a long conference table was bedecked with sodas, ashtrays, notepads, pens, and even a discreet flower arrangement befitting the anticipated big occasion. Through a partially open door, they could see a table on which were trays of champagne glasses and, standing by, a row of white-gloved waiters, poised at the ready to pick those trays on some given signal. That certainly set up the team's expectations for smooth sailing, but according to Stewart, that was not the way the meeting proceeded.

"Everything was going well until Thyssengas threw in the first of several monkey wrenches which came that day and not just from Thyssengas."

They were abruptly informed that Baron Thyssen wanted to call off the deal unless Esso and Shell would guarantee the $14 million bank loan needed for the initial pipeline investments. Stewart and the team stepped aside to discuss what to do with this astounding demand.

"Our team huddled over this new development, and after kicking around the pros and cons, we concluded that the deal was so important we thought we could sell it to our parent companies," said Stewart. "We told Thyssengas, 'Okay, we're ready to sign, but we have to check back with our shareholders.' I called Cox, and Schepers called Kruizinga. Both said they couldn't okay such a thing without first checking with our head offices. Before we had signed anything or heard back from headquarters, someone in Thyssengas gave a signal, and in marched those champagne-laden waiters with bottles, buckets, glasses, and cigars."

At almost the very same minute, Cox was on the phone. Jersey, in no way, would agree to guarantee a Thyssengas loan. Nor would Shell. Even with Esso and Shell as 50 percent shareholders, Thyssengas would have to float its own loans.

Red-faced, Stewart informed Thyssengas of this decision. The waiters turned on their heels and did a 180 with that champagne.

Stewart recalled how he and the team all were acting cool, trying to exude a "take it or leave it" attitude. "Now it was Thyssengas's turn to call headquarters. Baron Thyssen, who was apparently as anxious as we were to make the deal, now told his people to go ahead and sign without the loan guarantee. Half an hour later, we were all back at the signing table, and this time the waiters not only marched in. They popped the corks on that champagne. Esso and Shell were now on the way to owning half of that yacht, the artificial insemination plant, and last but not least, the gas business of Thyssengas. We now had our very big feet in the door of Germany."

With the acquisition of Thyssengas, Ruhrgas did lose half of its lucrative Dusseldorf market and no doubt saw more erosion on the way because Stewart and Schepers were publicly carrying on talks with the Bavarian and Southern German gas companies. The meetings with Ruhrgas now became more frequent.

In a 2005 meeting arranged by the authors with Stewart, Löblich, Mortimer, and Dr. Klaus Liesen, Ruhrgas's former chairman, Dr. Liesen acknowledged that the turning point for his company had been the Thyssengas agreement. "Although the Dusseldorf study caused some unrest among municipalities, those actions were not yet regarded by Ruhrgas as being truly dangerous. The united front of Ruhrgas and Thyssengas, if it ever existed, collapsed the moment Baron Heinrich Thyssen-Bornemisca decided to sell half of his stake in Thyssengas to Esso/Shell and to let Esso/Shell have the responsibility for industrial management of the company." The first real progress was made when Ruhrgas participated in a joint study to examine potential natural gas markets.

Löblich noted that their team was careful at that time not to discuss prices. "This approach, and the information the study revealed, must have opened up the eyes of Ruhrgas to new possibilities. In later years, our people were gratified that we received many compliments on the thoroughness of our work."

Dr. Liesen recalled that the Ruhrgas sales experts found the studies especially interesting in their methodology. "In the long run, the studies were convincing in their results, but it was felt that the study assumptions did not fully take into account the complicated combination of regional, local, and energy policy problems that would be encountered by natural gas on its market entry into Western Germany. On the basis of its own analyses, Ruhrgas was of the opinion that coke oven gas did not stand a chance against natural gas in the long run and that the future of Ruhrgas would depend on negotiating large natural gas deliveries with producers and then selling the natural gas in its traditional market and preferably beyond as well."

As a result of the NAM Gas Export/IGTM studies, Dr. Herbert Schelberger of Ruhrgas was convinced that the future of Ruhrgas lay with the conversion and expansion of the system to higher-calorie natural gas, but several obstacles lay in his way. One had to do with the plans of the oil companies to invade the Ruhrgas area with their own distribution lines. Another problem was that the coal mining companies were fearful about how natural gas would compete with their coal and coke oven gas supplies. This, of course, was a valid concern. According to Liesen, "The structure of Ruhrgas AG was shaped by over thirty shareholders (steel and coal companies) who simultaneously were, or had been, suppliers of coke oven gas. The purchase price of coke oven gas was largely determined by the revenue achieved by Ruhrgas in the market, less cost (netback)."

When the Ruhrgas supervisory board elevated Schelberger to chairman, it strengthened his negotiation position with the oil companies.

In a meeting in Essen in 2005, Dr. Liesen commended Schelberger's negotiation skills within Ruhrgas itself. "With his great foresight and ample communications skills, Dr. Schelberger was able to convince some of the large shareholders that importing large quantities of Dutch gas and diversifying with other supplies was the best prospect for Ruhrgas."

Dr. Liesen also noted his own involvement. "As personal assistant to Chairman Schelberger, I was involved in deliberations on the approach to be adopted, but the decisive aspects of preparing and conducting the negotiations were the responsibility of Dr. Jurgen Weise, who was the driving force behind the opening of Ruhrgas, in particular for his gaining the support of over thirty coal and steel shareholders."

Stewart remembered that Schepers had a particular love of negotiating and once played a game with Schelberger when he came to The Hague seeking to buy Dutch gas. "I'm not sure why we were still at odds then, but Krik decided to see how long we could talk without speaking about natural gas, and we went for almost an hour that way with nothing coming of it. I don't know what Dr. Schelberger thought."

Dr. Liesen recalled Schelberger being astonished in that meeting when Schepers casually popped his feet up on the desk to make a point. Paul Mortimer, an Esso analyst who later became an IGTM president, recalled that there were huge disagreements that had to be resolved before resolution was achieved. "It was highly uneconomical to fight against us and much more economical to go together with us."

"We had never had the idea to fight if we could come to an arrangement," said Liesen. "Our structure then was that the companies of which we were made gave us the coke oven gas, we sold it and tried to get as much as we could get for it. Then we deducted our costs, and they got the rest. We were paid no dividends, and they got the gas profit. So it was not difficult for us, in the first step, to imagine that we could do the same with natural gas producers in Germany, not in Holland but with German gas producers. We tried to get as much for their natural gas as the market and the competition of fuel oil allowed. That was the first step, and then step by step, things changed."

Dr. Liesen explained his company's thinking regarding Shell and Esso equity participation in Ruhrgas, which was ultimately what occurred. "From the outset, the Ruhrgas management considered such a structure for cooperation with the German gas producing arms of Esso and Shell (and other producers in Germany like Elwerath, Preussag, and Wintershall). This did not apply to Dutch gas, however, or for other gas produced abroad. Ruhrgas sought, in this case, a normal gas import contract (arm's length). At the end of the negotiations, the netback concept prevailed for production in Germany. Only several years later were the gas supply contracts with gas producers in Germany switched from netback to arm's length. This switch was proposed by the Ruhrgas management due to new legal and economic developments that occurred in the meantime and was accepted by all shareholders."

Part of the deal when Shell and Esso became shareholders of Ruhrgas was that Dr. Liesen would be sent to the United States on a training program prior to moving up into Schelberger's position. He visited Esso producing installations in Texas, spent time in Seattle with a gas pipeline and distribution company, and attended a management training course at Northwestern University's Business School in Illinois. After this, he spent time in the Far East, courtesy of Shell. Dr. Liesen was enthusiastic about the value this initiative had been to his career.

The lack of coordination between Brigitta and NAM, both shared enterprises of Shell and Esso, worked to the benefit of Ruhrgas. "The view held by all participants was that we would first have to sign a supply contract as quickly as possible with either Brigitta or NAM Gas Export in order to defend our sales area," said Dr. Liesen. "We feared that the sales policy of NAM and Brigitta would be coordinated and that we would come up against a united front of the two companies. To my surprise, this was not the case. It proved possible to reach agreement with NAM Gas Export, which reinforced our position in negotiations with Brigitta and its shareholders, Deutsche Shell AG and Esso A. G., so that we were then also able to convince Brigitta to join us in a cooperation model."

One distinctive aspect of these intensely complex negotiations was the consistency of the terms, which ultimately provided a pattern for negotiations decades into the future and were the foundation for contracts in France and Belgium.

Since all negotiations were being carried on for a business that had never before existed, inventiveness was their hallmark. Liesen explained, "There was a great deal of invention in these long-term contracts, which made two things happen. First, the gas price was so fixed that it automatically followed the trend of the competitive light and heavy fuel oil prices. Second, every three or five years, there was a negotiation for certain adjustments, if one party felt it necessary. This system is still alive today in many countries and contracts."

The path to such resolution in these years-long negotiations was certainly not always smooth. After Mortimer became president of IGTM, he recalled a meeting at which both he and Dr. Liesen were present. "It began about four in the afternoon, and we negotiated until five in the morning. It was awful. It went on and on."

According to Stewart, one of the major questions to be solved in the export of Dutch gas to the neighboring countries was to determine a price at the Dutch border. "On the one hand, the agreement had to allow gas distribution companies in Belgium and Germany to be able to sell gas into their premium markets and still receive a sufficient margin between the border price and what they charge their own customers. This would then provide capital for the construction of the expensive pipeline networks with still a reasonable profit."

Ultimately, NAM Gas Export was able to conclude a long-term gas purchase agreement with Ruhrgas, with the natural gas to be delivered in a separate pipeline system to various industries and cities that would be converted to natural gas.

Working with IGTM, Shell, and Esso, Ruhrgas invested and participated in the construction of several major trunk lines to bring natural gas into Germany. Ruhrgas developed a plan to redirect the coke oven gas and began converting town gas networks, residential appliances, and industries to natural gas.

Stewart was acutely aware of the massive investments that were before them. "There were millions of homes and appliances to be converted from low calorie gas to the natural gas, which had different characteristics than existing appliances could handle."

Löblich described the logistics of the changeover in both areas of supply as an undertaking of massive proportions. "The biggest pipelines had to be built. We fought with the grid gas companies about who should build them. Ruhrgas wanted to do everything under their own direction. Finally, we worked out a fifty-fifty solution with them. Huge compressor stations had to be built along the pipes. Each installation was the size of a big power plant."

In cooperation with the local gas distribution companies, Ruhrgas developed the means to expedite these conversions, and by the early 1970s, the major share of the towns and customers had been converted to natural gas. Coke oven gas was confined to a small area in the Ruhr.

The German grid gas companies also had to seal new contracts with their communities. "We were gratified at the transformation in the attitude of these companies when we took them to the States," said Löblich. "They were then convinced that the changeover was going to be profitable for them, even if they, as happened in some cases, had to shut down their own gas works."

Dr. Liesen explained that the shutting down of these gas works was not as disruptive as might have been expected. "They were able to develop a process of harmonizing the coke oven gas with the natural gas, decreasing the coke oven gas step by step."

In 1964, Esso A. G. determined that subsequent contract negotiations needed more of a legal expert rather than a technical expert, and Löblich was ordered back to Hamburg. To not disrupt his daughters, who had adjusted so well to the school and the community, Gisela and the girls remained there while Löblich once again set about the task of locating a new home, driving the long miles each weekend from Hamburg to his family.

For Löblich, his wife's extraordinary patience and steadfast support of him in the face of so many relocations was something he considered a decidedly significant factor in the success of his career. A year went by before he finally located a house in Hamburg, to which Gisela returned while the girls continued to board in the Catholic college for several more years to complete their schooling.

In Germany, by early 1965, Ruhrgas and NAM Gas Export/IGTM were near an agreement on a gas contract and a participation agreement. On May 26, a ververtrag (precontract) was reached with NAM Gas Export, and a joint press release from NAM Gas Export, Ruhrgas, and Thyssengas revealed plans for a joint trunk line. But it was not until the sixteenth of November 1965 that the first contract was finally signed. That year proved to be one of evolution and revelation for Doug Stewart and his family.

Left to right: Krik Schepers and Donald Mclean of NAM Gas Export and Dr. Dekker of Ruhrgas signing the first Dutch gas contract with Ruhrgas. Ruhrgas photo.

Below: Because of the advance planning by the oil companies and Gasunie, the gas trunk lines spread rapidly through the Dutch landscape carrying natural gas to the Dutch cities and to export at the Belgium and German borders. Gasunie photo.

In November 2005, Dr. Klaus Liesen, former chairman of Ruhrgas, hosted a luncheon at the new Ruhrgas building in Essen to discuss the early days of the Dutch gas negotiations to assist the authors in writing this book. Participants were Dr. Liesen, Douglass Stewart, Hans Löblich, and Paul Mortimer. Ms. Madsen recorded the meeting.

Above: Douglass Stewart and Dr. Klaus Liesen greeted each other.

Below: Stewart and Löblich with the bust of Dr. Herbert Schellberger, the former chairman of Ruhrgas who led the early Dutch gas negotiations with NAM Gas Export and IGTM. Ruhrgas photos.

Dr. Klaus Liesen and Engr. Hans Löblich at the 2005 luncheon meeting. Dr. Liesen recalled that the Ruhrgas sales experts found Löblich's studies especially interesting in their methodology, and in that the long run, the studies were convincing in their results.

Left to right: Douglass Stewart, Dr. Klaus Liesen, Eiaine Madsen Engr. Hans Löblich, and Paul Mortimer.

—Chapter 20—

Stewart Passages

During the years they lived in the Netherlands, Stewart and his wife, Jane, packed the wonders of Europe into their children's memory banks, and their own, as carefully as they packed away savings and investments for their children's future education. Jane's imaginative planning always made their summers memorable.

For Stewart, the summer of 1964 was exceptionally so. "Almost every weekend, we took off, trying to crowd in as much as possible before Doug Jr. had to return to school in Switzerland. We really loved going out on the network of canals because you could see Holland from a unique vantage point. The canals are frequently higher than the surrounding land, and there were brick paths alongside them that were originally intended for people or horses to pull barges before they became motorized. Now the paths are used for walking or bicycling, and we did both. For longer canal trips, we often took the boat that I'd bought in our second summer in Holland. After a few kilometers, you came to a lock, and there, the level of the canal changes by a few feet. To enter the lock, the lockmaster would lower a wooden shoe dangling on the end of a pole to collect the toll and then let you move on. There were so many little day trips we took this way, past picturesque little houses and gardens facing the canal. There seemed to be an endless variety of little restaurants and towns with street markets full of food and goods being offered by the endlessly cheerful and welcoming Dutch merchants."

There were also family car trips to Rome, Bavaria, Brussels, Paris, and Normandy. Stewart was pleased to be able to take the children and Jane to see the D-Day beaches and to visit the cemeteries honoring those who paid so dearly to claim them. He also loved the times Jane accompanied him on business trips out of town; she would shop while he attended the meetings.

"On one of the trips to France, Jane bought all these wonderful French cheeses and brought them back to the little old-fashioned hotel she'd found for us. These cheeses smelled so bad there was no doubt that they would taste good. However, by the time we got back from dinner, they had smelled up our whole room so badly that we had to put the package out on the balcony so we could sleep. Next morning, on the train, we were in one of those charming small compartments, and I put the bagful of cheese in the overhead rack. An elderly lady entered the compartment and quite soon was looking uncomfortable. By now, Jane and I were immune to the odor, but the cheese was announcing itself in the lady's wrinkling nose and scrunched-up eyes. When she left the compartment, I knew she would return with the conductor to inspect the source of her discomfort. While she was gone, I put our odiferous package in the passage between the cars. Soon, its presence drifted back into our car and, eventually, permeated the entire train. When we got off at our stop, we looked back, and there was the smelly cheese, going off without us."

Another extraordinary Stewart family adventure took place in Lascaux, the site of the celebrated cave dweller's drawings. The caves are no longer open, and visitors today have to be satisfied with looking at only an artful recreation of the caves. The Stewart family, however, were among the site's early visitors and were allowed to tour the original caves, walking on narrow boardwalks, the pathway lighted only by flashlights. Their tour was actually conducted by the man who discovered the drawings.

A decidedly awkward family adventure involved Stewart's beautiful but notoriously unreliable Jaguar sedan. "I'd put a trailer on the Jag, and we would haul our boat to a different location each time. On one weekend, we were going to launch the boat down the Rhine. In the middle of a tunnel leading into Rotterdam, the Jag conked out with the whole family in the car and the boat right behind. We were quite a sight and quite a problem to everyone behind us. We held up everybody for quite a good while until somebody managed to get in there to tow us out. The tow truck driver shrugged his shoulders at 'these crazy Americans.'"

So much of the export effort was on its way by mid-1964 that the possibility of an entirely different excursion was before the family. Jane planned what turned out to be the grandest family tour of all.

Stewart recalled that this one lasted for a whole month. "We flew to Czechoslovakia for several days and saw, for the first time, the effects of Soviet Communism on daily life. Our guide was a middle-aged lady, formerly a tourist agent before the war. We knew, of course, that she had connections with the government, or she wouldn't have been trusted with American tourists. I don't think she was really a committed Communist because when we moved back to the States, she came and stayed with us in Westport for several days and sold us some crystal she had brought along in lieu of money. Carrying money outside the country was then forbidden by her government. That was the only way she would have had any money with which to enjoy her visit in our country, and we were happy to have the things she brought. I'm sure she could never have even dreamed of the Velvet Revolution that so dramatically transformed her country in recent years.

"During our 1964 visit there, the guide and chauffeur who were assigned to us seemed absolutely stunned that we were bringing our children with us. I guess they expected 'the Stewart Group' to be businessmen. They were very courteous, but we were not free to wander about as we were able to do in other countries. We were allowed to see many of the famous places in Prague, including the home of Franz Kafka, as well as some of the wonders inside the walls of the ancient city, which had been spared the ravages war had brought elsewhere in the country."

A number of things stood out in Stewart's mind about Czechoslovakia at that time. There were almost no cars, and the family was watched all the time. He remembered vividly the condition of the plane on which they departed. "When we boarded the Russian-built plane to fly to Greece, it was dirty. The stewardess wore a grease-stained uniform, and the paper placemat was two paper napkins glued together."

The Stewarts spent a few days in Athens, had dinner on the rooftop of a small café in the Placa, and then took a seven-day cruise through the Greek Isles, winding up in Turkey on a ship called the *Stella Solarius*.

Stewart remembered this was the first time he saw young people dancing the Watusi. "That dance seemed quite striking to us at the time. In just a few years, the '60s would be in full swing, and the Watusi would be considered quite tame."

From there, the family flew on to Cairo. "In Cairo, we ran into the boxer Cassius Clay, who wasn't yet Muhammad Ali. The kids all got his autograph. I have one saved somewhere. Maybe it's worth something these days. We traveled by train to Luxor and saw the ruins on the east side and the tombs on the west side. It was so hot the kids got all excited and waded right into the water, but the guide warned them they had to get out immediately because of the Belasarius worm that gets between your toes and into your bloodstream, causing blindness."

The sight of the pyramids rising majestically from the desert floor moved Stewart profoundly. "I was struck by the feeling of how unimportant individuals are in the sweep of time. Those monumental structures had been there for thousands of years, as had the now ruined temples of Luxor. Yet the individuals who constructed them were there but for a fleeting moment. I wondered if someday some future generation would look at the system of natural gas we were working so hard to establish. Would they see it as an outmoded period lasting only a few generations, only to be succeeded in their day by another energy system, such as nuclear power?"

Stewart's 1964 prediction has emerged as a serious consideration for much of the world today. There is a growing recognition that the fossil fuels generating energy for the global economy are finite and have become a source of dependence for Europe and the United States. This recognition has set scientists, engineers, and economists racing against the inevitable for viable alternatives.

At the end of their world tour, the Stewarts returned to the Netherlands, just in time for Jane Ann and Mark to slide into their first day of school with a vivid collage of experiences to use in their "What I Did This Summer" essays. For the second time, they put Doug Jr. on the plane for his studies at La Rosey in Switzerland. Was it that he was taller this year that made it harder to see him go?

Stewart and Jane went home from the airport to catch up with the letters from family that had accumulated during the grand tour. Esso provided tickets back to the States every other year for executives on foreign duty, and the Stewarts had been stateside for a month just the previous summer. But somehow this stack of letters full of fresh news about the Fourth of July barbecues, family birthdays, Christenings, and cousins' weddings, along with the little packs of photos and folded-up news clippings about all the things for which Stewart and Jane had been absent, set off an awareness they didn't have time to name. The slippery creature called homesickness had come calling, as difficult to ignore as the shivery scent that lingers in the air after lightning strikes. At that moment, there was no time to examine its nagging tug. Jane was swept into the fall season's many activities with all the groups in which she participated or chaired. Stewart was immediately back into the rush of final negotiations in Germany and Belgium.

By Christmas, the Stewarts had encountered a new phenomenon. Somehow they had been transformed into a kind of official welcoming committee for new arrivals to the area. They actually couldn't quite recall who had served in that role when they arrived. They did, however, slowly realize that nearly everyone who had been there when they arrived had moved on, even the neighbors next door. They had enjoyed that family so much they put a gate in the hedge that divided their properties so that they didn't have to walk all the way round the road to go calling. The new neighbors didn't have children, so the gate hadn't been opened for quite a while.

The two of them had reached the moment that occurs in the life of everyone working out of their home country for any length of time. The novel, the exotic, and the amazing, which dominate one's arrival, gradually transmute into the daily background of the fact that you are always "the American" who only works there. Although the Stewarts certainly treasured the friendship of those native to the Netherlands, they could never be fully part of the political life of the community as they had always been when they lived in the States. They were simply not, and never would be, citizens there.

While they were beginning to recognize these shifts in their lives, January of 1965 brought them to a personal watershed. Everything came into sharp focus for them when it was time to put Doug Jr. on the plane back to his school in Switzerland. He was leaving full of his own plans. He was not coming home between semesters, he announced, as he would be skiing with friends. Driving back from Amsterdam, Jane's silence was pronounced. They knew each other too well to need explanations. When Jane said, "Doug . . .," he knew everything she was thinking and answered quietly, "Me too." What was before the two of them felt as heavy as the ice-storm-laden trees of their first Netherlands winter. What remaining in the Netherlands would mean to their family life finally insinuated itself past the closed door of the present. This was Jane Ann's last year at the American school. If Stewart continued with the Dutch gas project, on graduation, she too would have to be sent to school in Switzerland. Jane did not want to surrender her daughter's teenage years to an institution.

At the time, Stewart's smartest career move would have been to capitalize on his Dutch success by accepting the advancement that was open to him in Jersey's vast international operations. But the choice he and Jane had to make was not about his career. It was about their family life.

The two of them spent the next few hours putting words to the feelings that kept cropping up since their return from the family's summer tour. Although Stewart had kept his commitment to Jane to be home on weekends, the ease of travel that the job afforded the family on most of those weekends had not made up to Jane for all the days when he was away. And by now, there was very little of Europe they hadn't already seen. For the first time, Jane openly expressed her previously carefully shielded frustration with her husband's absences and her sense of loss about being away from her family in Texas. Stewart recounted to Jane his own unspoken frustrations about the demands of the job. One, about which he felt particularly bitter, had been a visit he'd expected to have with his parents. He'd gone back to New York for two meetings that were supposed to have been almost a week apart. He hadn't seen his parents for a year, and his mother had excitedly prepared for the visit, which he also had eagerly anticipated. Stewart arrived in Oklahoma around noon, but before the day was out, he had been summoned back to New York for Bill Stott's convenience. Forty years on, the capriciousness of it still stings.

The Stewarts' mutual decision emerged as easily as butter seeping through hot pasta. They were going home to America. Stewart would seek a position in the New York office. The two of them talked into the early hours of the morning about what the many aspects of leaving Holland were going to mean and about the logistics of shipping a whole household back to Connecticut.

The year 1965 also brought about the climax of the shared efforts of Schepers and Stewart. Like soldiers on parade, the successes of the Terrible Twins were marching to the finish line—with Distrigaz, in Belgium, and with Weser Ems and Thyssengas in Germany. Negotiations with Ruhrgas and the Southern gas companies were almost concluded, and Gaz de France was now eager for gas. The UK would be getting gas from its own North Sea discoveries. Everything Stewart and Schepers had done to bring pens to signature lines had been accomplished. Seeing those signatures set down in ink would only be ribbon cutting moments, acknowledging efforts already expended.

On Monday morning, Stewart told Schepers first about his decision. Schepers wasn't surprised. He and Stewart had talked recently about the chill wind of corporate micromanagement that had begun to descend. They acknowledged to each other that the fun just wasn't there anymore. The reason for their long and splendid ride on this roller coaster of negotiation was coming to its end.

Admitting that all the activity was ending was much easier than accepting they were now also losing the pleasure of each other's company.

Schepers's first thought was to dissuade Stewart from his decision, but they'd become so used to recognizing what the other was thinking that before Schepers even formed the words, he swallowed them. He knew better. Stewart would not even have broached the subject of departure without already having considered every angle of it. From their earliest days together, they'd pledged not to let the job get in the way of family.

Schepers simply put his hand on Stewart's shoulder. "We will . . . I will miss you sorely, my friend."

Sorting out the steps of transition would come later. Stewart headed over to the Esso building, amused at knowing Cox would make no attempt to dissuade him from going. This inaction would, of course, be for an entirely different reason from the restraint Schepers had just exercised. And indeed, there was no surprise. Cox did not protest or even ask what his future plans might be. It had been clear for too long that the Terrible Twin Cox probably regarded as the "Terrible Texan" would never deliver the salute to which Cox may have felt entitled.

Cox cabled Milbrath with the news, and regret was likely not part of that wire. Jersey replied that they would like to have Stewart return to New York as the manager responsible for their worldwide producing economics department. Shell, however, requested that he remain in The Hague for several more months to allow for a smooth transition, so Stewart's departure was scheduled for mid-April.

The supervisory committee of the designated delegates invited Stewart and Schepers one last time to the Castle Maurick, near Den Bosh. Stewart's Dutch had improved somewhat, and he worked diligently preparing a final short speech. At the castle, Stewart thanked the Dutch people and the members of the committee for their generous welcome and reception during all the many past negotiations. As a humorous thank-you, he acknowledged his appreciation for the years of courtesy during which meetings were conducted in English for his benefit by giving a brief speech in Latin. (Latin is the root of all the different languages represented by the different committee members and all its European customers.) As a memento of their years of working together, the committee presented Stewart with an antique map of the Netherlands, which still hangs on the wall of his Houston office.

At Smidswater, the staff gathered for a final goodbye party, at which Schepers presented Stewart with a silver cigar box upon which were engraved the signatures of each member of the staff. Stewart surprised them by presenting to each of them a game board he'd designed, similar to Monopoly, called the Funny Game of Gas Export, complete with "Cards of Disaster" and "Triumph," commemorating all the ups and downs they'd experienced together.

Stewart and Schepers took Dick Mariner, who would be the new general manager of IGTM, on a series of meetings to personally introduce him to Ruhrgas, Thyssengas, and Distrigaz. In Stewart's personal files today are a series of farewell appreciation letters from the principals of these companies as well as from the French presidents of Esso and Shell and Bob Milbrath, president of Esso International.

Stewart's goodbye to Distrigaz was delivered in French.

On his last visit to the Dutchman for whom he'd developed a great respect, Stewart presented Coen Smit a gilded scale model of a town gas holder, which is typically used to handle the hourly fluctuations in peak gas usage, along with the following presentation:

Presentation to Coen Smit, April 15, 1965

Four years ago, a small group from New York came to the Netherlands to look into reports that NAM (which is 50 percent owned by Esso) had found large gas reserves. Our task was not only to verify the story, but also to find ways and means of seeing that the gas would be put to optimum use. Not only did we find that the report was true, but we also found, here in the Netherlands, a man of stature who could lead the negotiations to a successful conclusion. He had a mind receptive to new ideas, the energy to put these into action, and the necessary sense of humor to carry the ship through the many storms. Today, he, and we, can see the physical results, as large gas lines cross the Netherlands, and industries and homeowners in the Netherlands benefit already from this new energy source.

All Europe is now watching Dutch Gas. Coen Smit, negotiator, entrepreneur, founding father of the Dutch gas business, it gives me great personal pleasure to present to you, as a token of our esteem, this reminder that four years in the gas business is like forty years in the oil business.

On April 15, 1965, Stewart said his final goodbyes to Schepers and the staff. Briefcase in hand, he stepped out onto the cobbled street along the canal. Jane hadn't yet arrived to pick him up in the Jaguar they were leaving behind. He strolled a few yards past Jagerstraat to the small bridge over the Smidswater Canal. Leaning on the rail, he looked back to No. 23 and then up the tree-lined canal. The trees were just turning green. A slight mist hung over the water, and a mother duck, looking for a handout, came "veeing" up, leading a small flotilla of ducklings.

Stewart's thoughts turned back four and a half years to the moment he'd first heard of Dutch gas in the Jersey boardroom and how he'd first seen the Netherlands with wild turkey eggs on his lap. He recalled the sound of the street organ at the De Wittebrug Hotel and his first meeting with Coen Smit and Jan van den Berg. There was that first icy meeting with Shell in Rotterdam and the vindication of being sent out to Oldenzaal.

He recalled the rush of realizing the possible magnitude of the gas find and the "eureka" moment spotting that gas pipe in Jan's house. The excitement of developing the premium market plan with Jan, Cees van der Post, and Orlean, and selling the idea to Milbrath, to the Jersey board, and to Shell, had been immensely satisfying. He had been there to see the protracted negotiations with de Pous and State Mines. With Shell's influence and cooperation, it had all come to final fruition. He was leaving the Netherlands with Shell and Esso owning 50 percent of Gasunie, 60 percent of the producing Maatschappij, and the rights to sell the gas in export for Gasunie with the full understanding that they would enter the gas business in the export countries.

Stewart's richest memories were of the fun it had been traveling with Schepers to joust with the entrenched gas companies. There were the first setbacks: thrown out of France, no dice in the UK, rejected in Belgium, unthinkable in Germany. Because he and Schepers had never lost their optimism, their perseverance had paid off. The stage had been set. Shell and Esso were in the gas business in the three key countries—the Netherlands, Belgium, and Germany. The premium value of natural gas was going primarily to householders and small businesses, with all its environmental benefits being established.

The detail of working out contracts, with the interminable meetings, would never be as appealing as the buccaneer days when he and Schepers had free reign. Stewart was leaving with no regrets. He looked down at the canal to see the ducks had sailed on, and he looked up to see Jane in the Jag to drive him to the hotel, where a limousine waited to take the family to the airport.

On the way to Schiphol, Stewart looked once more into the green fields, the canals, and the tulip fields. It had been a ride like no other. That there were other challenges before him, he was certain. The plane carrying Stewart and his family was lifting them off to the next one.

In 1992, Doug and Jane Stewart returned to Holland and renewed memories of the Dutch gas days with Krik and Louise Schepers at their home in 's-Hertogenbosch, Netherlands.

Above right: Doug Stewart and Millard Clegg in Houston, Texas, 2004.

Below: Stewart returned to the Smidswater bridge in 2005 and looked back once more at Smidswater 23. It had been forty years since he had last stood on the bridge. The canal and the buildings hadn't changed much, but the people's lives and the environment had improved, and it was satisfying to know that he had had a part in the changes.

Epilogue

Finishing the Kickoff

NAM Gas Export and IGTM were originally formed in 1963 to develop the initial export contracts and to set up the structure of Shell and Esso's participation in the gas business in Germany and Belgium. However, after a few years, these entities no longer served a useful purpose. After Shell and Esso obtained shareholdings in Distrigas, Thyssengas, Ruhrgas, and several trans-German trunk lines, IGTM was closed down. In November 1967, Krik Schepers resigned from NAM Gas Export and became a director of State Mines and a delegated commissar to Gasunie and Maatschappij. Following the nationalization of the oil companies in the Middle East, there was no reason to continue NAM Gas Export, and many of the personnel were transferred to Gasunie, which took over the export functions.

Esso established a gas coordination office in London to oversee Esso's growing interest in gas production from the North Sea as well as the interests obtained in continental Europe through the Dutch gas program. Don Cox, Jack Windham, and Martin Orleans moved to London with this new organization.

The following quote from Arne Kaijser in his 1996 article for the NEHA-Jaarboek, titled *"From Slochteren to Wassenaar,"* sums up the achievements of the Dutch Gas Project teams:

> *For both Shell and Esso, the exploitation of the Groningen field and participation in the Dutch gas industry has been a very important springboard. The exports from*

the Groningen field stimulated the building of trans-border pipelines that eventually became an integrated European gas network, encompassing most countries on the European continent. The strong influence over the gas sales from what was for a long time the largest single gas field in Western Europe, together with the competence generated in the building up of the Dutch gas system, enabled Shell and Esso to achieve control over strategic parts of the European gas industry in the 1970s and 1980s. In fact, the Groningen gas field was the catalyst for the transformation of the two giants from oil companies to energy companies.

The development of European natural gas markets and distribution systems kicked off by the Groningen discovery were further stimulated by the large gas discoveries in the North Sea, beginning in 1966 and later by the import of Russian gas. By the year 2005, natural gas supplied approximately 25 percent of the European energy market.

Back to the Uitsmijter Solution

For the thirty-five years from 1965 to 2000, the gas distribution companies in the Netherlands, Belgium, and Germany in which Shell and Esso had taken an interest flourished. Ruhrgas, under the leadership of Schelberger and Liesen, became a powerhouse in the German energy markets. Thyssengas and Distrigas rapidly converted their gas distribution systems to natural gas (see charts in appendix).

In 1998, the European Union, in line with its developing energy policy, passed a directive stipulating that third-party suppliers, that is, parties other than gas distribution company shareholders, were to have direct access to markets and have transportation use of existing pipelines. These directives brought about new complications and restructuring of the gas distribution companies. Exxon, which had sold out its share in Distrigas in 1975, also sold its one-quarter share of Thyssengas in 2000 to obtain the European Union's approval of its merger with Mobil. Later, Shell also sold out of Thyssengas. In 2002, both companies sold their holdings in Ruhrgas for approximately 2.8 billion euros, according to Exxon Mobil's 2002 annual report.

Gasunie was split up into two companies in 2004 so as to separate transportation and distribution from marketing. The Dutch government bought out Shell and Esso's interest in the Dutch pipeline transportation system for 2.8 billion euros. This system will remain under the name of N. V. Nederlandse Gasunie. The marketing entity was renamed Gasunie Trade & Supply, with Shell and Esso each retaining their 25 percent shareholding in this company. Thus, under the revised European Union system, gas purchasing and selling, separate from the transportation system, is back to the Uitsmijter idea as originally proposed by NAM Gas Export and IGTM.

Appendix Essay 2006

The Growth of Natural Gas Sales

Because of advanced planning and energy studies, the sales of Dutch natural gas increased rapidly once Gasunie had been established. As early as spring 1962, State Mines, Shell, and Esso had formed a planning group, anticipating that somehow the proposed new company and producing arrangements would take shape. Later, the State Gas Board and representatives of the municipal networks participated in the planning. NAM itself continued exploration drilling and made detailed plans for producing facilities. Almost immediately after, the charter of the Gasunie work began on the engineering and laying of new natural gas lines.

Export studies by Esso had started early in 1961, and Shell joined Esso in continuing this effort in mid-1962, and in the fall of 1963, the joint Shell/Esso study groups were embedded with Distrigas, Thyssengas, Ruhrgas, and Gaz de France. Because the export contracts were not finalized until late 1965 and early 1966, the conversion of the export countries was about two years behind the Netherlands.

The Groningen discovery provided the impetus for Europe's conversion to natural gas, and producers other than Shell and Esso also benefited greatly from the fact that there was an existing network and market for their gas discoveries. Quoting from *Natural Gas in the Netherlands* by Aad Correlje, Coby van der Linde, and Theo Westerwoudt:

Dutch gas exports played an important role in maintaining and developing the use of gas in Europe. Without Dutch gas the role of city gas in a number of regions would have been taken over by oil products and methane gas in bottles and containers. Moreover, the Dutch gas exports and the construction of the associated infrastructure created completely new regional and sectorial markets for gas. Most important, though, was the construction of a coordinated European gas infrastructure.

The existence of this gas infrastructure and the growing demand for gas created a need for additional imported supplies from the Soviet Union and Algeria and eventually from LNG sources in the Middle East and elsewhere.

Charts 1 and 2 that follow this page illustrate the growth of gas sales in the Netherlands as compared with the export sales. Because of the early start of conversion in the Netherlands, the domestic sales grew rapidly, but export sales eventually surplassed the demand for domestic Dutch gas. This data was obtained from annual reports of Gasunie.

Gasunie Sales
Domestic and Export
CHART 1

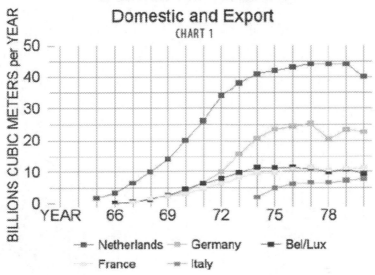

BILLIONS CUBIC METERS per YEAR

YEAR

- Netherlands
- Germany
- Bel/Lux
- France
- Italy

By 1974, Exports of Dutch Gas
Exceeded Domestic Use
CHART 2

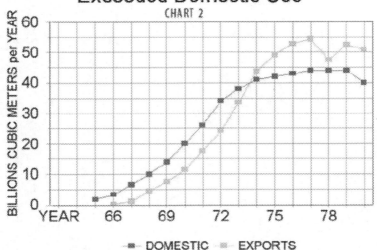

BILLIONS CUBIC METERS per YEAR

YEAR

- DOMESTIC
- EXPORTS

Afterword

A personal essay on natural gas in Holland by Emiel van Veen, resident of Rijksdorp, former CFO and vice chairman of the executive board of Royal Numico N. V.

The first natural gas reserves in Holland were discovered shortly after World War II. It took until 1959 before NAM (Nederlandse Aardolie Maatschappij), a fifty-fifty joint venture of Shell and Esso, found such amounts that one could think of starting an economically viable exploration. It was in the province of Groningen, around the village of Slochteren.

At that time, it was a huge discovery. It placed the country in the position of being the highest-ranked gas producer in Europe, gave the economy a great boost, and brought prosperity and convenience to the country. Almost all Dutch households are connected by a nationwide pipe system.

The Dutch State has earned around 150 billion euro from this so far. Today new and smaller fields are being found. Even in 2005, the exploration of the Waddenzee had started.

Currently, proven natural gas stores amount to 2,500 billion cubic meters. This looks inexhaustible, but with a gas consumption, including export, of approximately 75 billion cubic meters a year, Holland's natural gift will be over in twenty-five to forty years. Around 80 percent of the production is in the hands of NAM. The gas distribution is executed by the Nederlandse Gasunie, a company owned 50 percent by the state and the other 50 percent by Shell and Esso.

The positive side of the natural gas supply goes without saying. However, there are also two downsides. First, the level of the ground surface is gradually sinking. By 2040, Groningen will show a lowering of, say, forty centimeters. This caused, and is causing, small earthquakes (between 2.6 and 5.6 on the Richter scale). Ninety have been registered since 1980, fortunately, without too much damage.

Second, the revenues made Holland too prosperous. This sounds ridiculous, but it isn't. Indeed, many huge necessary infrastructure projects were easily funded without raising taxes. Wages rose dramatically, while the average working week was brought back over time to thirty-six hours, and six weeks vacation is seen as quite common. People, on average, want to be retired at an age of fifty-eight to sixty. Social systems are among the best, and most expensive, in the world. Without the benefits of natural gas, this all would never have been the case.

In light of the fact that in twenty to thirty years the gas supply will decrease dramatically, it is essential for the economy to become strong enough to do without that income. In an open economy, heavily dependent on exports, the competitive edge should then be found in innovative high-quality products and services at low-cost prices. The current economic downturn in Europe or, at best, lackluster growth makes it apparent that Holland has not invested enough in past years into fields such as first-class education systems and infrastructure. The people consumed too much by emptying a source of revenue that had no perpetual character. Salary and wage levels, in combination with less effective working hours, have made Holland too expensive. Social systems are too rigid. The Dutch society has to face reality.

Less gas has to be compensated for by a stronger economy. The people have to accept that wealth growth in the future will be lower and could even be temporarily negative. A new attitude must be born that accepts a more flexible labor market and less generous social systems, working harder and working longer. Prosperity cannot be taken for granted anymore.

Fortunately, there is still ample time. Government and society have opened their eyes. The lullaby of natural gas, which started around 1960, is over.

Reunion at the Stewarts' Fiftieth Wedding Anniversary Party

Douglass and Jane Stewart were feted at a fiftieth wedding anniversary party in Houston, Texas, in 1999, to which Jan van den Berg and Hans and Gisela Löblich came from Europe. The following are excerpts from their speeches. Van Den Berg:

> *You have heard that Doug was in Holland and Jane was running a household there. It was pure accident that we met each other. A lot of gas had been discovered in the Netherlands. I read it in the newspaper, and I wrote a note to the president of Esso Netherlands, and he asked me to write a report. The country was very poor, and we didn't have the standard of living we have today. I didn't know where to start. I had nothing on paper.*
>
> *Suddenly, some Americans came along, and I'll tell you what they did. Nobody knows about it really. Together, we made a fantastic plan. We would put everybody on natural gas. It was a very good and simple plan, but some people said it was impossible. We had no pipelines. Doug said, "Everything is possible. It is done in the United States. If you don't believe it, go there." Some Dutch people went there.*
>
> *Believe me, it was not that simple to connect all those houses and stoves and convert them to the new gas. It was a tremendous operation. The whole heating situation had to be changed. Doug was the man who pulled this whole thing off.*
>
> *Doug couldn't speak Dutch, yet he transformed the whole Dutch economy. I was there with him, a fellow in wooden shoes.*

The Dutch people have never officially thanked Jane and Douglass, so tonight, in the Dutch tradition, I want to officially thank Doug Stewart for what he did.

Hans Löblich:

About *thirty-five* years ago, Doug was on his way from New York to The Hague. There was a big problem because the Dutch had this gas in the ground. In 1963, he formed a company called NAM Gas Export, and this was the time that we were the first to make a study of the potential for natural gas in Germany. In 1963, there was no natural gas in Germany. We started the study, and we had no idea how to sell natural gas. Doug and Martin Orleans came and helped us. We had to convince the cokery gas people to convert to natural gas. Doug Stewart and Schepers pushed us. Every time they came, they had new ideas. We were successful because of the steady pushing.

Nowadays, thirty-five years later, natural gas is 32 percent of the energy in Germany. We are enjoying the gas in Germany, and we thank you for this. We wish you the same in the next decade and the same for you that you are in good health and enjoying your family.

Biographies

Douglass Stewart returned to New York to become manager of Standard Oil Producing Economics. In 1967, he was transferred to Esso Eastern to coordinate Esso's Far East producing division in Australia, Pakistan, and Indonesia. He took early retirement from Standard Oil to join Weeks National Resources Corporation as vice president, taking the company public in Australia. In 1973, he founded DMS Oil Company in Houston, Texas, in which he remains active with multiple interests in natural gas wells throughout the southwest area of the United States. Doug remarried in 2006, and he and his wife, Patricia, are living in Florida.

Jane Stewart, on returning to the States, became a volunteer at the Norwalk, Connecticut, hospital, enthusiastically resuming her role as community leader, becoming a deacon and one of the first women elders in the Norfield Congregational Church of Weston, Connecticut. She passed away in 2001.

Krik Schepers remained as managing director of Nam Gas Export until 1967, when he became a director and member of the Raad of Dutch State Mines, where he also served on the supervisory committee of Gas Unie Maatschappij Committee, retiring in 1988. He passed away in 1999.

Hans-Joachim Löblich continued with Esso A. G., becoming head of its department for environmental control and achieving such distinction in comprehensive scientific research on the emission of sulfur dioxide that in 1979, he was honored for his work by the German government with the German Order of Merits Class. When the government requested a massive study on the effects of sulfur emissions, he started his own company, Beratungsbüro für Umweltfragen (Consulting

Office for Environmental Matters), to carry out that study. When it was completed in 1985, he continued designing and conducting scientific studies in the environmental field throughout Europe until he retired. He and his wife, Gisela, reside in Hamburg and are avid world travelers.

Paul Mortimer became president of IGTM in 1968 and remained with Exxon until 1985. He is now the chairman of the board at Hardy Oil and Gas PLC, which has production and exploration operations offshore in India. He is also chairman of Rift Valley Holdings Limited, a privately held tea, coffee, coconut, and forestry company with plantations in Zimbabwe, Zambia, Tanzania, and Mozambique; director of the Gemini Oil and Gas Royalty Fund; and also director of Digital Ventures, a venture capital fund.

Dr. Klaus Liesen succeeded Dr. Schelberger as CEO of Ruhrgas in 1976, guiding the company's expansion in many pipeline and gas energy ventures in both Germany and other countries. In 1996, he became chairman of the supervisory board of Ruhrgas. In 2003, he left this position and became honorary chairman of the supervisory board. He is currently still a member of several supervisory boards of companies in the energy industry and other industrial sectors.

Martin Orlean transferred to the Esso office as an economist, later becoming a gas industry consultant, once representing the Gas Council against Esso. He is now retired and lives in London.

Harold Wright continued with Esso and retired as manager of Esso's United States producing department. He lived in Houston until his death in 2005. He and Stewart remained fast friends throughout their lives.

Jan van den Berg was educated as an economist at Erasmus University and served in that capacity with Esso Netherlands until he joined Gasunie's sales division, rising to the position of gas sales manager until his retirement in 1988. He passed away in 2003.

Neill "Cees" van der Post continued as a mechanical engineer with Esso Netherlands until 1972, when he became the head of Gasunie's Gas

Transport Laboratory in Groningen. He retired in 1987 and passed away in 1992.

Yves Monod's long international career with Shell included a post overseas as chairman of the board of Shell Chile. His assignment with NAM Gas Export and IGTM concluded in 1966, when he was appointed directeur a Shell Francoise until he became président directeur général of the Société TIPIAK in Nantes, France. He is a past president of the Paris YMCA, is now retired, and lives in Paris.

Rene Cozzi, following the closure of the NAM Gas Export/IGTM office in Paris, was transferred to the Esso coordination office in London and retired with Esso France. He resides in Paris.

Don Cox became the head of natural gas coordination when Esso moved its headquarters to London and later became an Exxon director.

Millard Clegg returned to the engineering division of Esso in Texas with worldwide assignments. He and his wife live in Houston, Texas.

Ciny van den Berg resides in Rodan in the province of Groningen, travels extensively, and enjoys her grandchildren.

Louise Schepers lives in 's-Hertogenbosch, travels widely, and enjoys her grandchildren.

Index of Persons Referenced by Country

AMERICA

Clegg, Millard, Esso pipeline engineer

Clegg, Dorothy, Millard's wife

Cox, Donald, Esso, Dutch gas advisor, later natural gas coordinator, London

Laufs, Jerry, Esso economist, IGTM

Mariner, Dick, Esso executive, succeeded Stewart as general manager IGTM

Miles, Paul, Esso pipeline engineer

Milbrath, Bob, Standard Oil (N. J.) marketing department, New York; Esso Export president

Mortimer, Paul, Esso economist IGTM, later general manager IGTM

Orlean, Martin, Standard Oil (N. J.), one of the "Esso Four," IGTM economist

Priestman, Dawson, Standard Oil (N. J.) manager producing economics, New York

Rathbone, Jack, Standard Oil (N. J.) chairman, chief executive officer

Stott, Bill, Standard Oil (N. J.) marketing vice president, New York

Stewart, Douglass M., Standard Oil (N. J.) deputy manager producing economics, New York, head of "Esso Four," general manager IGTM

Temple, Paul, lawyer Standard Oil (N. J.)

Vazquez, Siro, Standard Oil (N. J.) producing coordinator (Venezuelan citizen)

Windham, Jack, Esso pipeline engineer, succeeded mariner as general manager IGTM

Wright, Harold, Standard Oil (N. J.) petroleum engineer, Exxon USA executive

Weeks, Lewis, Standard Oil (N. J.) chief geologist

AUSTRIA

Kandler, Raymond, Esso executive, manager NAM Gas Export/IGTM Vienna office

BELGIUM

De Housse, Jacques, Esso Belgium, manager NAM Gas Export/IGTM Brussels office

De Brouwer, managing director Distrigas

Leemans, Victor, Belgian senator, member of European Parliament

Thys, Le Chavalier Albert, director Distrigas

FRANCE

Alby, Mssr., executive Gaz de France, later deputy general manager

Antoine, Mssr., lawyer Esso France

Bernard, Mssr., general manager Gaz de France 1964

Bijard, Mssr., executive Gaz de France

Bouriez, Mssr., economics advisor Shell France

Couture, J., energy general secretary French government

Chizelle, Kuhn de, general manager Gaz de France 1963

Cozzi, Rene, economist Esso France

Loizillon, Mssr., executive Shell France

Monod, Yves, Shell France, manager of NAM Gas Export/IGTM office in Paris

Monod, Solange, Yves wife

Shear, Serge, president Esso France

GERMANY

Dobmeyer, Herr, economist Esso A. G.

Geyer, Jerry, general manager Esso A. G. Hamburg

Kratzmuller, Herr, director Esso A. G.

Liesen, Dr. Klaus, succeeded Shelberger as chairman of Ruhrgas

Löblich, Hans, engineer, head of energy sales, Esso A. G., deputy manager NAM Gas Export/IGTM Frankfurt office

Löblich, Gisela; Monika and Gabi, Hans's wife and daughters

Scheffer, Herr, general manager Deutsche Shell Hamburg

Schelberger, Dr. Herbert, chairman Ruhrgas

Sottorf, Gert, Shell executive, manager NAM Gas Export/IGTM Frankfurt office

Swart, Herr, director Baron Thyssen's Bank voor Handel en Scheepvaart

Thyssen, Baron Hans Heinrich Bornemisca, owner of Thyssengas

Weise, Dr. Jurgen, executive Ruhrgas

NETHERLANDS

Boot, J. C., general manager Shell Nederland, 1962, delegated supervisor Gasunie

De Pous, J. W., Minister of Economic Affairs

Hoogland, Joop, legal department Shell and NAM Gas Export

Klosterman, A. H., Shell pipeline engineer, technical director Gasunie

Krazinger, Mnr., Shell advisor to NAM Gas Export

Schepers, J. P. (Krik), Shell general manager NAM Gas Export

Schepers, Louise; Jan Derk, Louise, and Willem, Kriks's wife and children

Schepers, Lykle, general manager Royal Dutch (BIPM), The Hague

Smit, Coen, general manager Esso Nederland, delegated supervisor Gasunie

Scheffer, Baren, general manager Shell Nederland, 1961

Stheeman, H. A., general manager NAM, discoverer of Groningen Gas Field

Van den Berg, Jan, manager Economics Esso Nederland, one of the "Esso Four," manager gas sales Gasunie

Van den Berg, Ciny, Jan's wife

Van der Grinten, W. C. L., chairman of de Pous's special committee

Van der Post, Cees, head LPG sales Esso Nederland, one of the "Esso Four," executive technical department Gasunie

Van Veen, Emil, Dutch executive, present owner of Stewarts' Wassenaar residence

Zilstra, J., prime minister Dutch government

UNITED KINGDOM

Corbett, Philip, Shell UK, deputy manager NAM/IGTM London office

Mclean, Donald, Shell executive, NAM Gas Export in The Hague and Frankfurt

Vale, Dennis, Shell advisor NAM Gas Export

Vizard, Vi, Shell gas department London

References

The Lamp by Shelley Moore, Exxon-Mobil Spring 2002 Publication

Frontline; History Today by Devra Davis, December 2002

Holland and Its Natural Gas by Gasunie, June 1994

Natural Gas in the Netherlands by Correlje, Van der Linde, and Westerwoudt

"A *New Mining Act for the Netherlands*" by Dr. Martha Roggenkamp and Dr. Christiaan Verwer

Ruhrgas—Highlights: the First 75 Years, anniversary publication

"*Striking Bonanza*," article by Prof. A. Kaisjer

Subterranean Commonwealth: 25 Years Gasunie and Natural Gas by Wolf Kielich

The Governance of Large Technical Systems, created for Routledge Studies in Business Organizations and Networks, edited by Olivier Coutard

"*The Transition from Coal to Gas: Radical Change of the Dutch Gas System*" by Aad Correlje and Geert Verbong

"*From Slochteren to Wassenaar,*" 1966 article by Arne Kaljser for NEHA-Jaarboek

The Embarrassment of Riches by Simon Schama

Patriots and Liberators: Revolution in the Netherlands 1780–1813 by Simon Schama

"*A New Mining Act for the Netherlands,*" 2003 article by Martha Roggenkamp and Dr. Christiaan Verwer

Mining Law: Bridging the Gap between Common Law and Civil Law Systems, from a paper presented at the Canadian Bar Association in April 1997 by Cecilia Slac, attorney-at-law at Tormina Consulting, Inc.

Mossadegh Conference: May 3 to May 6 2001, Northwestern University, in commemoration of the fiftieth anniversary of Dr. Mossadegh's government (1951–1953), © 1995, 1999, 2004 Alaa K. Ashmawy

Other Sources

New York Times archives

Original Douglass Stewart's narrative

Original Stewart's audio tapes with Hans Löblich, Krik Schepers, Jan van den Berg, Cees van der Post, and Yves Monod

2004–2005 personal interviews with Douglass Stewart, Hans Löblich, Dr. Klaas Liesen, Paul Mortimer, Henk Ensing, Gasunie, Louise Schepers, Louki Hoogland, L. Wansink, Yves Monod, Jane Ann Stewart, René Cozzi, Mark Stewart, Douglass Stewart Jr., Harold Wright, Mr. and Mrs. Millard Clegg, John Meeder, Wilma van den Berg de Brauw, Ciny van den Berg, Margaret van der Post, Josina Droppert, and Emiel van Veen

Acknowledgments

Except for the discovery of the Groningen natural gas field by Dr. H. A. Stheeman, none of the events in this book would have occurred. He early on recognized the value of natural gas and persevered against odds to make the discovery that revolutionized the European energy sector. His personal kindness and openness to Douglass Stewart on his first meeting with NAM in Oldenzaal is greatly appreciated.

Personal thanks and appreciation to Jane Ann Stewart for California office space and for her many courtesies and unflagging encouragement.

With gratitude to Hans and Gesel Löblich, Paul Mortimer, Louise Schepers, Yves Monod, and René Cozzi for their generous cooperation, frequent communications, and continuing encouragement and for lending their personal photographs and recollections; to Klaas Bens for his generosity of spirit, introductions, supportive critique, and many communications; to Ciny van den Berg and Wilma de Brouw for their photographs and hospitality; and to L. G. Wansink for his recollections and hospitality.

Without the enthusiastic cooperation of Dr. Klaus Liesen, much of "other side" of the export negotiations would be missing. Thanks for his hospitality and to Marianne van Schwartz, Dr. Liesen's assistant, for her very kind assistance; to Imelda Weizl, Jan van den Berg's secretary, for her work history of Jan; to Emiel and Liz van Veen and their daughter, Caroline, for their generosity in opening up their Rijksdorp home for visits and filming and to Emiel for his thoughtful afterword and his research on the history of the Rijksdorp house; to Margaret van der Post for Cees's work history; and to Louki Hoogland for her hospitality.

Special thanks to Gasunie's Henk Ensing and Bert van Engleshoven and their audio-visual department for generously opening their archives and giving permission to reproduce Gasunie photographs; to Profs. Geert Verbong and Arne Kaijser in Sweden and Prof. Martha Roggenkamp, University of Groningen, for permission to quote from their work; to Jo Linden of Dutch State Mines for photographs of Krik Schepers; and last but not least, to Dr. Liesen and Ruhrgas for permission to use text, data, and photographs from their rep.

For assistance with translations:

Dutch—Wilma de Brouw, Annelies Glen Teven, Klaas Bense
German—Elke Pusi
French—Yves Monod, René Cozzi, Molly Kidder Orts

About the Co-Author

Elaine Madsen is a published author, editor, and award-winning filmmaker. A native of Illinois, she was the books editor of Chicago's *Nit & Wit Cultural Arts* magazine. She is the editor in chief of *Felix Magazine* and the author of *Crayola Can't Make These Colors*, a collection of her poetry.

Her nonfiction book *The Texan and Dutch Gas*, written in collaboration with Douglass Stewart, has been a powerful and meaningful experience transporting her to historic moments in Stewart's World War II experience. Traveling with Stewart to locations in France, Germany, and the Netherlands, she gained a firsthand understanding of his partnership with three young men, all of whom had been on different sides of the conflict during World War II. A highlight of her writing career has been the privilege of bringing to life the story of how these young men were fatefully drawn together by massive natural gas deposits in the Netherlands, which heralded later massive North Sea discovery. Their business acumen and teamwork was significant and instrumental in the postwar transformation of Europe's energy industry.

As a filmmaker, Madsen is the Emmy Award winning director and producer of the documentary *Better Than It Has to Be* and also the director of the award-winning feature-length documentary *I Know a Woman Like That* produced by her Oscar-nominated daughter Virginia Madsen. Her play *Dear Murderess* will be on stage in the fall of 2020.

Printed in the United States
By Bookmasters